We, the Students and Teachers

We, the Students and Teachers

Teaching Democratically in the
History and Social Studies Classroom

Robert W. Maloy and Irene S. LaRoche

Published by State University of New York Press, Albany

For information, contact State University of New York Press, Albany, NY
www.sunypress.edu

Production, Jenn Bennett
Marketing, Michael Campochiaro

Library of Congress Cataloging-in-Publication Data

Maloy, Robert W.
    We, the students and teachers : teaching democratically in the history and social studies classroom / Robert W. Maloy and Irene S. LaRoche.
        pages cm
    Includes bibliographical references and index.
    ISBN 978-1-4384-5558-7 (pbk. : alk. paper)
    ISBN 978-1-4384-5559-4 (hardcover : alk. paper)
    ISBN 978-1-4384-5560-0 (ebook)
    1. Social sciences—Study and teaching (Elementary)   2. Social sciences—Study and teaching (Secondary)   3. History—Study and teaching (Elementary)
4. History—Study and teaching (Secondary)   5. Teacher-student relationships.
6. Democracy and education.   I. LaRoche, Irene S., 1984–   II. Title.

    LB1584.M28 2015
    372.83—dc23   2014015525

10 9 8 7 6 5 4 3 2 1

Contents

Tables

Acknowledgments

This book would not be possible without the ideas and perspectives provided by the students and teachers with whom we have worked at the University of Massachusetts Amherst and the Amherst (Massachusetts) public schools. We want to thank college students who collaborated and learned with us in Education 514, Education 592S, Education 510, Education 613, Education 743, and Education 497I (TEAMS Tutoring) at the University of Massachusetts Amherst. We are equally grateful to the students and teachers at Amherst Middle School in Amherst. All of you have shaped our thinking and inspired our teaching.

We particularly want to acknowledge Sharon A. Edwards for her questions, contributions, modeling of democratic teaching, and hours of reading and responding to the manuscript for the book; it could not have been finished without her steadfast support. Thank you to Marge LaRoche, David Hale, Teagan Hale, and Gavin Hale for their patience, understanding, and support for time spent on this work. We thank former students Julia Saari-Franks, Erica Winter, Kim Kench, Lou Proietti, and Gina Gacona for starting us down the path to this book in 2009.

For embracing democratic practices in schools, thank you to Heather Batchelor, Jessica Brehaut, Jessica Charnley, Kate Curtin, John Denmead, Joe Emery, Allison Evans, Allyson Furcick, Jeremy Greene, Jessica Johnson, Samantha Mandeville, Matt Mare, Kelly Marsh, Brenna Morrison, Lauren Morton, Nikki Pullen, Helen van Riel, Hilary K. Smith, and Samantha Whitman.

Over the years, we have been inspired and guided by the broad visions for better schools set forth by Byrd L. Jones, Irving Seidman, Richard J. Clark Jr., Atron Gentry, David Schimmel, Howard Peelle, Portia Elliott, John Fischetti, Jodi Bornstein, Dwight Allen, Joye Bowman, and Ruth-Ellen Verock.

We acknowledge the staff at the W.E.B. Du Bois Library, the Nahman-Waston Library, the Mason Library, and the New Castle Public Library. They provided wonderful writing spaces and answered our every question. Thank you to the wait staff of Bertucci's Restaurant in Amherst as well as the Bridgeside Grille in Sunderland for providing nourishment and a warm environment for countless dinner sessions processing and pondering the ideas for the book.

We also want to express our thanks to Beth Bouloukos, our editor at the State University of New York Press, who was always available with guidance and support. She believed in this project and that has helped make this book a reality.

Ideas do not take shape in a vacuum and to think so would be undemocratic. The countless interactions and experiences that influenced our thinking about democratic practices would be impossible to capture. In naming people who contributed to this work, we undoubtedly will leave out some to whom we are indebted. We apologize and express our gratitude to them.

To our readers, thank you for being interested in the ideas put forth in the book. We hope for and anticipate a future partnership with you through hearing the many ways you bring democratic teaching practices to life in schools.

Preface

The 7 Cs of Democratic Teaching

The schoolroom is the first opportunity most citizens have to experience the power of government. Through it passes every citizen and public official, from schoolteachers to policemen and prison guards. The values they learn there, they take with them in life.

—Supreme Court Justice John Paul Stevens
(New Jersey v. T.L.O, 1985)

"What does it mean to teach democratically?"

We pose this question every year to college students entering history and political science teacher license programs at the University of Massachusetts Amherst. They, in turn, ask elementary, middle, and high school students taking history and social studies classes in local schools. These inquiries encourage everyone to consider the multifaceted roles of history and social studies in preparing students for civic roles and responsibilities as members of American democracy. It is an expected goal of K–12 education that students learn about democracy in school in order to act democratically in society.

What does it mean to teach democratically introduces powerful dynamics that emerge each year in the behaviors of teacher candidates and K–12 students when new democratic practices are introduced in school classes. Graphic artist M.C. Escher (2000) once noted that he sought to "awaken astonishment" in those who viewed his art. Similarly, by asking the meaning of democratic teaching, we seek to awaken the power and importance of democratic experiences in schools. Repeatedly, history/social studies teacher candidates describe their amazement at the culture, tone, and substance of transformed classes when democratic practices are introduced and sustained. Many explain they will never think about teaching or history/

social studies in the same way again; their pedagogy will firmly be grounded in democratic principles and practices.

Introducing the 7 Cs

We, the Students and Teachers explores how to teach democratically in history and social studies classrooms, with an emphasis on middle and high schools. We argue that history/social studies classes at all grade levels can play a unique and essential role in how students learn about democracy and their roles as engaged members of a democratic society.

The book envisions classrooms as laboratories for democratic learning, places where students and teachers together build frameworks for future citizenship through their lessons and actions. It proposes practical and concrete solutions to the fundamental contradiction of students learning about democracy in undemocratic ways. It offers ideas for involving students directly and purposefully in their own learning, a way to re-energize a commitment to education among many youths today who find school in general, and history/social studies in particular, uninspiring and disengaging.

Seven chapters, each beginning with the letter "C," present different dimensions of teaching democratically in the history/social studies classroom:

1. Contrasting: Curriculum Coverage and Uncoverage

2. Conducting: Student Engagement and Flipped Classrooms

3. Collaborating: Decision Making and Power Sharing

4. Conversing: Conversations, Discussions, and Student Voice

5. Conferring: Student Feedback about Teaching Practices

6. Co-construction: Digital Technologies and Student Inquiry

7. Connecting: Civic Learning and Community Engagement

We use the "7 Cs of democratic teaching" to establish a framework for thinking about the potentials and possibilities of democratic teaching in schools. Each "C" features practical alternatives to traditional curriculum content, teacher-centered instructional practices, adult-directed decision making, one-way teacher–student interactions, minimal student input about teaching practices, non-innovative uses of digital technology, and separation of schools from communities.

The term *7 Cs* is a wordplay derived from the phrase "seven seas," which has been used to refer to bodies of water at different times in history. In ancient Rome, the seven seas were lagoons that were separated from open water by land. During the Age of Exploration and Transregional Encounters, early geographers listed the Red Sea, Mediterranean Sea, Persian Gulf, Black Sea, Adriatic Sea, Caspian Sea, and Indian Ocean as the seven seas (Woods Hole Oceanographic Institution Information Office, 1997). Although not commonly used today, the seven seas refer to the world's major oceans (National Oceanic and Atmospheric Administration, 2013).

Our image of the 7 Cs of democratic teaching is derived from math rather than history. Imagine a seven-sided polygon with all even sides. It is called a regular heptagon. The sum of its angles is 900 degrees and each of its seven points is equidistance from the center. In this way, *Contrasting, Conducting, Collaborating, Conversing, Conferring, Co-Constructing,* and *Connecting* are equally connected parts of a vision for classroom teaching and student learning. Students and teachers may choose to emphasize certain of the Cs over others, but all of them will transform education when used to organize history/social studies learning in schools.

About This Book

Our vision for readers' use of this book is inspired by the inherently democratic, never the same, always changing compositions of jazz music. The improvisational structure of jazz emerges from the combinations of musicians performing in groups, each bringing their individual designs of color, tone, rhythm, and harmony that convey melody through instrumentation, generating a unique rendition of a composition. Ralph Ellison (2003, p. 267) once observed that jazz "is an art of individual assertion within and against the group." A composer's piece is given to group of musicians to present through the technique and form they design. As Wesley J. Watkins, founder of the Jazz and Democracy Project in Oakland, California, noted: "Jazz musicians have the ability to balance individual freedom and what is best for the group, which I think is a struggle for any democracy" (NPR Staff, 2013).

In this spirit, we provide adaptable and adjustable outlines and frameworks for democratic teaching to fit the realities of multiple schools and classes. Offering neither formal recipes or absolute arrangements, we invite students and teachers to express ideas and perspectives, blend talents and visions, to create meaning and substance instructionally, experientially, and democratically.

As you enact democratic teaching using ideas in this book, we invite you to read the chapters as you choose, depending on your interests and goals. Proceeding from the front, each chapter has a similar structure. A brief story introduces the chapter's "C," followed by background material designed to situate each "C" in the work of educational researchers and policymakers. A section called "Voices of Teacher Candidates" presents first-hand perspectives of college students who have been preparing to become history/social studies teachers at the University of Massachusetts Amherst. These first-person comments show new teachers going about integrating democratic practices in classrooms today while dealing with how schools are organized as well as their own evolving conceptions of the roles of history/social studies teachers.

The balance of each chapter is devoted to ideas and strategies for using each "C" in history/social studies classes, primarily at middle and high school grade levels. Teachers new to the field or veterans of many years in the classroom can implement these teaching and learning approaches with students. These strategies connect theoretical and policy ideas with practical approaches to make classrooms more democratic places and spaces. These strategies are intended as starting points to launch further explorations and expansions of democratic practices in all classrooms at all grade levels. We invite readers to add their own ideas to create a broader framework for democratic teaching in schools.

Alternatively, we begin each chapter with "Building Democracy" strategies and activities to focus on practical ideas for the classroom. As you implement these democratic practices, consult the earlier sections of the chapter to compare those perspectives with your own experiences.

We hope you find the book inspiring to you as a teacher, student, or community member interested in making schools more democratic. We are guided by a certainty—born anew every year among the teacher candidates in our program as they begin implementing the 7 Cs in classrooms—that initial doubt and reluctance will melt away to be replaced by the transformative effects that teaching democratically has on students and schools. In democratic classes, traditional practices are upended by approaches where students have substantive opportunities for voice, participation, and responsibility in the study of history and social studies topics. Such changes support the fundamental reality that if elementary, middle, and high school students are to be actively engaged with democratic structures and responsibilities in society, they must regularly and meaningfully experience democratic structures and responsibilities in schools.

Introduction

Defining Democracy and Democratic Teaching

Our decision to focus this book on democratic teaching and learning in schools is grounded in democracy's central place in the intellectual, social, and political lives of students, teachers, and everyday citizens. Democracy is America's most cherished concept, the cornerstone of our system of government and way of life. As voters, Americans think of democratically held elections—choosing presidents, senators, congressional representatives, and state and local officials who will represent the will of the people in the making of laws and policies. As individuals, we cherish our rights to life, liberty, and the pursuit of happiness, resisting whatever is perceived as threats to those protections and guarantees. As members of an international community, we see protecting democracy as a paramount goal of the nation's foreign policy.

Thinking about democracy and education, we imagine that schools, primarily through classes in history and social studies, will teach children and adolescents the roles and responsibilities needed to become engaged members of our political, social, and economic systems. Through experiences in schools, we trust, students will learn the meaning, roles, and responsibilities of democracy and democratic action, readying themselves to be productive, participating members of society.

Yet, across the grade levels in many schools, students remain uninspired by their history and social studies education. Teachers lecture to passive listeners. Classroom discussions emphasize reciting correct answers rather than asking critical questions. Rules are set without input from the students most affected by them. Textbooks and curriculum frameworks shortchange the struggles and accomplishments of people of color, women, workers, and other dispossessed groups. Daily instruction remains disconnected from the world outside the school building's walls. The issues that children and teenagers face in their daily lives, and their historical ante-

1

cedents, are rarely talked about, reinforcing an impression that history and social studies is about events that happened long ago, far away, and irrelevant to present-day lives.

At the same time, and in marked contrast to prevailing patterns of history and social studies instruction, there are teachers who engage students in learning about democracy by thinking and acting democratically. One of those educators, Heather Batchelor, a finalist for the 2010–2011 Massachusetts teacher of the year, recalled that she became a teacher out of frustration about people's inability to "affect political change." She believed her educational role was democratically based, to give students "the power and the skills to affect change in life" (Albertini, 2011, p. C4).

Voice and participation by all members of a classroom community is a common theme in these visions of democratic teaching. In democratically based places and spaces, teachers and students learn together cooperatively and productively. Everyone plays a substantive role in the processes of learning—voices are expressed and heard; rights are acknowledged and respected; backgrounds, cultures, and values are affirmed. Such democratic experiences in individual history/social studies classrooms reveal the multiple ways democracy can be practiced in schools and society. We have written this book to advance those ideals with strategies for democratic teaching.

Democracy in National and State Frameworks

Preparing students for democratic citizenship in history/social studies classes has been a preeminent theme in national and state curriculum frameworks and policy statements. "The main purpose of social studies," said the National Council for the Social Studies (1994, p. vii), "is to help young people develop the ability to make informed and reasoned decisions for the public good as citizens of a culturally diverse, democratic society in an interdependent world." That organization renewed this focus in its latest policy document, "College, Career, and Civic Life (C3) Framework for Social Studies State Standards," a report designed to help states strengthen social studies education in K–12 schools. "Engagement in civic life," the report states, "requires knowledge and experience; children learn to be citizens by working individually and together *as* citizens" (National Council for the Social Studies, 2013, p. 7).

In curriculum frameworks designed to guide K–12 education, states have declared that students should not only learn about democracy as a form of government, but learn how to act democratically in society. In its

"History-Social Science Curriculum Framework," California declares students should "realize that only a small fraction of the world's population (now or in the past) has been fortunate enough to live under a democratic form of government, and we want them to understand the conditions that encourage democracy to prosper" (California Department of Education, 2005, pp. 1–2). At the youngest grades, South Carolina expects students need to learn "the values of American democracy as reflected in the traditions and history of the nation" (South Carolina Department of Education, 2011, p. 7). Oregon expects students at every grade to "examine the relationship between government and citizens to distinguish and evaluate the ways that civic participation occurs in local, state, tribal, national and global governments" (Oregon State Board of Education, 2011, p. vi).

State and national standards, for all their emphasis on the importance of preparing students for democracy, are less clear about how teachers should achieve such learning goals within the day-to-day worlds of K–12 classrooms. Although most frameworks identify specific academic information for students to learn, they leave open the instructional strategies and interpersonal experiences that best convey those attitudes and information to students.

Democracy in the Words of New Teachers

To stimulate the thinking of the future teachers about democracy in schools, we ask history teacher candidates for written responses to the following questions: "What is democracy?" and "What is democratic teaching?" Their responses reveal a still-being-formed portrait of how future educators are thinking about democracy in schools and classrooms at the outset of their teaching careers. We invite you to answer these questions as well.

Overwhelmingly, teacher candidates in our program define democracy in terms of political and social systems. A democratic society, they conclude, is one where voices are heard, rights are protected, and participation is essential for the system to succeed. Familiar concepts of freedom, equality, and decision making strongly resonate with these soon-to-be classroom teachers, as in the following comments:

- "Democracy is a social system that promotes equality. Democratic principles ensure that people's voices are heard and the majority's beliefs are represented accordingly. In a democracy, people's choices and opinions are valued and respected."

- "I see democracy as the practice of taking all opinions into account when making decisions in a community. . . . Most of us are willing to go unheard and unrepresented some of the time so long as we can be heard on issues that matter to us."

- "I go back to a simple idea when thinking about democracy—everyone has a say in decision making, and everyone is considered equal, with the same rights."

- "Democracy is a philosophy that encourages all opinions to be heard but can't necessarily assure everyone will be happy with the end result."

Asked to define democratic teaching, many teacher candidates initially expressed skepticism and uncertainty. "What do you mean?" they asked.

- "Let the students run the classroom?"

- "Relinquish my responsibility and lose my authority as a teacher?"

- "Allow students to set the rules such as no homework and [only] easy exams?"

- "Isn't teaching about democracy the same as teaching democratically?"

Our country's political system is democratic, these candidates seemed to be telling us, but in the classroom, the teacher must be the dominant authority in charge.

Initially, some thought it difficult to begin creating a democratic classroom. One high school student teacher recalled how "offering to incorporate direct democracy into the classroom" resulted in "students attempting to take the easy way out, do less work, or find an option that allows them to focus on socializing." Although "I do not believe that the classroom should be a strict dictatorship at all times . . . the option of a direct democracy in the classroom may not be the best one." Another high school candidate found "when I give students the chance to pick what assignment they would like to do they are overwhelmed and tend not work as productively as they would if I give the assignment and say 'It's due in 20 minutes.' "

As we encouraged beginning teachers to continue refining goals and expectations for students and to explain why they were implementing changes in the classroom, candidates began focusing on the idea that democratic teaching depends on adults supporting student voice and participation in class. "Democracy should be represented in educational practices." "Students have the right to be heard and need to have an active role inside the classroom," noted one high school candidate. A second high school candidate believed that "democratic teaching allows students the choice to participate in the construction of the classroom" and a middle school candidate proposed "democratic teaching would include students having a say in the classroom."

Other candidates believed democratic teaching to be less directly tied to student voice and participation. One high school candidate hoped students would "contribute their unique abilities and personalities to create a stronger community, rather than focusing on one's own outcomes." A second high school candidate said, "True democratic teaching does not just incorporate student opinions but also the opinions of teachers, administrators, and parents." A few candidates remained firm in their belief that a classroom is not a democracy: "Democratic teaching should not be confused with teaching as if it were a democracy," observed one. "Democratic teaching should have democratic qualities, but not be a democracy . . . democratic teaching simply means allowing students to have access to some power in the classroom."

Each year, a small number of candidates define democratic teaching as fundamentally changing—and expanding—the roles of students in the classroom. "I believe it is not enough to just teach students about our democratic process," stated a middle school candidate. "They must experience it for themselves." Students need opportunities to "take some ownership and responsibility for their own learning experiences." A high school candidate remarked that "democratic teaching seems like it should include input from everyone in the classroom regarding what is to be studied, how it is to be studied, how the classroom should function, and under what rules the class will proceed."

As candidates proposed their definitions of democratic teaching, some recalled practices from their own schooling that they felt were democratic in nature. Classroom rule making was an often cited example, as one high school history candidate stated, "if students are given the choice to make their own class rules that they agree upon, or help decide what they want to learn, students will take an active role in their own education."

Although most of the future teachers expressed a broad vision of democratic teaching featuring student voice and participation, they did not agree on how teachers can make that vision a reality within the day-to-day operation of history/social studies classrooms. Many saw, in the words of one high school candidate, "abundant obstacles" to democratic teaching, including mandated curriculum frameworks; limited time for exploration of interesting topics and ideas; the demands of grades, credits, and graduation; and expectations for attendance, behavior, and appearance that limit how students can express themselves individually.

For many college students at the beginning of their careers, democratic teaching seemed to require "a kind of magic," framed by two questions:

1. "How can we give responsibility and ownership to students in an environment as undemocratically structured as a public high school?"

2. "How can we give students the feeling of power and control when everything they see as important remains outside of their control?"

Democracy in History/Social Studies Education

The idea of democratic teaching has given rise to a rich and varied literature about schools where students learn to be critical and creative thinkers, committed to fairness and equity in society. We draw on this literature, especially the writing of Michael Apple (2004, 2013; Apple & Beane, 2007), Sam Wineburg (2001), Walter C. Parker (2002), Diana E. Hess (2009), Beth Rubin (2011), Joel Westheimer (2007), Ronald Evans (2004, 2011a, 2011b), and Linda McNeil (1988) who have set forth frameworks for making schools more democratic places for teaching and learning using critical theory, social justice, student-centered teaching methods, and inquiry-based approaches to the study of the present and the past.

These scholars also have documented how visions for democratic schools have been frustrated by efforts begun in the 1980s for more prescribed curriculum, increased standardized testing, and greater measures of teacher accountability, all of which became more fully established with the No Child Left Behind Act of 2001. Today, under the influence of conservative policymakers, ultraconservative evangelicals, and representatives from both political parties, that movement has sufficient political power to affect the design of curriculum content in many states and communities. In response, progressive educators and scholars believe that developing more democratic values and practices in classrooms reverse these trends "while developing in students not only basic knowledge and skills, but also a critical facility and broad understanding of the social world" (Evans, 2011b, p. 4).

In our subtitle and throughout the book, we use the term *history/social studies* to refer to classes taught as part of the K–12 social studies education curriculum. Depending on the school or school district, these classes may be called social studies, history, government, politics, economics, geography, global studies, or some other historical or social science-related name. All of these classes can become spaces for democratically engaged learning.

We recognize that history and social studies education in schools is a hotly contested political topic. In U.S. education, different visions of what should be taught in school classes have gained and lost prominence as competing groups have achieved power at different times in the past, as historians Ronald W. Evans and Larry Cuban have well documented. Using *history/social studies*, we do not privilege one term over the other.

In recent years, conservative groups, including the Thomas J. Fordham Foundation, have mounted a vigorous opposition to a social studies-based approach to curriculum and instruction. In reports written after the September 11 attacks, *Where Did Social Studies Go Wrong?* (Porter-Magee, Leming, & Ellington, 2003) and *Terrorists, Depots and Democracy: What Children Need to Know* (Rodriguez, Weinstein, Hanson, & Mead, 2003), conservative-minded commentators decried the failure of social studies education in schools. In 2013, the National Council for the Social Studies responded to calls for policy change by issuing its C3 framework. Leaving decisions about academic content to individual states, the C3 document highlights the development of inquiry-based skills in the classroom while supporting "students in learning to be actively engaged in civic life" (National Council for the Social Studies, 2013, p. 6).

C3's publication served only to heighten criticism from conservative groups about the academic content of school curriculum. Against the backdrop of such contentious politics, new history/social studies candidates make decisions about what to teach, how to teach, and how to incorporate democracy and democratic practices in the classroom and the curriculum. Many find themselves, in Cuban's (2008) term, *hugging the middle* between competing visions of history teaching, moving tentatively one way or the other from year to year, needing concrete strategies for realizing democratic goals with students.

For us as authors, what is important here are academic topics, teaching methods, and critical thinking skills. Apple, an eloquent advocate of democratic schools and democratic teaching, contends that schools legitimize knowledge through whatever curriculum is and is not taught in classrooms. We would add that teaching methods as well as student and teacher interactions also deliver powerful messages about roles and power in schools and society. We believe teachers make learning more democratic by giving students opportunities to examine and propose solutions to meaningful problems, by providing students with relevant resources for learning, and by offering students consistent feedback that holds them accountable for their decisions and actions. We seek to enact that vision through ideas and strategies for teaching democratically in history/social studies classrooms.

Chapter 1

Contrasting

Curriculum Coverage and Uncoverage

> To me, contrasting content means content that tells an opposing story.
> It's content that tells the untold story, one that traditionally has been
> left out of the history books. It's content that is multicultural and
> includes many perspectives, particularly the perspectives of people who
> have been historically marginalized and oppressed. It's taking the tradi-
> tional viewpoint or story and directly contrasting it with the untold.
>
> —Middle School Teacher Candidate

For many students and teachers, the history of the American West is framed
by images of the Gold Rush, the transcontinental railroad, and violent
conflicts between native peoples and White settlers. In Hollywood movies
and the popular imagination, the story unfolds in similar ways—European
settlers in wagon trains tamed the frontier, bringing civilization, religion,
and progress to the wilderness. Yet, the American West is a far more complex and problematic concept than most imagine, filled with the hidden
histories and untold stories of women, native peoples, African Americans,
and immigrants from Asia and Mexico, all waiting to be included so history
can be more fully understood.

"The West is a land of infinite horizons and unimaginable distances.
But it was never empty," said filmmakers Stephen Ives and Ken Burns
(1996, p. vii). For emigrants from eastern states, the West offered opportunities for wealth, land, and/or community. For powerful politicians it was
a place to fulfill visions of Manifest Destiny and new statehood. For many
others, "the West" did not exist in such terms. It was "the East" for those
who came from China and Russia; "free land" for African Americans; "el
Norte" for Spanish settlers from Mexico; "South" for British and French
settlers moving down from Canada; or simply "the Land," "Home," or "the

9

Center of the Universe" for the Native Americans who had lived there for thousands of generations.

History is multiple realities, not singular occurrences. There is not one American, Asian, African, or European story. There are parallel, overlapping, intersecting pasts, forming mosaics of human experience. This multiple and varied view of history stands markedly in contrast to the collection of names, dates, and places taught straightforwardly in many K–12 history/social studies classes. Students or teachers thinking in terms of a single reality or a single account of events privilege a dominant viewpoint or repeat a prevailing metanarrative rather than expressed nuanced views of national or regional history.

Contrasting, the first of 7 Cs of democratic teaching recognizes that students develop ideas and understandings about democracy from the academic content expressed in their school's history/social studies curriculum. Textbook reading assignments, teachers' lesson plans, classroom discussions, and learning assessments are important in terms of what curriculum content they include or leave out. In our highly politicized, media-driven society, deciding what will be taught is a difficult and contentious process. Ideological disagreements, party politics, and competing television news channels have diminished informed discussions among scholars. Teachers, and then students, are at the center of controversy about the nature of history education in schools.

Debating History Content

The academic content of K–12 history curriculum has long been the subject of intense political debates (Foner, 2003). Questions of what, when, and how much history should be taught in schools create "flash points" as conservative and progressive educators seek to structure educational standards to match ideological agendas. University of Georgia historian Peter Charles Hoffer (2004, pp. 1–2) refers to the current state of American history teaching as "two-faced," consisting of the importance of celebrating the ideals of democracy, justice, and equality and the importance of critiquing how far short of those ideals has been the experience of people of color, women, and other groups. For teachers at every level, there is "an almost intolerable burden: to balance a critical approach and a rightful pride."

Common ground can be enormously difficult to find. Exploring the role of historic places in American culture, for example, students and teachers will encounter the competing perspectives of James W. Loewen's (1999) *Lies Across America*, which details how national parks and monuments distort the actual events that happened in those locations and Newt Gingrich's *Recovering God in America* (2006), which presents a walking tour of Christian religious symbols displayed at the Supreme Court, the Library of Congress, the White House, and other locations in the nation's capitol.

As the wide expanse between the Loewen and Gingrich books illustrates, progressive and conservative groups have sharply competing and contrasting visions for what content should be taught at each grade level. Conservative commentators call for a renewed emphasis on the values and institutions that Americans share in common. Minimizing the differences among us, they urge more in-depth study of the founding fathers, the Constitution, America's technological and scientific progress, and the civic responsibilities of citizens. Progressive educators, citing the multicultural nature of American history and contemporary society, want more instructional time spent addressing the experiences of women, Blacks, Native Americans, Latinos, and other groups that are typically left out the curriculum. Studying diverse histories of many groups enables students to understand how existing patterns of class, race, and gender have evolved over time, and might change in more equitable directions in the future.

Teaching Traditional American History

In 2002, the U.S. Department of Education began administering a Teaching American History (TAH) grant program. The purpose of TAH was to "raise student achievement by improving teachers' knowledge and understanding of and appreciation for traditional American history." The authorizing statute, Title II, Part C, Subpart 4, was vague in its definition of traditional American history, stating only that the TAH recipients must carry out activities to promote the teaching of traditional American history in elementary and secondary schools as a "separate academic subject (not as a component of social studies)."

The reference to history as a separate academic subject rather than a component of social studies in the TAH legislation reflected a longstanding concern on the part of many educators that historical thinking and analysis is diluted when history is grouped together with psychology, sociology, anthropology, economics, political science—the fields of the social studies. However, by 2002, traditional American history had become a politically charged term, one that held great meaning to political and social conservatives who sought to move the history curriculum away from what they regarded as too much multiculturalism and not enough core values and heritage.

Debates over the content of history frameworks illustrate how conservative political groups have coalesced reform efforts around the concept of traditional American history. Pennsylvania State University historian David Warren Saxe (2006) defined traditional American history as:

> The installation of patriotism and love of country as the norm, not the exception; Textbooks proudly reflected America as THE exceptional nation; "One nation, one people" defined American heritage; and a common American history provided admiration for national heroes, reverence for America's founding, promotion of America's seminal documents; acceptance of America's founding principles, and respect for America's law and Constitutional heritage. (p. 12)

In an essay entitled "Reviving Traditional American History in an Age of Social Justice," Saxe (2006) asserted that since the social upheavals of the 1960s, public school classrooms are no longer providing students with the "knowledge, skills, and tools of American heritage for citizenship" (p. 12). Classrooms are "more like little political activist camps not places of education," with too much emphasis on social change and the contributions of diverse groups instead of America's founding documents and principles (p. 12).

Other conservative commentators, calling for the teaching of "traditional" American history in sometimes politically less strident terms, cite consistent themes: a focus on founding documents and principles, the vital role of religion in society, an emphasis on American exceptionalism, the criticism of multicultural education and teaching about dispossessed groups in history, and the importance of a capitalist economic system. There is a strong effort to defuse criticism of American foreign and domestic policies, past and present. The effect of these proposals, concluded two history educators, has had less to do with changing instructional practices in schools than returning the "social studies curriculum to its place as a battleground in the culture wars where debates over American values can be staged" (Williams & Maloyed, 2013, p. 26).

State of the State U.S. History Frameworks

Reviewing the academic content in history and social studies curriculum frameworks in 49 of the 50 states in 2010 (Rhode Island has no statewide curriculum), the Thomas B. Fordham Foundation, a conservative-oriented policy organization, graded each standard on its historical quality (Stern & Stern, 2011). The report was a follow-up to an earlier review of state standards in 2002 of which David Warren Saxe was one of the authors.

South Carolina earned an A, whereas Alabama, California, Indiana, Massachusetts, New York, and the District of Columbia received A-minuses. All the other states received very low ratings, mainly "mediocre to awful," for a national average of D, leading the report's authors to conclude that our schools are "creating a generation of students who don't understand or value our own nation's history" (Finn & Porter-Magee, 2011, p. 5).

What shortcomings produce "weak" standards? A main culprit, in the view of the Fordham Report, was "states' ill-considered decision to embed history in 'social studies'" (Finn & Porter-Magee, 2011, p. 8). As a collection of social science disciplines—sociology, psychology, geography, anthropology, political science, and history—social studies lacks the explanatory power of historical thinking. Using a social studies perspective, "teachers and students fail to grasp why history unfolded as it did," relying instead on "trans-historical (and often ahistorical) interpretive 'concepts' over historical facts and context" (pp. 8, 12).

Concerns about history content have also become part of the debate over what to teach at the college level. "The Vanishing West," a 2011 report from the National Association of Scholars, criticized the "decline and near extinction of the Western Civilization history survey course in America's top colleges and universities" (Ricketts et al., 2011, p. iv). Examining history requirements at 50 major institutions of higher education plus 75 additional state universities, the authors found a "parallel decline of the American history survey requirements" and the "emergence of 'world history' as a substitute for the history of the West" (Ricketts, Wood, Balch, & Thorne, 2011, p. iv).

Throughout the 20th century, argue the report authors, the Western history survey course provided a coherent narrative for all college undergraduates, whatever their academic major. "Studying the history of the West brings a student to grips, as nothing else can, with the roots, the shaping events, the underlying causes of the process and substance of globalization, indeed of the creation of modernity itself" (Ricketts et al., 2011, p. 19). Now, as the survey course requirement moves to the wayside, there is no substitute in place. Lacking a Western history survey, "the curriculum spins out into an all-things-to-all-people cornucopia of offerings, many of them exceptionally narrow in scope and many of them trivial in character" (Ricketts et al., 2011, p. 8).

Repeating familiar conservative criticisms, the report's authors define multicultural history as a major problem in the college curriculum: "Multiculturalism leaves students ill-equipped to understand the context of their own lives or the world around them." Without a deep knowledge of

Western civilization, continued the report's authors, because it is so interconnected with the histories of the world's civilizations and cultures, students can "achieve at best only a superficial knowledge of the larger picture" (Ricketts et al., 2011, p. v).

Progressive educators and historians, by contrast, see state and national curriculum frameworks as insufficiently historic, multicultural, and educational. In books and articles, they urge a dramatic refocusing of the history content that is taught in schools: Howard Zinn presents a "people's history"; James Loewen seeks to "teach what really happened"; Ronald Takaki looks through a "different mirror"; Ray Raphael reveals "founding" and "constitutional myths"; Henry Louis Gates explores African American "life upon these shores"; Ellen Carol DuBois and Lynn Dumenil view history "through women's eyes"; and Ray Suarez honors Latino Americans' "500-year legacy that shaped a nation."

These writers and many more directly resist calls by conservative commentators for a greater emphasis on teaching traditional American history in schools. Acknowledging the importance of the founding documents, they envision curriculum that emphasizes the ways in which the principles of freedom, justice, and equality have been systematically denied to African Americans, Native Americans, women, and other groups in society throughout American history. They urge thorough examination of our capitalist economic system to reveal historical disparities of wealth and poverty and the destructive contemporary impacts of economic and social inequality. They stress the expansionist nature of American foreign policy and its uses of armed force around the world. As Ray Raphael (2009) noted at the beginning of his book *Founders*, "if the American nation is about 'the people,' our national narrative must be too" (p. xiii).

Collective Memory and the Cultural Curriculum

Employing the concepts of "collective memory" and the "cultural curriculum," Stanford University historian and teacher educator Sam Wineburg explores how everyday people develop views of history apart from the school classroom. In one study, Wineburg and his colleagues (Wineburg, Mosburg, Porat, & Duncan, 2007) followed a group of 15 high school students from three very different schools (an inner-city high school, an elite college preparatory academy, and an Evangelical Christian school) during their 11th- and 12th-grade school years. Presenting iconic photographs from the Vietnam War era, the researchers interviewed the students about their historical knowledge of the time period. Despite the differences among the students, their families, and their schooling, the researchers found a common narrative in the responses: "How America entered the conflict, what happened on the battlefield, and how a cloud of despair hung over the nation in the war's aftermath." Among White and non-White, affluent and poor, native-born and immigrant, Christian and nonpracticing individuals, these "young peoples' narrative bore a remarkable likeness" (Wineburg et al., 2007, p. 173).

Little information from high school history/social studies classes were part of the students' narratives, even for youngsters whose teachers discussed the 1954 Geneva Conference that partitioned Vietnam, the parallels between the American "Declaration of Independence" and the "Declaration of Independence of the Democratic Republic of Vietnam," or the role of the Vietnam Veterans Against the War in reversing American public opinion about war policies. Nor did the students mimic the views of their parents, who had lived through the time period and had sharply divided views about the purpose and effect of American involvement in Vietnam. These students had developed their own perspectives from their own societal experiences.

To explain common narratives among students the researchers turned to the ideas of "collective memory" and "the cultural curriculum" (Wineburg, 2001). Collective memory refers to what someone has learned, as opposed to what is remembered from lessons at school. Discussing the Vietnam War era, these youngsters' collective memory included "soldiers fighting" and "hippies protesting." There was no recall about prowar demonstrations or George McGovern's defeat as the "peace candidate" in the 1968 presidential campaign.

The students' collective memories are a product of what Wineburg calls a "cultural curriculum," a compelling, memorable set of assumptions, influences, and generalizations, largely conveyed by the media and the popular culture. Not a formalized or agreed on collection of standards or lesson plans, the cultural curriculum is a "'sensitizing concept' that points to the distributed nature of learning in modern society" (Wineburg & Monte-Sano, 2008).

As a cultural artifact, the 1994 movie *Forrest Gump* was one of the key influences on student impressions about the Vietnam War. Most students had seen the film; in two of the three schools in the study, it was required viewing in history/social studies classes. *Forrest Gump* presented an uncomplicated narrative of the Vietnam era with the complexities and nuances of the time glossed over by the movie's compelling narrative thread. The movie's main character flows in and out of the key historical events of the time, but those events have little meaning beyond the film's images.

Yet they generate long lasting, strongly held impressions for viewers about what happened historically during that time.

The cultural curriculum has a profound effect on how students think about history. Hollywood movies, television documentaries, school-sponsored trips to national monuments, or rap artists "may be far more powerful in shaping young people's ideas about the past than the mountains of textbooks that continue to occupy historians' and educators' attention" (Wineburg et al., 2007, p. 176). The cultural curriculum produces widely shared common knowledge about the past despite the economic, social, and political experiences that divide many Americans. Youngsters who are rich or poor; urban, suburban, or rural; and White or non-White have learned certain ideas from the culture; ideas that Wineburg suggests need no "proof text nor justification" (2007, p. 176).

In another revealing study, Wineburg asked high school students and ordinary adults aged 45 and over to list the most famous figures in American history, not including presidents or first ladies. Eight of the 10 most-named figures were the same for both groups, suggesting the reach of shared information and shared assumptions across generations (Wineburg & Monte-Sano, 2008). The challenge, concluded Wineburg et al. (2007), is for teachers and students to find "new ways to engage the cultural curriculum that engulfs them" by identifying "the history that does or does not 'seep into cultural pores'" (p. 177).

Voices of Teacher Candidates:
Teaching Academic Content to Students

History and social studies teaching candidates in our program, like many experienced classroom educators, are struggling to negotiate their way through politically intensified debates about the teaching of history as well as broad, sometimes competing, sets of academic curriculum standards. Not surprisingly, given all of the information and controversy surrounding the teaching of history, candidates have strong opinions about curriculum frameworks, textbooks, and what history teachers should teach.

When asked "What does contrasting content mean to you?" candidates repeatedly defined contrasting content in terms of opposing and untold stories. One candidate said, "contrasting content means to see both sides of the story," whereas another stated, "contrasting content means looking at history from multiple perspectives." Still another new teacher saw contrasting content as a teacher serving as a point/counterpoint or devil's advocate, "to deliberately go against what your students will most likely rationalize as 'normal.' "

Some candidates divided history content into two, mostly mutually exclusive categories, the traditional and the untold, as in this statement by a high school teacher candidate: "contrasting content includes seeing pro and con sides of arguments, good and bad effects of certain events, and the perspectives of those people that are not included in the 'majority.' " Others expanded the idea of content to feature many or multiple categories: "Contrasting content means exactly what it says—introducing different perspectives so that students can compare and contrast lessons from multiple perspectives. It includes providing competing narratives, untold stories, and ideas that may not be widely known with respect to a topic."

Asked to describe how contrasting content happens in the classroom, teacher candidates cited the importance of multiple sources of information as a way to provide students with many ways to look at people and events: "I like to give students primary and secondary sources other than the textbook," noted one high school candidate, "so that they can see the differences in how each source presents history." She went on to say, "I also ask students to find examples of bias in what they read as well to discuss which histories and herstories are often written out of history textbooks."

Other candidates stressed the importance of discussion and debate as a way to broaden the content that is being taught. Discussion and debates assured candidates they were being fair-minded and neutral rather than giving their own opinions about historical matters. As one middle school intern noted, "If we push the views we believe upon students, we are not giving them the opportunity to explore their own creativity and critical thinking skills."

Following along with the idea that discussions and debates are essential components of expansive teaching, a high school candidate indicated "contrasting content looks like classroom discussions that are not directly related in the learning targets." He told the story of how a lively debate had occurred in a world history class about the rights of Western archaeologists and museums to remove artifacts from countries such as Egypt and Greece—both in the past and in the present. Although this topic was not in the lesson plan for the day, he found pleasure in how "students shared their feelings pro and con about disturbing ancient tombs and burial sites for the sake of academic knowledge."

Having expressed a high level of commitment with the idea of contrasting content, candidates struggled with how to implement this democratic teaching practice. Citing the ever-present constraints of covering the curriculum frameworks and following the school's chosen textbook, they felt there was too much to teach and too little time to do so. Accompanying this view was a prevailing fear of losing control of the class when raising controversial or untold topics. They were not sure how students might react to serious discussions about North American slavery, the atomic bombing of Japanese cities, McCarthyism, Iran/Contra, or the current wars in Iraq and Afghanistan.

Candidates were perplexed about how curriculum frameworks required by school systems could include contrasting content for students. A middle school geography teacher told us that she was "confused as to how contrasting content plays out in my world geography classroom where the standards are so bland and particularly people-centric. It's not as though the standards tell me to teach one dominant viewpoint. There really isn't a viewpoint. The standards are basic, dry, and uninspiring." It took time and trial and error before she found ways to teach required material in contrasting ways: "I turn dry standards such as locating countries on a map or studying population statistics or basic economic concepts such as supply and demand into content and lessons that put people and their needs at the forefront." She also noted that while studying the Middle East as a geographic region, she included examining stereotypes about Arabs, Muslims, and the Middle East in general.

Several candidates expressed ideas about methods to integrate contrasting content in teaching. A high school candidate noted that in his plans, "contrasting content shows as either a discussion or a debate." Another candidate at the same school stated: "Democratic teaching doesn't just mean allowing students greater voice in rules, classroom structures or in how they learn. It's also about the content that is taught. It's about creating student-centered lessons where students are exposed to and analyze many different viewpoints (many of which have been left out the history books) and then allowing students to come to their own conclusions and solutions." Also seeing a direct connection to democratic teaching, a middle school candidate stated "contrasting content can make students see things that they may not have noticed before and allowing them to air their thoughts promotes a democratic classroom by giving students a chance to share their feelings/views."

Contrasting Strategies for Building Democracy

At the beginning of his book, *A Different Mirror: A History of Multicultural America*, and as part of his speaking engagements at colleges and conferences around the country, historian Ronald Takaki (2008) tells the story of a cab ride he took from the airport to a meeting in Virginia Beach, Virginia more than three decades ago. Takaki, a slender man of Asian descent, was gazing out the window when the cab driver, a White man in his 40s asked, "How long have you been in this country?" Momentarily taken back, Takaki, whose grandfather had come to America from Japan more than 100 years earlier, replied "All my life."

Recalling the experience later, Takaki realized that an Asian man traveling from the airport to the Virginia seashore, did not fit a conception of "looking American." "What had he learned about Asian Americans in courses called U.S. history?" Takaki (2008, p. 4) thought of the driver's intent to begin a conversation. The cab driver, using the frame of reference he possessed, did not consider the long history of Asian Americans struggling to achieve status and place in American society because this may never have been part of his cultural or historical knowledge.

This chapter's "Building Democracy" activities focus on ways that teachers and students can use the content and language of school textbooks and curriculum frameworks to uncover and discover hidden histories and untold stories of the multicultural past. We start with textbooks and how they become sources to be analyzed rather than collections of facts to be memorized for a test. We introduce the idea of "curriculum uncoverage" to show that teaching democratically involves accessing hidden histories and untold stories to build curriculum that integrates multicultural content in substantive and transformative ways. Finally, we propose that teachers and students examine language use in curriculum materials to understand the ideas and assumptions contained in academic terms.

Strategy: Analyzing Textbooks

Large and lengthy, textbooks present the past chronologically, acknowledging "important" names, dates, events, and places through a particular lens of historical analysis or point of view. Many history/social studies teachers rely on textbooks to transmit common ideas, assigning pages as required reading and testing students to assess recall and understanding of information. Students lament the linear, text-based presentations in textbooks, finding them uninteresting, or, with newer editions, densely packed with overwhelming amounts of visual images, graphs, and related sidebars on each page.

Researchers have been critiquing public school history textbooks for decades. Francis Fitzgerald (1980) documented the ways textbooks presented different periods of American history, actually revealing more about the time period when the books were published than about the historical topics discussed. Diane Ravitch (2003, p. 8) has argued that textbook publishers, in an effort to eliminate bias against different societal groups, have intentionally narrowed and diluted the presentation of historical topics, stripping "away everything that is potentially thought-provoking and colorful."

Examining disputes over the content of history textbooks since the Civil War, Joseph Moreau (2004) found that publishers concentrated on "unifying myths" at times in the past when Americans were struggling to "reinterpret the past and forge a new consensus about it" (p. 24). As Moreau noted, "a bit of historical amnesia can make it easier for people to imagine themselves as a single body," but "repressing truths about subjects central to a country's identity, like slavery or racism . . . makes it impossible to construct a version of the past that doesn't collapse under its contradictions" (pp. 337–338).

Shortcomings and distortions in textbooks are not restricted to American history. Examining five popular world history textbooks in light of recent scholarship, researcher Michael Marino (2011) found that although the book titles promised "world history," the content emphasized "Western civilization." At least 55% of page content (and in some texts more) focused on European history. Although many historians argue that "world history is about defining a version of historical chronology that transcends the history of any one geographic region and creates a global vision of the past," the textbooks being used in schools are "firmly ensconced in a Western version of historical chronology and evolution" (pp. 441–442).

Exploring How Textbooks Present the Past

James Loewen, an outspoken critic of history education in K–12 schools, suggests that students and teachers analyze each textbook for its strengths and weaknesses as a presentation of the past. Loewen's books include *Lies My Teacher Told Me: Everything Your American History Textbook Got Wrong* (2005) and *Teaching What Really Happened: How To Avoid the Tyranny of Textbooks and Get Students Excited About Doing History* (2010).

Examining the lives and works of Helen Keller and Woodrow Wilson as representative case studies, Loewen finds that textbooks offer biographical facts while omitting controversial political realities. Students read how Helen Keller as a blind and deaf girl who overcame her physical disabilities, but they do not learn that she was a radical socialist who worked tirelessly to improve the lives of poor and disenfranchised Americans, contributed to the NAACP, helped to found the ACLU, championed birth control, and protested outside a theater showing a movie of her life because the film focused on her disabilities and not her political activism.

In textbooks, Woodrow Wilson is presented as a courageous president who led the country during World War I, but not as the commander in chief who sent troops to intervene in Latin America more often than any other time in American history. Nor do textbooks capture the complex nature of the man who wept at his White House desk after asking Congress to declare war on Germany, a speech in which he declared: "It is a fearful thing to lead this great peaceful people into war, into the most terrible and disastrous of all wars, civilization itself seeming to be in the balance."

For Loewen, the examples of Helen Keller and Woodrow Wilson reveal a fundamental problem with textbooks. Caught between "the conflicting desires to promote inquiry and to indoctrinate blind patriotism," the vast majority of history textbooks reflect historical facts and perspectives in selective slices, not in fluid panoramic views (Loewen, 2010, p. 6). They compress the past into bits on timelines, leading students to think, in a simplified context, of history as sequential information to be memorized rather than people's actions, decisions, and choices to be analyzed and understood.

Instead, Loewen (2010) urges "schools to help us learn how to ask questions about our society and its history and figure out answers for ourselves" (p. 356). Students can act as editors of their textbooks, adding historically accurate information about the struggles and accomplishments of individuals and groups while locating examples of bias, inconsistency, and inaccuracy within the text (Ward, 2010, p. xv). This will generate a wider view of historical experience, for as African American poet James Baldwin observed: "history is longer, larger, more various, more beautiful, and more terrible than anything anyone has ever said about it."

Introducing Students to Alternative Texts

Beginning in 1980 with the publication of the first edition of *A People's History of the United States* (1980/2010), historian Howard Zinn has produced a host of materials that challenge traditional textbooks while providing teachers and students with alternative content for the study of history. *A People's History* alone has sold more than 1 million copies.

Zinn's writing crosses multiple genres: young adult: *A Young People's History of the United States* (Zinn & Stefoff, 2007); primary sources: *Voices of a People's History of the United States* (Zinn & Arnove, 2004); graphic comix: *A People's History of the American Empire* (Zinn, Konopacki, & Buhle, 2008); memoir: *You Can't Be Neutral on a Moving Train: A Personal History of Our Times* (Zinn, 2002), and anthology: *The Zinn Reader: Writings on Disobedience and Democracy* (Zinn, 2009).

All these books present voices that "have mostly been shut out of the orthodox histories, the major media, the standard textbooks, the controlled culture" (Zinn & Arnove, 2004, p. 24). Standard curriculum and traditional teaching create what Zinn calls a "passive citizenry, not knowing its powers" to enact change in society. Students need to learn when and where people rose against oppression to remake society, for "history looked at under the surface, in the streets and on the farms, in GI barracks and trailer camps, in factories and offices, tells a different story" (Zinn & Arnove, 2004, p. 24).

Zinn's critically minded history books for student readers, notes media critic James Heflin (2011, p. 20), offer an approach that is very different from the "sober, distanced analysis" of mainstream history textbooks, viewing history "from a broad perspective, discussing how events impact nations and societies." Other writers have followed Zinn in exploring the experiences of everyday people, notably *A People's History of the American Revolution* (Raphael, 2002), *A People's History of the World* (Harman, 2008), *A People's History of Christianity* (Bass, 2010), *A People's History of the Supreme Court* (Irons, 2006), and *A People's History of the Sports in the United States* (Zirin, 2009). Although mainstream textbooks can be useful teaching tools, they "ride along on waves of dates and numbers and non-gripping narratives" (Heflin, 2011, p. 20). By contrast, alternative texts enable students and teachers to see history "up-close and personal" through first-person narratives and compelling stories.

Alternative texts present an important point/counterpoint to mainstream textbooks. As they read and discuss the textbook, students and teachers can examine different presentations about a topic and compare it with what the textbook tells them. Further information can be added using primary sources and historical studies. This mixture of information from different perspectives creates a more nuanced, historically complex portrait of people, places, and events where students must make informed judgments about cause and effect, motivation, and power, probing deeply into events to understand their meaning and impact.

Exploring Hidden Histories and Untold Stories

Hidden histories and untold stories refers to the experiences of individuals and groups who are mostly absent from textbooks and curriculum frameworks, particularly women, African Americans, Native Americans, Mexican Americans, gays, lesbians, and workers. As a guide for contrasting curriculum content, students and teachers can use national or state curriculum standards to explore hidden histories and untold stories from different historical time periods.

Table 1.1 shows how students and teachers can connect hidden histories and untold stories to curriculum frameworks, using examples from both the U.S. History advanced placement (AP) and Massachusetts learning standards.

Any learning standard from any curriculum framework can be a starting point for uncovering the hidden histories and untold stories of diverse individuals and groups. The goal is to first see what the state or national standard expects teachers to teach and students to learn. Then, students and teachers collectively identify and learn about individuals, groups, and events that have been omitted or neglected by the standard.

Many excellent resources support the hidden history/untold stories research process. *The Secret Histories*, an anthology of documents assembled by John S. Friedman (2005), is a useful companion for exploring the untold stories of the recent past. It features the work of courageous journalists who lifted the veil of government secrets including I. F. Stone's expose of the Korean War, Edward R. Murrow's report on Sen. Joseph McCarthy, and Seymour Hersh's investigations of the My Lai massacre and torture at Abu Ghraib. These secret histories enlarge often told textbook accounts by offering students more complex historical understandings.

Ray Raphael, a history researcher at Humboldt State University, writes about the hidden histories of the American Revolutionary era. His recent books include *Constitutional Myths: What We Get Wrong and How To Get It Right* (2013), *The First American Revolution: Before Lexington and Concord* (2011), *Founders: The People Who Brought You a Nation* (2009), and *Founding Myths: Stories that Hide Our Patriotic Past* (2004). Eric Foner's *Voices of Freedom: A Documentary History* (2010) has an impressive collection of primary sources for use in the classroom while his historical writing focuses on Civil War and Reconstruction periods in American history, notably T*he Fiery Trial: Abraham Lincoln and American Slavery* (2011). "If We Know Our History," a regular column on the Zinn Education Project website, features articles by teachers and researchers explicitly challenging myths and stereotypes found in mainstream textbooks.

The films of Ken Burns are a compelling source of contrasting content. His made-for-television documentaries, notes media scholar Gary R. Edgerton (2001, p. vii), have focused on "epic events, landmarks and

Table 1.1. Hidden Histories and Untold Stories by Learning Standards

Learning Standard	Hidden History/Untold Story Topic
Massachusetts Grade 5.31: Describe the significance and consequences of the abolition of slavery in the northern states after the Revolution and of the 1808 law that banned the importation of slaves in the United States.	**Benjamin Banneker:** A free Black astronomer, mathematician, surveyor, author and farmer whose opposition to slavery was published in *Benjamin Banneker's Almanac*, a collection of scientific information (compared with Benjamin Franklin's *Poor Richard's Almanac*), published annually between 1792 and1797.
Massachusetts United States History I.4: Analyze how Americans resisted British policies before 1775 and analyze the reasons for the American victory and the British defeat during the Revolutionary War. *AP United States History Theme 4:* The American Revolutionary Era, 1754–1789	Seeking freedom from slavery, Blacks fought on both sides of the Revolution; an estimated 5,000 served in the Continental Army (including the First Rhode Island regiment) or at sea, whereas others resettled in Sierra Leone, Australia, and Nova Scotia.
Massachusetts United States History I.28: Explain the emergence and effect of the textile industry in New England and industrial growth throughout antebellum America. *AP United States History Theme 6:* Transformation of the Economy and Society in Antebellum America	**Lowell Mill Girls:** Women and young girls in the textile mills were part of the development of the Factory Girls Association and the Strike of 1836 in Lowell, Massachusetts.
Massachusetts United States History II.9: Analyze the post-Civil War struggles of women and Blacks in gaining basic rights *AP United States History Theme 17:* Populism and Progressivism	**Ida B. Wells**: Wells, an early civil rights activist, journalist, and anti-lynching campaigner refused to give up her seat in a Jim Crow-era railroad car, setting in motion a seminal court case that challenged segregation.
AP United States History Theme 19: The 1920s	**Tulsa Race Riots:** Rioters burned Oklahoma's second largest Black community in 1921, destroying more than 1,000 homes and businesses and killing as many as 300 people.

Massachusetts United States History II.17: Explain the important domestic events that took place during World War II.	**Zoot Suit Riots**: Race riots in Los Angeles in 1943 directed against Mexican Americans and involving racial profiling by the police.
AP United States History Theme 22: The Home Front During the War	**Navajo Code Talkers**: The role of Native Americans in creating a military communication code based on the Navajo language that the Japanese forces could not break during World War II.
Massachusetts United States History II.24: Analyze the roots of domestic anti-communism as well as the origins and consequences of McCarthyism. *Advanced Placement United States History Theme 24*: The 1950s	**The Lavender Scare**: Persecution and criminalization of gay and lesbian federal employees during the 1950s.

institutions of historical significance . . . understood through the popular mythology of America's collective memory." Weaving throughout the films are the often hidden histories of African Americans, women, and other dispossessed groups, all framed in terms of American ideals of democracy and justice for all.

In the classroom, every Burns film connects historical people and events to contemporary audiences in emotionally empathetic ways. As a biographer, Burns is able to "stimulate powerful feelings of intimacy in audience members as they watch and relate to the featured characters' life stories" (Edgerton, 2001, p. viii). The "American Lives" series (Thomas Jefferson, Lewis and Clark, Frank Lloyd Wright, Elizabeth Cady Stanton, Mark Twain, Horatio's Drive, and Jack Johnson) is now available on iTunes. In 2014, Burns released an iPad app that enables students and teachers to view mixtapes drawn from more than 8,000 minutes of film from 23 award-winning documentaries, organized by themes of innovation, race, politics, art, hard times, and war. In the classroom, with handheld cameras or smartphones, students and teachers can write, document, and film their own videos about historical topics, adding music, and using the "Ken Burns effect" of zooming in and out of still photographs to sustain interest and involvement by viewers.

Writing a "post-Loewen" view of history for students is a complex process, notes Scott L. Roberts (2013) about his efforts to write a revised version of the Georgia state history book, *Time Travel Through Georgia*. At the outset, Roberts (2013) had six Loewen-inspired goals for his revision, each intended to address the inaccuracies and biases found in other state textbooks:

1. remove unnecessary information/focus on the standards;

2. remove heroification;

3. make the text relevant to the lives of students;

4. remove the tone of an omniscient/noncritical narrator;

5. incorporate more historical sources; and

6. limit the assumption that Georgia's history and culture was superior to those of other states.

Meeting these goals proved difficult for Roberts. The publisher deleted critical assessments of some historical figures (e.g., an analysis of Woodrow Wilson's presidency) to meet page-limit requirements. Colleagues and teachers criticized sections of the book as not informative enough about the Battle of Gettysburg or Hernando de Soto's cruelty toward native peoples. History book authors, concluded Roberts (2013), have to compromise about what to include in a text while, most importantly, students and teachers have to "learn how to locate and use different sources in order to prevent the overuse of textbooks" (p. 57).

Strategy: Uncovering and Discovering the Past

In 1968, Bill Cosby narrated *Black History: Lost, Stolen or Strayed?* a CBS News television special critiquing the absence of African Americans in history textbooks. Andy Rooney wrote the Emmy Award-winning script. As the film opens, Cosby, then a young actor and humorist, enters an elementary school classroom while the children are exiting for recess. When the room is empty, he begins recounting stories of African Americans who have accomplished great things in history, but who are not in textbooks, before pointing out it is less important whether a few Black heroes were lost, stolen, or strayed from the textbooks than why they were left out. Societal and institutional racism systematically fails to give credence or agency to the actions of African Americans in American history.

Key to going beyond mainstream histories is understanding the words *coverage* and *uncoverage*, note Grant Wiggins and Jay McTighe (2005, p. 16), the authors of the *Understanding by Design* approach to curriculum development. In the authors' view, coverage is a "negative term (whereas introduction or survey is not)." When teachers put an emphasis on covering the material, "the student is led through unending facts, ideas, and readings with little or no sense of the overarching ideas, issues, and learning goals that might inform study" (p. 16). Uncoverage involves "guided inquiry into big ideas, where knowledge is made more connected, meaningful, and useful" for students (p. 104).

Historian Lendol Calder also champions "uncoverage" as an approach to curriculum development. In a 2006 *Journal of American History* article, Calder contrasted the scholarly work of practicing historians with the realities of teaching history to students. The structure of basic history survey courses (Calder was discussing courses for college undergraduates but his points apply to public schools as well) "require professors to pass on essential information about a time period." Covering curriculum in a "facts first" framework involves lectures, assigned readings, and written exams; what Calder characterizes as the "signature pedagogy" for teaching history to beginning students. All too often, the result is disengaged, disinterested students who feel overwhelmed by the amount of information they must remember. Similar student responses happen in public schools when history classes resemble college survey courses where teachers try to cover as much content as possible within the school year.

Calder proposes challenging the "signature pedagogy" of coverage. Coverage, he notes, has many meanings from "to go the length of" all the way "to conceal." Many lecture-based survey courses stressing dates over information embody this second meaning, keeping students from experiencing the "inquires, arguments, assumptions, and points of view" that encompass the work of historians and social scientists. Students need to examine primary sources and draw conclusions about the causes and consequences of events based on historical evidence. Without opportunities to do this, students do not experience debates. Instead, they assume that the meaning of the past has already been decided when in fact it is constantly being revisited and revised.

Examining Historical Events Thematically

The National Council for the Social Studies (NCSS; 1994, 2010) organizes curriculum standards around 10 themes drawn from different social science fields to create interdisciplinary approaches to the design, delivery and assessment of instruction:

1. Culture and cultural diversity,

2. Time, continuity, and change,

3. People, places, and environment,

4. Individual development and identity,

5. Individuals, groups, and institutions,

6. Power, authority, and governance,

7. Production, distribution, and consumption,

8. Science technology and society,

9. Global connections, and

10. Civic ideals and practices.

Using the academic concepts and tools of different social science disciplines, curriculum topics can be studied from multiple perspectives. One example is King Philip's War of 1675–78 (also known as Metacom's War or Metacom's Rebellion), a brutal and bloody struggle that occurred between Native Americans loyal to the Wampanoag tribal leader Metacom and English settlers and their Native American allies throughout New England. In Massachusetts schools, King Philip's War is studied in fifth grade as part of the learning standard: "Explain the early relationship of the English settlers to the indigenous peoples, or Indians, in North America, including the different views on ownership or use of land and the conflicts between them (e.g., the Pequot and King Philip's Wars in New England [Massachusetts Department of Education, 2003])." King Philip's War might also be taught in U.S. History AP Theme 2: "Transatlantic Encounters and Colonial Beginnings, 1492–1690."

King Philip's War was a seminal event in colonial North America; it "cleared southern New England's native population from the land, and with it a way of life that had evolved over a millennium" (Schultz & Tougias, 2000, p. 1). Native peoples were "slaughtered, sold into slavery, or placed in widely scattered communities throughout New England after the war." Over time, the war has been largely neglected in textbooks and curriculum frameworks. But there is much for students to learn from this struggle. Contrasting the popular view of native peoples feasting peacefully with

Pilgrims at the first Thanksgiving with the violence of King Philip's War and the public display of Metacom's severed head in Plymouth after the war, two historians conclude the "real tragedy is how we came to embrace one image and lose the other" (Schultz & Tougias, 2000, p. 2).

Table 1.2 shows how students and teachers might use the NCSS themes to construct a wide-angle view of King Philip's War. Such an NCSS theme-inspired collage of historical and social science viewpoints can be constructed for any historical event to reveal how individuals, groups, and nations respond to events while showing the effects of culture, geography, politics, economics, and technology on people and places.

Table 1.2. NCSS Themes and King Philip's War

Theme 1: Culture and cultural diversity	Depictions of Native American culture in U.S. history textbooks
Theme 2: Time, continuity, and change	Timeline and outcomes of native/settler conflicts throughout the colonies
Theme 3: People, places, and environment	Land-use patterns by native people and colonial settlers
Theme 4: Individual development and identity	Motivations of native leaders in opposing or developing alliances with settlers
Theme 5: Individuals, groups, and institutions	Social organization of native and colonial communities
Theme 6: Power, authority, and governance	Nature of colonial governments and charters
Theme 7: Production, distribution, and consumption	Trading relationships involving native peoples and European settlers
Theme 8: Science, technology, and society	Native longhouses and colonial cabins as environmental adaptations
Theme 9: Global connections	North American empires of England, France, and Spain
Theme 10: Civic ideals and practices	Decision making and governmental systems within native tribes and colonial towns and villages

The Civil Rights Movement offers another opportunity for thematic teaching using contrasting content. As the Southern Poverty Law Center (SPLC) has documented, the great 20th-century African American struggle for justice and equality is poorly taught in the nation's schools. On balance, "students are likely to remember only two names and four words about the Civil Rights Movement: Martin Luther King Jr., Rosa Parks, and 'I Have a Dream'" (Teaching Tolerance, 2014, p. 9). Evaluating state curriculum frameworks, the SPLC gave an overall average national grade of D with 20 states earning an F and only 3 states—Louisiana, South Carolina, and Georgia—receiving an A.

What is needed, according to the SPLC, is for students and teachers to understand the civil rights struggle as a national, not a regional event that remains unfinished and unfulfilled, with issues of race and inequality continuing to dominate and distort our national experience. Teaching civil rights thematically enlarges how students and teachers see these issues, establishing a broad historical context that extends throughout the nation's history and still resonates today as communities become re-segregated and voting rights are challenged by restrictive state laws. Outstanding teaching and learning resources are available from the departments of education in Alabama, Louisiana, South Carolina, Georgia, Maryland, Virginia, Pennsylvania, North Carolina, and Utah, notes the SPLC.

Integrating Multicultural Content

James A. Banks, professor and director of the Center for Multicultural Education in the College of Education at the University of Washington, is the author of well-known books and more than 100 articles examining multicultural learning. He was the first recipient of the American Educational Research Association (AERA) Social Justice in Education award in 2004. Banks focuses on how teachers can incorporate hidden histories and untold stories in curriculum and instruction. He argues for the necessity of shifting the learning lens from the mainstream to the margins as a way to bring the broader stories of history and society into classes.

To expand multicultural K–12 curriculum and instruction, teachers and students can use Banks's (1991, 2007) framework for "Integrating Ethnic Content.

> Level 1: "Contributions" focuses attention on heroes, holidays and events associated with different racial or ethnic groups in American society.

Level 2: "Additive" contributes multicultural material to the curriculum throughout the school year without broad explorations of the experiences of people of color in history or society.

Level 3: "Transformation" diverts attention from a traditional emphasis on majority culture and history to examine events from the perspectives of people of color and social groups usually omitted from textbooks and curriculum materials.

Level 4: "Social Action" extends the transformational approach from examining the experiences of people of color academically to students and teachers engaging in community-based steps to address longstanding social problems and inequities.

Banks' four levels establish a broad framework for integrating hidden histories, untold stories, and multicultural content into history/social studies classes. It shows teachers and students ways to expand and deepen studies of past and present, by generating contrasting content and promoting curriculum "uncoverage."

As a class activity, groups of students can "Banks-ize" historical topics, envisioning how curriculum might be expanded across the four levels of content integration. Exploring the history of African American soldiers, for example, a contributions and additive approach might feature the stories of the First Rhode Island Regiment (Revolutionary War), the 54th Regiment of Massachusetts Volunteers (Civil War), the 92nd and 93rd Divisions (World War I), and the Tuskegee Airmen (World War II). A transformation approach would add the voices of soldiers and political leaders that document patriotism and heroism in the face of discrimination and prejudice. Frederick Douglass's call for Black soldiers during the Civil War is one notable primary source example. A social action approach could focus on how fully integrated organizations where men and women of different races and sexual orientations can function effectively.

Strategy: Understanding Academic Language

Asking students and teachers to analyze how textbooks and curriculum frameworks use words, vocabulary, symbols, phrases, and other language conventions promotes critical thinking about language use in every type of social or political situation. Textbooks and frameworks are written in "academic language," a formalized presentation of information common to scholarly writing and standardized tests. Academic language has been defined as "the language needed by students to do the work in schools" (Herr, 2007).

Academic language is different from the conversational language used by students and teachers in everyday life. Words and phrases used informally with family and friends have different meanings and implications in academic settings. Students need to know how English varies in different contexts. Public documents, primary sources, political speeches, television advertisements, online blog and commentaries, and corporate reports are examples of language contexts that students will need to read and understand in a democratic society.

Analyzing the Language of History Textbooks

Students and teachers can begin their study of academic language by making history textbooks sources to be analyzed. As one case study, we use the building of the transcontinental railroad, a momentous event in American history given how the railroad business would transform the economy, politics, and collective identity of not only the West, but the entire nation as well. In *Out of Many: A History of the American Nation*, historian John Mack Faragher and his co-authors (Faragher, Buhle, Armitage, & Czitrom, 2001) discuss the Transcontinental Railroad under the subheading, "The Age of Capital." In the 1999 edition of the book, railroad building receives about one page of densely packed two-column text; the 2001 edition adds a color picture of the celebrated meeting of two locomotives at Promontory Point, Utah on May 10, 1869.

Sophisticated academic language and complex sentence structure present the book's information: ""Railroads required huge outlays of investment capital, and their growth increased the economic power of banks and investment houses centered in Wall Street"; "Railroad promoters, lawyers, and lobbyists became ubiquitous figures in Washington and state capitals, wielding enormous influence among lawmakers"; and "A new breed of aggressive entrepreneur sought to ease cutthroat competition by absorbing smaller companies and forming 'pools' that set rates and divided the market" (Faragher et al., 2001, p. 323).

The text focuses on key industrialists and entrepreneurs (Cornelius Vanderbilt, Jay Gould, Collis P. Huntington, James J. Hill, Leland Stanford, and John D. Rockefeller), the Credit Mobilier scandal, and the National Mineral Act of 1866 as well as the role of federal government in funding the expansion of the nation's industries. The book briefly mentions that Irish American and African American workers along with Chinese laborers laid the track and that workers earned little money during physically crushing workweeks, but does not analyze the effect of the railroads on native peoples or Western society and culture. Many students find such textbook presentations dry and distant—removed from their lives and their interests—difficult to read and understand.

How does the academic language of textbooks shape students' understanding of history? Using the Cherokee Removal from Georgia and the Great Depression as case studies, two University of Georgia researchers found that textbook language actually may block students from understanding why events happen (Achugar & Schleppegrell, 2005). The use of abstract nouns, a passive voice, and the lack of explicit language about cause and effect leave an impression that what happened was inevitable rather than the results of people's decisions and actions.

One textbook analyzed by the Georgia research team mentions Cherokee "resistance" but does not define or explain it; whereas another textbook refers to an "uneven distribution of wealth" in the years before the Stock Market Crash of 1929 without providing any additional information about the financial differences between the rich and the poor. Lacking further explanation or more in-depth investigation, students see events simply happening on their own, the product of unseen forces beyond human intervention or control.

The National History Education Clearinghouse recommends that teachers proactively approach the language complexities of textbooks. Teachers and students read textbook passages together, unpacking the academic language and examining how cause and effect may be obscured by the vocabulary and the sentence structures. Pictures, charts, and graphs can be examined separately—students describe first what they see in the images, without trying to "correctly" explain the meaning. From these descriptions and analysis, connections between visual information and written text can emerge.

Other analyzing strategies include asking class members to write alternative versions of the text to provide a more complete picture of events. Primary source materials can be included to reveal participants and their motivations for action. In the words of educator Stanley L. Pesick (2011), the history classroom becomes a conversation between the teacher, the students, and the textbook, collectively and interactively building more complete understanding and knowledge.

In *Reading Like a Historian: Teaching Literacy In Middle and High School History Classrooms*, Wineburg et al. (2011) urge teachers and students to formulate thought-provoking questions about historical events, thereby redefining history as topics to investigate and reinterpret during class activities rather than memorize and regurgitate on a test. For example, when learning about the settlement of the Virginia colony, students might explore the question "Did Pocahontas save Captain John Smith from mortal danger or was this a figment of Smith's supple imagination?" (p. ix). Questions become the vehicle for in-depth historical study, sending students "back to original sources to formulate arguments that admit no easy answer. Each question requires us to marshal facts to argue our case" (p. v).

Through questioning, teachers and students examine historical context and decision making as historians do. Wineburg and his colleagues use the Lincoln–Douglas debates to illustrate the question-asking process: "What was the context for Lincoln's words? (A debate with Stephen O. Douglas for a fiercely contested Senate seat) When and where were those words uttered? (On September 22, 1858 in Ottawa, Illinois, a hotbed of anti-Black sentiment.)" (Wineburg et al., 2011, p. vi). Questions and evidence-based responses lead to further explorations and additional questions as students build thinking skills by analyzing and understanding history in context.

Analyzing the Language of Curriculum Frameworks

State curriculum frameworks, issued by all states except Rhode Island where learning standards are locally set, are another opportunity for academic language analysis and curriculum uncoverage. Teachers and students, expected to cover the frameworks, may use the standards as a launch for historical study. As with textbooks, students begin by expressing ideas and assumptions about key topics in the standards while teachers introduce primary sources and historical studies to expand knowledge and challenge commonly believed information.

Student viewpoints set the stage for meaningful historical questions; for example, "Did Rosa Parks refuse to give up her seat on a Montgomery, Alabama city bus because she was tired or because she was part of organized set of protests against White segregation throughout the South?" Exploring the historical evidence in primary and secondary sources, students can refute the often repeated myth that Rosa Parks was acting on her own, motivated by being tired after a long day at work. As Herbert Kohl (2007, p. 171) remarked at the end of his classic essay about the politics of children's literature: "As a tale of social movement and a community effort to overthrow injustice, the Rosa Parks' story opens the possibilities of every child identifying himself or herself as an activist, as someone who can help make justice happen."

A 2012 exhibition of Native American art hosted by the Berkshire Museum in Pittsfield, Massachusetts offers another example of analyzing the language and content of curriculum frameworks. The museum wanted visitors, including students from local schools, to question their assumptions and understandings about the histories of the native peoples of North America. The late 19th-/early 20th-century experiences of Native Americans are in the Massachusetts curriculum frameworks under U.S. History II.4: "Analyze the causes of the continuing westward expansion of the American people after the Civil War and the impact of this migration on the Indians." The U.S. History AP standards include native peoples in "Topic 9: Territorial Expansion and Manifest Destiny" and "Topic 14: The Development of the West in the late Nineteenth Century."

In pamphlets for visitors, the curators noted that in the early 20th century, the Berkshire Museum (like many museums around the country) began collecting different forms of Native American art, including clothing, headdresses, moccasins, pottery, bead work, pipes, and other artifacts. The intention was to document the "vanishing" cultures of North American Indian tribes. This museum has proudly displayed items from its collection for more than a century.

The problems with this approach to artifact collection and display were multifold, the museum frankly acknowledged. Native American cultures have not vanished, and although they remain vitally alive in this century as in they did in the previous ones, they are largely hidden from the view of mainstream American society. However, museum collections have tended to present the work of selected tribes as representative of all tribes, a view of culture and art that built and sustained White stereotypes of Native Americans and the settling of the West. Additionally, native artists at the time, aware of what museums and other buyers wanted, produced those items that would generate sales, further entrenching the idea of a unitary and fixed Native American culture.

The Berkshire Museum's exhibition, curated by half a dozen Native American artists and historians from different parts of the United States, brought into focus the richness and diversity of Native American life and art as well as the effects of cross-cultural encounters between native people and Euro-American settlers—historical realities not mentioned in the generalized language of curriculum frameworks. Euro-Americans, for example, adopted Native American materials to survive on the frontier (rawhide for clothing), whereas Native Americans adopted European materials for their own purposes (glass beads and wool making). Life for native people and settlers was transformed through these encounters.

As a way to start critically analyzing the language of state and district curriculum frameworks, we suggest teachers write responses to the following statements:

- The state (district's) curriculum frameworks are a positive development for teaching and learning because _____ .

- The state (district's) curriculum frameworks are a problematic development for teaching and learning because _____ .

- One key concept that teachers must teach from the state's (district's) curriculum framework is _____ .

- One key concept that teachers must teach not from the state's (district's) curriculum framework is _____ .

- If I were revising the frameworks, students would spend more time learning _____ .

- A major problem I have with how history is taught in schools is _____ .

- I expand history/social studies teaching beyond a recitation of names, dates, battles and famous people by _____ .

- I foster critical thinking and inquiry learning in history/social studies by _____ .

Answers to these questions generate ideas and assumptions about how to teach history in schools. Teachers might ask students to respond to the same questions. Teacher and student comments can be compared and discussed to provide further insights into how unexamined curriculum frameworks can push teachers and students toward covering rather than uncovering and discovering history/social studies content.

Conclusion

In this chapter, we explored the connections of contrasting history content and democratic teaching and learning in the history/social studies classrooms. Contrasting as a democratic teaching strategy means that teachers and students honor democracy's central premise that knowledgeable citizens thoughtfully assess multiple sets of information before making informed judgments about policy and society. It does not mean replacing one set of "truths" or explanations with another one.

Curriculum uncoverage is at the center of contrasting content, emphasizing untold stories and hidden histories that Zinn, Loewen, and other historians seek to bring into discussion and debate for students and teachers. Studying history by covering historical content minimizes the stories and struggles of individuals and groups left out of the history frameworks and textbooks. Broader viewpoints uncover people, events, and movements long ignored that provide contrast to mainstream knowledge and reveal a more democratic history for students to learn.

In society, broad and diverse information is essential. Democracy cannot function if democratic decision makers learn only one view of a story or event. Similarly, students have little opportunity to understand the choices of people and the causes of events if teachers provide access only to facts and interpretations contained in textbooks and curriculum frameworks. Democratically inclined teachers and students together must examine scenarios of "contrasting content" that mix the traditional and often told presentations of textbooks and curriculum frameworks with the hidden histories and untold stories of the past. Students' own presumptions, assumptions, and culturally formed notions can be contrasted with the official school curriculum to make a powerful mix of ideas and information leading to new understandings. Juxtaposing traditional and often told presentations with hidden histories and untold stories, students and teachers build frameworks for democratically inspired change in history/social studies education.

Chapter 2

Conducting

Student Engagement and Flipped Classrooms

> When I started teaching, everyone said I was good at lecturing: Students, colleagues, department chairs, and deans. And I liked lecturing. However, early in my teaching, it gnawed at me that the focus was on me and my teaching, not on students and their learning.
>
> —High School Teacher Candidate

Musician and theater critic Terry Teachout has written two acclaimed, but very different works about the life of the great jazz trumpeter Louis Armstrong: a biography, *Pops, A Life of Louis Armstrong* (2009), and *Satchmo at the Waldorf*, a one-man stage play memorably performed by actor John Douglas Thompson in 2012 at Shakespeare and Company in Lenox, Massachusetts. In Teachout's (2012) author's note for the *Satchmo at the Waldorf* playbill, he candidly discusses the difference between writing an historical biography and constructing a play for the stage. Book writing is a solitary process, "spending countless hours sitting alone in a room, shaping a mountain of research into a manuscript that I then delivered to my publisher." A stage play is a far more collaborative endeavor, the original script serving "more like a recipe" to be shaped into an onstage production by the director, actors, playwright, stage personnel, and ultimately the audience. Through many rehearsals, "all intellectual concepts must be translated into the language of concrete intention" (p. 1).

Teachout's distinction between a book and a stage play introduces *Conducting*, our second C of democratic teaching. Conducting refers to how the instructional methods and classroom practices that teachers use to deliver academic lessons to students—in both face-to-face and online settings—convey messages and lessons about democracy. Like writers or biographers, teachers must create lesson plans and curriculum units, often by themselves, before they can bring their material to an audience of students. It is in the classroom, through their use of instructional methods, that teachers translate their historical knowledge, intellectual concepts, and instructional lesson plans into what Teachout refers to as the "language of concrete intention."

Choices of instructional methods by teachers have enormous consequences for how students view their educational experiences. Classes dominated by teacher lectures convey the certainty of adult control, whereas classes featuring more interactive discussions promote greater student agency. Students make lasting judgments about their role in learning processes and their opportunities for voice and participation from how much class time is devoted to teacher-directed presentations in contrast with how often students are asked to evaluate primary sources, work together in groups, express their own ideas in writing, discuss controversial topics, integrate art or music into their learning, or experience other interactive and inquiry-based learning strategies.

Facing the day-to-day complexities of teaching, new teachers tend to teach the way they were taught, using teacher-directed lessons, whole-group instruction, desks arranged in rows, students listening/taking notes/completing worksheets, grades determined by scores on multiple-choice tests, and other practices familiar to them from their own experiences as middle and high school students. Such teaching practices, however, fail to engage many students who experience more active, engaging, informal learning environments in other parts of their lives. This chapter presents ideas to create more lively and inspiring teaching in classrooms for students from many backgrounds, learning styles, and levels of interest in the curriculum.

Transmission and Constructivist Approaches to Learning

In many schools today, as it has been historically, there is a deep division between teacher-centered (transmission) and student-centered (constructivist) approaches to teaching and learning in classrooms. In a transmission approach, teachers convey information to students who are expected to learn it and use it. "Knowledge is conceived as discrete facts commonly understood by everyone, and knowledge is fixed, something we can all point to and understand in the same way" (Coppola, 2004, p. 19). The teacher's goal is to "instruct" quickly, efficiently, and effectively so students learn the information. Students are the audience for planned presentations and are expected to learn through remembering material from a fixed curriculum and by completing class and homework assignments.

In history/social studies classrooms, teacher-centered methods most often happen through lecture and PowerPoint presentations by teachers, with historical content focused mainly on majority White culture and outcome expectations that students recall names, dates, and places on paper worksheets and multiple-choice tests. John Goodlad (1984) characterized such practices as a "frontal" approach to teaching—ideas and information flow primarily from the teacher to the students. Critics of teacher-centered instructional methods contend this type of adult-dominated communication obstructs engaged participation by members of a classroom community where all voices are heard and all ideas matter.

Transmission approaches foster interrogational interactions between teachers and students. For instance, in a teacher-centered classroom, teachers ask 95% of the questions, most of them requiring short answers and factual recall (Hmelo-Silver, 2003). In such situations, a small number of students answer teacher questions while much of the class remains passive, uninvolved with the academic material.

Constructivist approaches make the active engagement of students with academic material and real-life situations the dominant learning goal (Donovan & Bransford, 2000, 2005). Constructivist methods, also called "inquiry-based" or "experiential," present students with assignments, projects, and resources that raise questions about taken for granted or unexamined beliefs and assumptions. As students encounter, discuss, and investigate such questions and puzzles, they enlarge and reframe understandings, views, and values. The goal of the teacher is to create and sustain active learning, minds-on problem solving, and thoughtful reflection. In these methods, student talk is essential to the processes of assembling knowledge and discovering interconnections between different sets of information to construct new knowledge.

Student-Centered versus Teacher-Centered Learning

Education reformers from as far back as John Dewey in the 1930s have urged active, student-centered learning in schools. Summarizing what they call a "progressive consensus," researchers Steven Zemelman, Harvey Daniels, and Steven Hyde (2012) urge less whole-class, teacher-directed instruction, less student passivity, less reliance on standardized tests, and less time spent with textbooks or basal readers. They recount how educational research repeatedly shows students' learning flourishing from experiential learning activities, emphasis on higher-order thinking, time spent reading and discussing fiction and nonfiction books, opportunities for creative and analytical writing by students, and performance-based evaluations of student achievement.

In student-centered history/social studies classrooms, the goal is to build a "culture of inquiry" where teachers and students work together to investigate problems, pose solutions, and reflect about what they are learning (Doyle, 2008). Students are active participants in all elements of teaching and learning from planning lessons to conducting activities and experiments to engaging in discussions to participating in assessing learning outcomes. Students are engaged in "doing" history by analyzing sources and evidence, evaluating competing historical interpretations of events, and making informed judgments about past events and future policies. The role of teachers changes too, as educators "stop seeing themselves as curriculum *deliverers* and start seeing themselves as curriculum *creators*" (Wolk, 2008, p. 122).

Student-centered approaches view history/social studies learning extending from the active engagement of students with academic material and real-life situations. To implement the basic framework of constructivist and constructionist approaches, teachers create learning activities where students participate in minds-on problem solving and thoughtful reflection about academic experiences. Teachers raise questions about students' taken-for-granted, unexamined beliefs and assumptions about who did what and why in the past and in the present society. As students encounter and resolve meaningful questions about historical and contemporary situations, they incorporate new knowledge and understandings into their views and values.

Conservative reformers basically dismiss the usefulness of student-centered approaches, preferring instead direct instruction by teachers, strict discipline by school organizations, and assigned individual learning tasks for students as ways to improve learning outcomes as measured by standardized tests. In a 4-year study in nine low-performing schools in Los Angeles County, California, a team of researchers from Claremont Graduate University listed the key characteristics and qualities they found in the classrooms of 31 elementary, middle, and high school teachers whose students had done well on standardized achievement tests. Those teachers had "the highest percentage of students moving up a level on the English/language arts or math subtests of the California Standards Test for two to three years" (Poplin et al., 2011, p. 40). Among the students, 51% moved up a grade level, 34% maintained their grade level, and only 15% dropped a grade level.

According to the researchers, "traditional, explicit, teacher-directed instruction was by far the most dominant instructional practice" in these classrooms (p. 41). Lessons were based directly on state standards and drawn from official curriculum materials. Teachers gave "energetic content presentations and demonstrations," they "always *pushed* students" to do better, and instruction was followed by independent practice" (pp. 41–42). What the researchers found "least" effective in improving student test scores were constructivist practices; the student-centered methods they did observe were "used more for practice or a reward for learning rather than a route to it" (p. 41).

Constructivist or student-centered instruction stands in marked contrast to teacher-centered instructional methods. Student-centered classrooms emphasize interactive discussions, small-group work, cooperative learning, primary source analysis, creative writing, dramatic read-alouds, use of children's and adolescent literature, and a reliance on individual and group performance assessments rather than test-based assessments. Student-centered methods also promote democratic values of engagement and participation by making students active creators and shapers of school learning, precursors of the roles they will play in the future as members of a democratic society.

How Teachers Teach History

What is history and social studies teaching really like in elementary and secondary classrooms? In *How Teachers Taught: Constancy and Change in American Classrooms, 1890–1990,* historian Larry Cuban (1993) used photos, lesson plans, written reports, and other primary source data to document 100 years of classroom instruction in urban and rural K–12 schools. He found the contrast between teacher-centered and student-centered instruction has been longstanding and strident as has been the differences between what he called "incremental" and "fundamental" reforms. Incremental reforms "aim to improve the efficiency and effectiveness of existing structures" while fundamental reforms "aim to transform—alter permanently—those very same structures" (Cuban, 1993, p. 3).

To mark the differences between teacher-centered and student-centered classrooms, Cuban (1993) used six key indicators: arrangement of classroom furniture; ratio of teacher talk to student talk; whether most instruction occurs individually, in small groups, or with the entire class; the presence or absence of learning centers that are used by students as part of the normal school day; the degree of physical movement students are allowed without asking the teacher, and the degree of reliance on texts and use of varied instructional materials.

Over the decades, a typical teacher-centered classroom has consistently featured teachers transmitting knowledge and skills to students according to the teacher's plan with authoritarian management by adults. Student-centered instruction, by contrast, "means that students exercise a substantial degree of responsibility for what is taught, how it is learned, and for movement within the classroom" (Cuban, 1993, p. 7).

As one of his examples, Cuban described the physical arrangement of furniture and people in different classrooms. In a teacher-centered room, desks are placed in rows with the teacher at the front talking while students listen and take notes. In a student-centered class, the furniture is spread out around the room so students can work collaboratively while the teacher guides their studies. In addition to flexible furniture patterns, student-centered instruction featured learning settings where student talk was at least equal to teacher talk, small-group and individual instruction happened as well as whole-group activities, students participated in setting classroom rules, teachers used a variety of teaching methods, and students were involved in choosing instructional materials to read and view.

What actually happened was more of a hybrid of both instructional approaches, a pattern Cuban found lasting more than a century whereby teachers adopted combinations of "familiar and new practices" (p. 8). In the 1960s and 1970s, classrooms incorporated more student-centered components into the teacher-centered instruction of the past. Teachers tended to fall somewhere along a continuum between teacher- and student-centered, rather than demonstrating a pure form of either practice. For example, the physical environment of classrooms has transitioned from fixed desks in rows to movable furniture configured for small- or large-group instruction. With different physical arrangements, student projects became a feature appearing in social studies classes. Still, despite the increasing use of student-centered practices during this time period, the majority of classes fell more toward the teacher-centered than the student-centered in most schools.

Cuban initially reported his findings in the early 1980s, before the current movement for standardization and testing in schools. Since that time, many observers have concluded that standardized tests have forced teachers to use more teacher-centered practices in the classroom (Grant, 2003, 2007; Ravitch, 2010). Cuban conducted a follow-up to his original research to determine if a shift to more teacher-centered instruction in the current testing era were accurate. In *Hugging the Middle: How Teachers Teach in an Era of Testing and Accountability*, Cuban (2008) found that the earlier hybridization of teacher-centered and student-centered instruction had continued. He also found more student-centered classes in the elementary grades rather than in secondary classrooms.

Although Cuban acknowledges that each practice draws on a different set of beliefs, teacher-centered approaches tend to view students as "empty vessels," whereas student-centered approaches regard students as knowledge "constructors." Despite these stark differences, Cuban finds debates between the two models to be unproductive: "Yet the accumulated evidence on how actual classroom practices produce particular student outcomes has been mixed and unconvincing" (Cuban, 2008, p. 6). At all grade levels, concluded Cuban, "most teachers hugged the middle of the continuum, blending activities, grouping patterns, and furniture arrangements to create hybrids of the two traditions" (p. 76).

Teaching Methods in an Era of Standardized Testing

The rise of the accountability movement of education reform has led researchers to examine teaching practices in the era of standardized testing (Cuban, 2008; Ravitch, 2010, 2013). Summarizing some early findings, S.G. Grant (2007) found teachers largely adapting to high-stakes testing without making "wholesale instructional change." Instead, standardized tests were seen as just one more complexity that teachers must respond to while still focusing on the day-to-day realities of classroom instruction.

Academic content (what to teach) was the biggest area Grant found changed by high-stakes tests, meaning pedagogical decisions (how to teach) were still an area in which teachers were exercising considerable autonomy. Grant proposed the term *ambitious teaching* to capture the nuanced ways in which teachers are dealing with mandated education reform. Ambitious teachers fold high-stakes tests into other factors affecting how they teach their classes, such as their own knowledge of the subject and historical knowledge of students. Ambitious teachers "understand the challenges that state tests pose and they factor those challenges into the mix of ideas and influences they consider" in their teaching (Grant, 2007, p. 255).

To explore how teachers' perceptions of high-stakes testing effected the decisions they made about teaching methods and instructional practices, Kenneth E. Vogler (2005) studied the survey responses of 107 Mississippi social studies teachers who were teaching historical material that was included on the state's mandated test for high school graduation. Vogler was interested in discovering what instructional practices these teachers used and how the Mississippi state high school graduation examination influenced their choice of teaching methods. Teachers were given a survey asking them about their instructional practices, influences on those practices, and demographic information.

Vogler used the survey data to compute frequency and means of the questions asked in the survey. The most common instructional practice used by the teacher was the textbook (94.4%). All but one open-response question (84.1%) of the top seven instructional practices used was catego-rized as teacher-centered methods. Furthermore, according to Vogler, the instructional practices that teachers reported using the least were primarily student-centered, with the exception of the use of true–false questions.

An additional comparison was made between teachers who spent between 1 to 2 months preparing students for the graduation examina-tion and those who spent more than 2 months explicitly focusing on the test. In this comparison, those teachers who spent the most time preparing students for the test used the most teacher-centered methods of instruc-tion. In looking at the influences on teaching practice, Vogler found that teachers focused on the high-stakes graduation examination had a strong influence with 96.3% agreeing that their choice of instructional method was influenced by an interest in helping their students pass the test. At least in the case of these social studies teachers in Mississippi, the presence of a high-stakes test did limit the amount of time spent on student-centered instruction in social studies.

Vogler (2008) extended his original study of Mississippi social studies teachers to include teachers in both Mississippi and Tennessee in a follow-up comparative study. In this study, Vogler again found that teachers were teaching with more teacher-centered instructional methods and that they attributed the test and the state standards as the reason for this choice. More teachers in Tennessee than in in Mississippi cited personal-related factors such as "personal desire" as their reason for their choice. This may have attributed to the fact that the standardized test in Tennessee is not as high stakes as the one in Mississippi, allowing teachers to feel freer to exercise some control over their classroom practice.

More recently, William Benedict Russell (2010) conducted a national survey of the instructional practices used by a sample of 281 social studies teachers. The teachers were asked to rate on a Likert scale how frequently they employed different methods. He found no method or practice was skewed so heavily toward the more frequent scale than the lecture method with 90% of the teachers using this approach at least 50% of the time. There was also a strong preference among the teachers for student note-taking (87% of teachers reported using this method at least 50% of the time) as well as a reliance on textbooks as the main source of information. Eighty percent of teachers asked students to complete written assignments from the textbook at least 50% of the time, whereas only 40% had students read from other sources besides the textbook at least 50% of the time.

Despite calls for more active learning to prepare students for life as 21st-century citizens, the study found teachers not increasing engagement and participation by students. Teacher-led discussions greatly outnumbered student-led discussions, whereas only 25% of the teachers had students regularly participate in debates. Less than 20% of the teachers had students engage in role-playing activities or historical simulations. Technology, too, remained underused—only 7% of teachers reported regularly using videos or other multimedia resources, whereas only 19% had students use the Internet at least 50% of the time. Teaching practices, concluded the study's author, do not align with the literature supporting "more authentic learning strategies" (Russell, 2010, p. 70).

Voices of Teacher Candidates: Teaching Methods in School Classrooms

The history and social studies teacher candidates in our program reported being unsure about what teaching and learning practices to use in their classrooms. They tend to begin teaching as they were taught when in secondary school, which generally means emphasizing more teacher-dominated instructional methods. But, at the same time, they express support for the ideals of student-centered instruction in democratic settings. Their comments reflect their confusion about how best to organize teaching and learning in school classrooms for the achievement of all students.

Every year, one of the first assignments in our teacher preparation program asks history teacher candidates to "shadow" a middle or high school student for a day. The goals are twofold:

1. To experience what a middle or high school student's school schedule is like on a daily basis

2. To examine where candidates see democratic teaching practices in students' academic and classroom experiences.

Shadowing consists of following not a student, but a student's schedule. Middle and high school students were informed that a college student was going with them to observe different classes that students take, but not to monitor anyone's behavior. With the shadowing day over, teacher candidates posted their reflections on our course online discussion board where everyone could read and comment on each other's thoughts.

Shadowing experiences vary from school to school, depending on college schedules (some were only able to stay for a half rather than a full day), the particular activities of various classes on the day of shadowing (some classes were giving exams), and which student's schedule the teacher candidates were following (AP and honors students had different schedules than non-AP or non-honors students).

Following a student's schedule even for half a day was an eye-opening, often exhausting experience for most teacher candidates. Their reflection papers highlighted the theme of just how regulated and time-driven the school day felt to them. Class periods have tightly fixed times, students must move quickly from one class to another, lunch is short, and there is barely time to go to the bathroom or get a drink of water. At one high school, students had 3 minutes to move from class to class, and were expected to use the bathroom during this time. However, the bathrooms were locked between classes as a punishment because some students were caught smoking in a restroom. Not everyone was aware of the policy and confusion resulted.

Teacher candidates, not long removed from being secondary school students themselves, felt amazed by the intensity of the school day. A student might begin early in the morning in his or her homeroom before going to classes in social studies, math, and science, all before lunch, with language arts and an elective course filling out the rest of the school day. There is no time to think and reflect as students must make the mental shift necessary to take notes, do seat work, answer questions, and manage assignments in compact amounts of time. Then, for some students, extracurricular activities such as sports or music or after-school jobs extend the school day even further.

Repeatedly, the candidates commented on the disengagement of many students when teachers used traditional approaches to instruction. One candidate summarized her morning in school as follows:

> Mr. O primarily lectured during class. It was typical of his teaching style. He encourages student participation, but primarily lectures from the specific section of the textbook. While he does ask for questions periodically, there is not much student choice or opinion in his lessons. Her [the student the candidate was shadowing] next class was physics. The teacher went over the lab that the class had done during the previous class. The teacher lectured, while he incorporated student interaction by using the Socratic method. It did not appear that students had much say. The answers appeared to be right or wrong. Students seemed disengaged and at times confused. One student was playing with her lab partner's hair for most of the class.

Perhaps not surprisingly, given how schools structure daily learning around class periods and time blocks, seemingly routine matters like bathroom passes and classroom seating plans caught the attention of the teacher candidates. Some teachers had firm policies. Students sat in the same seats every day and no one was allowed to leave the classroom during instructional time. Other teachers had more flexible systems. In one teacher's class, students sign themselves out for bathroom or water breaks and are expected to self-regulate the system. The teacher and the students had worked out this system at the beginning of the school year, and they modify as a decision-making group only when problems arise.

When asked about democratic practices in schools, most candidates found occasional examples. One high school intern said he "saw a definite attempt of having democracy in the classroom. Students were often given choices of activities and/or when assessments would be given." However, this new teacher wondered if the students did not appreciate or understand what was happening when choice was given: The students "often met options with blank stares." Another high school intern appreciated how a veteran teacher gave students "many opportunities to voice their opinions about the subject being taught and how things operated. He gave the students many chances to choose what they wanted to do."

Several candidates commented on how democratic practices they observed were connected to rule-making and classroom management. One recounted how a teacher whose class had had a major discipline incident the day before "allowed the students to choose whether to resume activity given the disturbance the day before." The students choose to do so. It was interesting, the candidate continued, "to see the students take control of the classroom and productively engage in a lesson that had proven difficult previously."

For some candidates, the presence of democracy or democratic practices depended on the teachers and classes they observed. One candidate noted after his shadowing day was over: "Overall, my thinking of democratic teaching has not changed. . . . Math, science, and gym are hard classes to be democratic in for they just simply are not based around those concepts. However, in history and sociology the classes were very democratic, and I think that goes along with the material taught in those classes, as well as with the teacher." Another candidate agreed, stating, "it is hard to incorporate it [democracy] into the 'traditional' classroom because sometimes teachers have to give lectures or reviews for certain subjects."

A third candidate, who saw the possibilities for democratic teaching, remarked: "In a math class, a teacher can choose to accept multiple approaches to problem solving, allowing students to show their work and justify their methods. I would say that the concept of 'partial credit' for showing work in math is a form of democratic teaching, because it honors a student's effort and attempt to explain his or her response."

Other candidates saw few examples of democratic input and student voice in the daily flow of academic experience. Instead, noted one candidate: "I did observe plenty of non-examples of school-based democracy that seemed to transcend the particular class activities I observed on Wednesday. In general, students have very little control over their daily actions at school. Everything from the location of their seats in the classroom, to when they may use the bathroom or get a drink of water, to the content of their curricula, are assigned to them."

That same candidate highlighted an occasion she called "pseudo-democracy" in one social studies class studying different world religions. The teacher selected 25 noteworthy historical figures representing a wide span of time periods and religious traditions. Students were allowed to "choose" one person to research, but they were not actually allowed to look at the list before making their decision. In this way, no one, in the words of the candidate, could "make an informed decision and thus have a meaningful impact on the content of their assignment."

Interestingly, that candidate found one compelling example of democracy during her day at the school. "Students may also choose where to sit in the cafeteria. Though these lunchtime examples might seem trite, I think it provides a window into why students are so protective of their lunch period: it seems to be, unfortunately, one of the most democracy-rich segments of their school day."

Conducting Strategies for Building Democracy

No teaching method or instructional practice generates learning success for all students all the time, as beginning teachers quickly discover. An approach that produces engagement and involvement one day may not succeed the next, whereas an initially unpromising method energizes thoughtful investigations of historical topics. This variability is what gives teaching tremendous challenge and excitement. Every class, every day, is a new experience and a new experiment. Teachers start with an instructional plan, but must be ready to adjust what they are teaching and how they are teaching it at a moment's notice in response to student interests or concerns. At the same time, students are not passive actors waiting for teachers to implement different strategies in the classroom. Students are must-be-included partners, and their learning, or lack of it, is the crucial outcome of any educational endeavor.

This chapter's "Building Democracy" activities are designed for students and teachers to identify the strengths and complexities of active learning, student-centered and flipped teaching methods, and then envision changes that can turn potential problems and student resistance into learning success. We begin with ideas for flipping the classroom to create new opportunities for student engagement with and analysis of historical materials. Next, we offer strategies for overcoming resistance from students and teachers to more active, student-centered, flipped learning models. Finally, we present an approach called "Ideas, Issues, and Insights" where teachers and students collectively assess the advantages and disadvantages of interactive instructional methods while proposing ideas and strategies to make teaching and learning more successful for everyone in a classroom.

Strategy: Student-Centered Flipped Instruction

As broadly described by its advocates, "flipped" or "flattened" classrooms involve reversing the learning activities students traditionally do in class with those they are expected to do for homework. In a flipped classroom, students spend outside-of-class time viewing teacher lectures, watching video clips and PowerPoint presentations, taking notes, completing worksheets, and doing other assignments on their own time. During in-school class time, students engage in individual research, group project development, and meetings with teachers for individual assistance, all activities that used to be done for homework. The assumption is that what students need most from teachers is individualized and small-group learning support; learning academic content can be done on one's own outside of class (Bergmann & Sams, 2012).

Because teacher-centered content presentations, textbook assignments, and worksheets are no longer primarily the focus of in-class time, teachers and students are able to organize classes around a workshop-like setting where individuals and small groups explore topics in greater depth using multiple technology-based and paper resources. Students analyze primary source materials, visit interactive websites, and develop and present group projects. By observing the work students do during class, teachers can better understand and respond to individual learning needs.

Flipped classrooms would not be possible without the capacity of computers and the Internet to create anywhere/anytime learning for students through vodcasts and podcasts, interactive websites, and access to many other multimedia resources. Technology enables teachers to shift much of the information presentation function of teaching to online materials. Plus, the use of computers and the Internet connects directly with the interests of today's students in digital environments. Students repeatedly tell anyone who will listen that they want more opportunities to use new technologies in school. Flipped classrooms provide teachers with ways to connect student interest in technology with the academic content that teachers want to deliver.

Flipping the classroom changes everyone's roles and responsibilities in the direction of more student-centered instructional approaches. The teacher, no longer the sole director of what and how students learn, pivots from dispenser of information to manager of individual and group learning experiences. Students, no longer expected to be mainly passive recipients of curriculum content, become active researchers, analyzers, and presenters of ideas and information. Teachers and students alike use technology for learning on a regular basis and the effect can be huge. Studies have found that students are more likely to develop interests in science, technology, engineering and math fields when teachers use instructional practices that feature digital technology, social media, and student-driven learning (Project Tomorrow, 2012).

HATs as an Approach to History Learning

The concept of flipped classrooms invites students and teachers to envision many different ways to reorganize history and social studies teaching using student-centered learning principles. Moving the focus of instruction away from a reliance on teacher-centered instruction, however it is done, creates a "flip" in the experience of students and teachers alike. Working together in groups, sharing ideas orally or in writing, analyzing primary source materials, reading a wide variety of texts, and accessing multimedia and multimodal materials, students find learning more engaging and more substantive. Whereas group work, primary source analysis, and other smaller scale changes may not seem to be as radically different as a full-fledged flipped classroom model complete with computers and online websites, students and teachers can still transform learning through how they use historical materials in classes.

Historical Assessments of Thinking (HATs), based on digital materials from the Library of Congress and developed by Sam Wineburg and his colleagues at the Stanford University History Education Group (2011), offer a compelling way to change the way history is taught in schools. HATs are also found on the Stanford History Education Group's website, *Beyond the Bubble: A New Generation of History Assessments.*

To use HATs in the classroom, students are given primary source materials and then asked to "go beyond factual recall to apply information in a specific historical context" (Stanford History Education Group, 2013). For example, students might view Dorothea Lange's famous 1936 "Migrant Mother" photograph and then asked to assess the purpose of the document at the time it was published by responding to the following question, taken from the *Beyond the Bubble* website: "Was Lange's photo taken to dramatize the misery of the Dust Bowl or to drum up support for Roosevelt's social programs—or both?" (Stanford History Education Group, 2013). They can then explore the history of the photograph as well as the life of the woman in the picture, Florence Owens Thompson, who said she posed for the camera to help people in poverty, although she and her children were not living in the pea-pickers camp where the picture was taken.

An example of a HAT that we use every year with new teacher candidates in our history methods class features a letter written to President Dwight Eisenhower on May 13, 1958 by the baseball player and civil rights advocate Jackie Robinson. Typed on stationary from the Chock Full O'Nuts Coffee Corporation where he was an executive, Robinson was responding to the Little Rock school desegregation crisis and the actions of Arkansas Governor Orville Faubus in trying to prevent nine students from entering the city's high school. From 1956 to 1972, every president received letters from Robinson urging faster federal action to ensure civil rights for Blacks. We give the teacher candidates a copy of the letter without the signature and ask them to imagine who wrote it and why, before expanding on the issues surrounding the Civil Rights Movement of the time. The letter can be found on the featured document website of the National Archives and Records Administration.

HATs give students the opportunity to show what they know and what they can do with that knowledge, providing teachers with immediate formative assessments of student learning. Teachers can then use that information to target further instruction more directly to student needs and interests. The class benefits from exploring historical scenarios along with the conflicting motivations and complex choices facing people at different moments in the past.

HATs also teach students to be more active readers of historical materials. To illustrate this point, Wineburg describes how students and historians read primary sources differently. Students tend to plunge right in, reading from beginning to end, trying to determine the meaning of the text. Historians "flip" the reading process, starting at the end, not the beginning, to determine the type and source of the document, developing meaning from context. In this way, "sourcing transforms the act of reading from passive reception to an engaged and passionate interrogation" (Wineburg et al., 2011, p. vi). For Wineburg, primary source materials are prerequisites to engage students from all reading levels to engage them more deeply in history learning. Indeed, those youngsters who find textbooks challenging are precisely the students "who most need to be exposed to historical questions and the documents that address them" (p. vi).

Developing Interactive Online Activities

Using online spaces for history/social studies learning is challenging for students and teachers alike. Students are used to accessing the Web for entertainment and information, not academic learning. They need guidance about how to respond to materials they are asked to read or view as part of online homework. Teachers, used to asking questions, conducting discussions, and responding to students in face-to-face settings, need ways to best organize the content and structure of virtual assignments. Everyone needs to guard against defining online experiences as automatically good or poor pedagogy. Based on our experience, here are key approaches for developing effective online instruction.

Online activities featuring multimodal resources are essential to sustaining student interest and involvement in Web-based learning. Many students do not use online text-based readings well; they skim over the content without considering key points. They respond more positively and thoughtfully when online materials are interactive and visual—charts and graphs, infographics, videos, podcasts, websites, and learning games. "Picturing the 1930s," a website from the Smithsonian Art Museum, illustrates this idea. This site has sound, music, artwork, video clips, three-dimensional objects, newsreels, photographs, and other resources for learning about the Great Depression and the New Deal. Students can explore this resource individually or in small groups and then share their impressions in class. Combining the interactivity of "Picturing the 1930s" with primary and secondary source materials and in-class discussions can generate memorable learning experiences.

Teachers can incorporate many highly interactive online experiences into history/social studies classes: "Immigration Explorer" from *The New York Times* shows the movement of different groups of people throughout

American history; the "NAACP Interactive Historical Timeline" presents milestone events in civil rights history for the past 100 years; "Stop Disasters" from the United Nations International Strategy for Disaster Reduction" engages students in trying to prevent devastation from wildfires, earthquakes, tsunamis, or other natural calamities; "A History of the World in 100 Objects" explores social and political developments associated with historical artifacts in the British Museum; the "National Priorities Project" lets students reallocate the federal budget to promote greater social and economic justice; PBS has a series of experiential history websites focusing on houses in American History, including "Colonial House," "Frontier House," "Manor House," and "The 1900 House."

Interactive multimodal resources work well when accompanied by thoughtful questions that students can answer as part of online assignments. Students use writing to focus their thinking and clarify their learning. Teachers get evidence that documents students' work and academic thinking. In formulating thoughtful online assignments, we ask two types of questions: descriptive information questions (to demonstrate that students did the assignment) and reflective response questions (to show what students have learned from the experience), as displayed in the following examples:

- In a lesson on the powers of the president in our political system, students view State of the Union addresses by Barack Obama, Lyndon Johnson, Franklin D. Roosevelt, Abraham Lincoln, and George Washington in word clouds as well as in full primary source text. Students are first asked to list the eight largest words of each of the speeches. Then, using their list, they answer these questions: "How do the largest words in each address reveal issues being faced by the president at the time?" and "How can a word cloud help you understand the text of the speech before reading the speech or hearing it aloud?"

- In a lesson on poverty in America in the second half of the 20th century, we feature the work of documentary photographer Milton Rogovin, whose entire photographic archive is held by the Library of Congress. Online, students read a 2011 NPR obituary that includes a slideshow, watch a biographical short video, listen to a podcast based on his photographic work, and then respond to the following questions: (a) Before you did this assignment, what you would have done to learn about Milton Rogovin and what he did in history (include URL addresses of where you would go online and/or book titles you might have used in the library)? (b) How would you describe Rogovin's contributions to documenting the struggles of poor and impoverished people in America? (c) Which of the multimodal resources in this assignment did you prefer as a learner and describe what you learned from it?

- For a lesson on immigration, we have students take a series of practice questions from the U.S. Naturalization Test. We then ask them how many questions they knew and didn't know; which questions they would keep as important for conferring citizenship and which ones would they eliminate; and what two new questions would they add to the test.

To continue learning how to formulate effective questions for online assignments, we invite students to join us in writing and revising Web-based homework activities. We have a Google group where students post feedback about resources on each week's assignment page, including questions to be included in future lesson plans, preferences for certain types of activities, and additional resources that would help teach about a topic.

Strategy: Overcoming Resistance to Change

Historian Larry Cuban (1993) compared efforts by education reformers to make classroom learning more student-centered to the effect of a hurricane on ocean waters: "Winds sweep across the sea, tossing up 20-foot waves, a fathom below the surface turbulent waters swirl, while on an ocean floor there is unruffled calm." For Cuban, traditional or teacher-centered teaching practices are like the ocean floor during a storm, relatively unmoved by the waves of change brought on by the latest reform ideas.

As they consider ways to improve history/social studies teaching in schools, advocates and skeptics alike are pondering how active learning, student-centered, and flipped history/social studies classes might function in day-to-day practice. To succeed, these new approaches require greater technological resources and stronger stakeholder commitments. Teachers and students need up-to-date technology tools—teachers to generate online content and students to access what teachers have generated. There must be sufficient buy-in from teachers, administrators, family members, and students themselves. Beyond resources and commitments, new approaches must overcome lingering resistance from two sources: students and teachers themselves.

Gaining Student Support

Many teachers have told us, and multiple researchers have confirmed, how difficult it can be to implement student-centered teaching methods in school classrooms. There are many reasons why this is so. Teachers benefit from professional development workshops about new approaches, but there is not enough time or money for these supports to happen. School administrators or veteran teachers may not provide the leadership needed to guide new approaches forward. Top–down change mandates often fail to address the day-to-day priorities of teachers and thus are ignored by the very practitioners those proposals seek to motivate. But student-centered teaching practices also fall short of their intended goals because of resistance from students.

Student opposition to student-centered methods is a perplexing problem. On the one hand, many students say they do not learn well in traditionally taught history and social studies classes. They complain about teacher lectures and the isolated facts and dates they must remember, asking, "What does learning this have to do with me?" Yet, when teachers try to implement interactive, inquiry-based and student-centered teaching, many of those same students react unenthusiastically. Educators John Kornfeld and Jesse Goodman (1998) have characterized this type of student response as the "glaze," a pattern that includes staring silently at the teacher, avoiding eye contact, and giving muffled monosyllabic responses to questions.

Why do many students resist instructional activities where they are asked to express opinions, draw informed conclusions, and conduct historical investigations, preferring instead more traditional classroom practices? Kornfeld and Goodman (1998) believe students fear the new, particularly if they might be perceived as making mistakes or not giving the "right" answer. Students who have been rewarded for the memorization and regurgitation of information are not "immediately ready to experience school as a democratic sphere." Teachers must gradually shift students from "their dependence on teacher control over the curriculum and the question–answer mode of knowledge transfer to which they were accustomed" (p. 309).

Another answer to student resistance focuses less on the methods themselves and more on how the methods are implemented by teachers (Felder, 2011). In this view, student reluctance toward group work, creative writing, or other active learning strategies is tied to how teachers go about using these strategies in their classes. Unknowingly, teachers leave unaddressed key issues or dynamics raised by an active learning method that must be dealt with for students to embrace rather than resist that approach.

Active learning researchers Richard Felder and Rebecca Brent (2009) offer a telling example of this point. When teachers always ask volunteers to share results of cooperative learning/group-work activity, students pay less attention to the assignment because they are likely not to have to speak in front of the group. They imagine someone else will give a suitable response and they can free ride on those students' answers. By contrast, when teachers let it be known that everyone in the group might be asked to respond orally or everyone must provide a written reflection, students focus on the activity more intently.

The overriding challenge of student-centered instruction is students' familiarity, and in many cases, comfort with traditional teaching practices. They are used to the routine of learning individually, being held responsible for assigned work whether they clearly understand the academic material or not. At the same time, students want meaningful learning experiences that connect academic material to their lives, interests and goals. Implementing student-centered instruction begins with teachers discussing with students what they intend to change about instructional practices and classroom routines, and why these changes are being proposed. Student input and participation at this stage is essential so that any change away from traditional teaching has been explored with the class.

Once under way, new practices need ongoing student feedback about their effectiveness to generate mutually agreed on improvements in how future activities will be conducted. Students need to feel as though their voices have been heard, even if not every idea can be implemented with a school schedule. Additionally, changes in instructional practices may need to happen incrementally; it may not be possible to move from a teacher presentation/student worksheet model to a team-based teaching approach or flipped classroom all at once. Everyone needs opportunities to experience new practices and make them part of their daily experience.

Furthermore, student-centered activities must be challenging and meaningful. Students recognize the difference between what they perceive as "busy work" versus substantive academic learning. Challenging and meaningful student-centered instruction means, for example, that group work must have clear goals for the group to achieve, student writing must have genuine audiences who will read what students have written; Web-based activities must have open-ended opportunities to explore topics. Teachers must not allow students to think of learning as something that happens to them, but rather, like democratic practices in society, learning is a process that teachers and students are actively engaged in together every day.

Recognizing Teachers as Innovators

In every school, certain teachers (as well as administrators and support personnel) seek innovation and change more quickly than others; these change-oriented early adopters eagerly integrate new ideas and novel approaches into their practice. There are other professionals who follow these leaders, more or less rapidly, whereas there are still others who wait to see if a proposed change is lasting.

Sociologist Everett Rogers (2003) characterized these different responses to change among members of organizations in a classic book, *Diffusion of Innovations*, first published in 1962. The "Rogers innovation curve" depicts that with every new idea, there are always a small percentage of innovators (3%) and early adopters (13%) followed by a sizable majority of followers (68%) who sooner or later will adopt new practices. A small group (16%) tends to avoid or resist change as well. Applying Rogers' model to education, teachers divide this way:

- A small group of innovators eager to integrate new approaches into their teaching.

- A somewhat larger group of skeptical and cautious adopters worrying about the problems presented by new approaches before appreciating the potentials to engage student learners.

- A majority of undecided observers who would use new approaches more readily if they felt more confident about how to do so in the classroom.

The challenge for change advocates is to find ways to recognize and support the majority of teachers as they consider new directions while still sustaining the enthusiasm and commitment of early adopters. This begins by recognizing how every teacher, even those who emphasize traditional instructional practices, can be an educational innovator. A teacher might design a new instructional unit, add new primary sources to an existing lesson, or restructure how students present their historical inquiry projects. When acknowledged as genuine efforts to improve instruction, these individual change initiatives create a foundation for those teachers to undertake further development and change efforts. Students can be part of this process when they are invited to be partners in plans for change.

Strategy: Exploring Ideas, Issues, and Insights

An approach we call "Ideas, Issues, and Insights" provides an opportunity for teachers to become more comfortable making changes to their instructional practices. Standing back from the immediacy of the moment, any teaching method or instructional approach can be seen from three different perspectives:

1. *Ideas* refer to the strengths or advantages of a teaching method when used to explore history/social studies content with students. Every method, even the most traditional or teacher-centered, offers certain positive elements in some instructional situations. Cooperative learning groups, for example, are a powerful learning approach where the collective energy and talents of the group can produce remarkable results. The key is to be able to activate those positive elements when using that method in class.

2. *Issues* refer to the problems or disadvantages of a teaching method when used in history/social studies classes. Even the most active learning/student-centered approach produces uncertainties that can short circuit its instructional potential. These problems may arise in any group situation; the key is to collectively identify an issue and envision ways to overcome it.

3. *Insights* refer to the results of teacher and student problem solving about how a teaching method is going to work in the classroom. Insights come from a synthesis of ideas and issues in which advantages meet disadvantages and thoughtful solutions emerge.

An Ideas, Issues, and Insights framework allows teachers and students to discuss with each other the potentials and problems they see with any educational change approach. Every instructional approach generates a range of responses from students and teachers. Some students are enthralled, inspired, bored, or discouraged by what happens during a class; the same is true for teachers. Such responses may be explicit or implicit, and can vary from individual to individual. A teacher may think that no one is listening, whereas students feel they are enjoying what they are learning. Everything from the time of day to personal health to the latest shifts in interpersonal relationships can influence student or teacher responses. The challenge is for teachers and students to openly communicate with one another to realize the potential advantages and positive results that can follow from the use of new, student-centered, active learning, flipped instruction approaches to history/social studies learning.

In our teacher preparation program, we ask history candidates to first teach and then reflect on lessons using different best practice, student-centered teaching methods (Maloy & LaRoche, 2010). The term *best practice* has been defined as "serious, thoughtful, informed, responsible, state-of-the-art teaching" (Zemelman et al., 2012, p. 2). Commonly used active learning instructional methods include strategies for engaging students through large- and small-group discussions, active note taking, visual learning, materials other than the voice of the teacher, and other student involvement strategies—in effect, as two researchers summarized it, "anything course-related that all students in a class session are called upon to do other than simply watching, listening and taking notes" (Felder & Brent, 2009, p. 2).

After each classroom lesson, candidates write a two- to four-page reflection paper using the following questions to focus on the Ideas, Issues, and Insights generated by a teaching method:

- Describe *ideas* you had for using this teaching method in the classroom.

- Describe *issues* that arose from your lesson, including obstacles that may have blocked student understanding and learning.

- Describe *insights* you gained about how to use this teaching method for promoting student learning including and how do you plan to overcome any issues in the future.

Students too can participate in an Ideas, Issues, and Insights reflection activity by expressing ideas, identifying issues, and generating problem-solving insights. There are many ways to implement student participation. Students might give written or oral responses for an Ideas, Issues, and Insights list or a teacher might ask them for specific comments about an ongoing issue. Then collectively, students and teachers develop plans that will promote engagement and improve learning. The key is to ensure that everyone has the opportunity to reflect on their experiences, to offer suggestions for more productive use of class time, and to implement collectively agreed upon changes in response to purposeful and thoughtful reflection.

To show how an Ideas, Issues, and Insights approach works in practice, here are summaries of how future history teachers viewed three active learning, student-centered teaching methods: group work and cooperative learning, primary sources, and children's and young adult literature.

Conducting Group Work and Cooperative Learning

Group work and cooperative learning are much discussed teaching methods for history/social studies classrooms. Proponents contend these approaches break the one-way flow of teacher lectures while promoting teamwork in the classroom (Cohen, 1994; Schul, 2010; Stahl, VanSickle, & Stahl, 2009). But, some teachers are reluctant to use group work and cooperative learning because of classroom management and student participation issues.

Table 2.1 presents how history teacher candidates from our program have envisioned the Ideas, Issues, and Insights raised by group work and cooperative learning. They saw the potential of engaging students, but also recognized the complexities of doing such activities in a class. The insights column includes the most common candidate suggestions for making these methods work successfully.

Integrating Primary Sources

Primary sources are one of the most widely used teaching methods in the history/social studies classroom. In written and visual language, primary sources show real people dealing with complex issues and problems of their times (Barton, 2005; Schur, 2007). Some sources are essential documents of the crafting of democratic institutions—the Magna Carta, Declaration of Independence, Bill of Rights, and Declaration of Sentiments. Other documents reveal everyday life and material culture of ordinary people from a first-person point of view.

Table 2.2 shows how new history teacher candidates envisioned the Ideas, Issues, and Insights raised by primary sources. These candidates saw the unique capacity of primary sources to engage students in the study of the past, but also how the challenges of reading and interpreting make many materials difficult to use in the classroom. As with group work/cooperative learning, candidates offered a series of insights for successfully using original materials with students.

Table 2.1. Ideas, Issues, and Insights for Group Work and Cooperative Learning

Ideas	1. Groups gain the attention of students and get them to start thinking, whereas lecturing may lose their interest. 2. Group-work activity can ground abstract ideas in more concrete terms that are easier for students to understand. 3. Group work simulates the roles of citizens in a democratic society where collective action is essential to effective government.
Issues	1. Some students refuse to participate, do not work well together, or one person does all the work for the group. 2. It is not immediately clear how to assign students to groups, how long to let groups work together, and how to let groups share what they have done with the rest of the class. 3. Students may be loud and animated and spend time talking about unrelated topics, possibly distracting classmates (build "down time" into activities). 4. Standing in the front of the room and urging students to stay focused on group work is not sufficient for keeping students on task.
Insights	1. Develop focused academic activities that can be finished in a reasonable amount of time. 2. Each group member needs to be responsible for a portion of an activity. 3. Develop systems for moving students from large to small groups and back. 4. Assign grades to students for participation to focus energy on group activity. 5. Develop extension activities to involve individuals or groups who finish an activity before others in the class.

Reading Picture Books and Historical Fiction

Reading picture books and historical fiction can be a compelling learning experience in the history/social studies classroom. Students at every grade level relate to the way stories reveal important issues and themes in history. After all, the word "story" rests inside the word "history," and many teachers see great value in making "his stories" and "her stories" an integral part of the curriculum.

Picture books encompass multiple visual formats.

Table 2.2. Ideas, Issues, and Insights for Primary Sources

Ideas	1. Firsthand accounts offer a more enriched understanding of how life was lived in the past, giving students the sense of "being there" as events happened.
	2. Primary sources teach students that there are many different viewpoints that must be taken into consideration when analyzing events.
	3. Visual sources (maps, photographs, political cartoons, art, drawings) engage the interest of many students.
	4. Sources connect modern-day events to historical ones; for example, prohibition and marijuana repeal or the wars in Vietnam and Iraq.
	5. As students read primary sources more frequently, their ability to interpret the material and draw out important information increases.
Issues	1. Language in sources can be difficult for students to read; students become bogged down and frustrated by not just individual words, but syntax and language structure as well.
	2. Students may not have developed their abilities to draw conclusions, think critically, and carry on a conversation about what they are reading or watching.
	3. Students, used to multimedia materials may be uninspired by written documents.
	4. Students do not connect the formal writing style of sources to the lives and times of the writers, making the sources remote and hard to understand.
Insights	1. Provide primary source texts in larger fonts with plenty of space for students to write comments and responses.
	2. Use stimulating openers to get students engaged with sources; for example, the Peters Projection Map as a way to start looking at historic maps.
	3. Have specific questions for students to answer while reading sources.
	4. Develop an ongoing vocabulary list of unfamiliar terms and concepts from sources with student-authored modern everyday language translations.
	5. Preview sources before handing them to the students to set context for the material and to identify potentially confusing language and concepts.
	6. When students struggle with primary source material, stop a reading activity and discuss the source as a whole class.

1. No-word books convey historical stories without printed text as in *Anno's USA* where an immigrant travels west to east rather than east to west through a landscape of blended historical and contemporary images.

2. Storybooks combine words and pictures to transport readers emotionally into historical settings as in *Baseball Saved Us* by Ken Mochizuki that tells the story of a young Japanese-American boy in an internment camp during World War II who finds purpose in life by playing baseball, the book's artwork shifting from dark and somber images when the families arrive at the camp to more colorful drawings as the baseball field is constructed to full color when the boy hits a game-winning home run.

3. Historical biographies reveal the lives of famous and forgotten people in history, expanding our understanding of the past, as in *Bad News for Outlaws: The Remarkable Life of Bass Reeves, Deputy U. S. Marshall* by Vaunda Michauz Nelson that recounts the life of an African American lawman whose life may have been the inspiration for the original "Lone Ranger" radio show.

4. Graphic books examine historical events using the style and conventions of comic books. Howard Zinn's *A People's History of American Empire* is an example of this approach as are the cartoon histories of American and world history by Larry Gonick.

Historical fiction includes both adult and young adult novels. As literature, historical fiction can bring history alive for students through memorable characters who must face great challenges during times of historical conflict and change. Although historical fiction writers may not present the past with complete factual accuracy, they convey the themes and nuances of different time periods, letting readers imagine what they would do if they too had to make hard choices with difficult consequences. Laurie Halse Anderson's *Chains* tells the fictional story of a 13-year-old slave girl, Isabel, fighting for her freedom in the midst of Revolutionary War preparations in New York City where her existence becomes increasingly perilous with her efforts to pass information she has heard about British maneuvers to the American rebels.

"Notable Social Studies Trade Books for Young People," a yearly list published by the National Council for the Social Studies is an informative resource for locating history/social studies-themed literature to use in the classroom. Other resources include "OurStory" from the Smithsonian's National Museum of American History, the "Reading & Writing Project" at Teachers College, Columbia University, and the "Young Adult Historical Fiction Society Discussion Section" at the social cataloging website, Goodreads.

Table 2.3 shows how history teacher candidates envisioned the Ideas, Issues, and Insights raised by picture books and historical fiction. As with group work/cooperative learning and primary sources, candidates identified strategies for successfully using literature with students.

Table 2.3. Ideas, Issues, and Insights for Picture Books and Historical Fiction

Ideas	1. Engage students in stories that are more than just the facts of history: a. French Revolution: *Revolution* by Jennifer Donnelly. b. Industrial Revolution: *Frankenstein* by Mary Shelley. c. Holocaust: *Night* by Eli Wiesel and *Maus: A Survivor's Tale* by Art Spiegelman. d. The Civil War: *Rifles for Watie* by Harold Keith and *Killer Angels:* *A Novel of the Civil War* by Michael Shaara.
Issues	1. Students with special needs may struggle with language in fiction books. 2. Some students may be uninterested in reading book-length stories. 3. Some schools engage in subtle or overt censorship of controversial material. 4. Historical fiction is a blend of fact and imagination and some students are unsure how to draw the distinctions.
Insights	1. Use picture books and literature as part of an interdisciplinary curriculum with other teachers. 2. Approach history study thematically and use picture books and literature to show different aspects of life during various time periods 3. Make the effort to continually teach with picture books and literature so students gain confidence as readers and interpreters 4. Use teacher read-outs and other group reading experiences to make stories come alive in the classroom.

The examples of group work/cooperative learning, primary sources, and picture books and historical fiction only begin to illustrate how a thoughtful examination of the strengths and complexities of different instructional methods by teachers and students can improve learning experiences for everyone in a classroom. Individual teachers can use Ideas, Issues, and Insights as a form of personal self-reflection, groups of teachers can assembled these lists as a professional development activity, and teachers and students can build these reactions as a collaborative learning process. All three approaches support democratic teaching and learning in history/social studies classrooms.

Conclusion

In this chapter we focused on how democratic teaching can be built around the ways that teachers and students go about conducting history/social studies classes. A reliance on teacher-centered instructional methods, as Cuban among others has shown, has long dominated the field of history/social studies teaching. Lectures, PowerPoint presentations, worksheets, student note taking, and multiple-choice exams have been the preferred mode of instruction. This kind of teacher-centered approach limits historical thinking and reasoning by students. Communication flows mainly one way from a teacher giving historical information to students who are expected to receive it and then do with it what the teacher demands. There is little dialogue or few opportunities for students to make sense of the information in their own ways or connect it to other things they know.

Student-centered instruction with a focus on conceptual and analytical thinking and "flipping" the classroom generates alternative approaches to teaching and learning history/social studies material. Traditional practices are turned upside down by flipped instruction. A teacher's lecture becomes the homework that students do outside of class while the readings, primary source materials, worksheets, and group projects that used to be homework become the activities that teachers and students do together during class time. In effect, the classroom becomes a democratic space for doing education rather than a lecture hall for listening to presentations of information by teachers.

No teaching method meets every learning challenge. Instead, every instructional approach generates Ideas, Issues, and Insights among students and teachers. Ideas refer to the advantages or gains that can happen when an instructional approach is used in class. Issues are the complexities that arise whenever a method is used instructionally. Insights represent the synthesis of ideas and issues, the realizations and understandings that students and teachers create as they interact in a classroom learning community.

Focusing on Ideas, Issues, and Insights mirror democratic decision-making processes in other settings where members of a community or organization must thoughtfully consider the advantages and complexities of different proposals and then chart a course of action together. As teachers and students individually and collectively discuss and then act upon the ideas, issues and insights that are generated by student-centered and flipped instructional practices, they build democracy in classrooms while creating frameworks for democracy in society.

Chapter 3

Collaborating

Decision Making and Power Sharing

I believe the goal for collaborating is to make students not only have an opinion, but allow them to see their opinion play out in the classroom.

—High School Teacher Candidate

As part of a unit teaching the structures of American government, Samantha, a middle school history teacher candidate, organized an assembly-style meeting where students in each of five classes could discuss and propose new rules and policies for their school. Samantha's goal was for students to envision, draft, and present proposals for improving their school, and then, practicing the skills they would need as future voters and community members, decide which ideas to support or reject. Teachers who do similar activities call them a town or community meeting, school assembly, model Congress, or model United Nations.

Samantha had an ambitious agenda for students' democratic learning within these class assembly meetings. Each class had to decide democratically how they would deliberate together in an open and transparent manner as they proposed rules and policies to be endorsed by the group. For Samantha, what students decided and how they went about making those decisions were equally important.

The first thing she did was ask students to brainstorm the structural framework of how they planned to vote on the rules and policies proposed by each class assembly; for example, the seating plan they wanted in the classroom; what personal behavior and conduct rules they planned to follow during the assembly; and whether presenters would speak at a podium or stand at their seat when discussing issues under consideration. She explained that her role as teacher was also open for negotiation about whether she should intervene if students seemed to be stymied by lack of progress in making decisions or remain silent and let the process of student decision making continue to a point of resolution.

Deciding how to conduct the assembly prompted lively discussions among students in each class. Proposals were written on the smartboard in the front of the room, then discussed and revised before everyone voted to determine which approach they wanted to use. Surprising to Samantha, each of five classes voted a different meeting format. Three chose circular seating, while two preferred a horseshoe arrangement; none wanted to sit alphabetically in rows. One class put speakers at a podium in the front of the room; the other four allowed students to address the group from their seats.

Discussions about how to vote on proposals—show of hands, secret ballot, voicing aye and nay, or Congressional-style roll call of names in alphabetical order—produced different procedures adopted by different classes. One class decided to vote by secret ballot with students going to the hallway individually to cast votes; another chose the alphabetical roll call format with an oral aye or nay response. Deciding rules for personal behavior produced active discussion and decision making. Students defined acceptable and unacceptable behaviors, identifying what everyone should or should not do during the assembly.

Once under way, the assemblies flowed according to their rules with each of the five classes adopting different proposals for change:

- Period 1: Permitting the use of cellphones in the classroom and improving school lunches.

- Period 2: Bringing back an ice cream machine and having two recess breaks instead of one.

- Period 3: Installing a swimming pool and renovating the existing locker rooms.

- Period 4: Buying new baseball and softball team uniforms and equipment, and improving school lunches.

- Period 5: Offering more late bus service for students and installing artificial turf on the football field.

Samantha's uses of class assemblies introduce *Collaborating*, our third C of democratic teaching. Collaborating evolves from the idea that students learn about democracy by the ways that teachers and students make decisions and share power in classrooms. Every democratically inclined group must adopt procedures for how its members will decide issues or questions that come before them. Those choices, however, may be made without considering the inherent differences and unintended consequences present in any decision-making approach. By examining different ways that groups make decisions, students and teachers learn about key power-sharing dynamics that may support or frustrate democratic outcomes. Understanding those multifaceted issues makes it possible to envision and to implement structures where teachers and students collaborate productively, and democratically.

New and Emerging Decision-Making Structures

Citizen participation in democratic decision making is a hallmark concept in history/social studies curriculum at every grade level. For example, under the broad standard of the "role of citizens in the United States," the Massachusetts History & Social Science Curriculum Framework declares that students should learn about "voting in public elections, participating in voluntary associations to promote the common good, and participating in political activities to influence public policy decisions of government" (Massachusetts Department of Education, 2003).

Ask Americans about the meaning of citizen participation in a democracy and most will say voting. They have been taught from elementary school that voting is the quintessential democratic action. Alone in a voting booth, citizens express their preferences for candidates and policies, supposedly unfettered by public opinion or political pressure. In schools, teaching students about voting and elections is a mainstay of history and social studies classes. State and national curriculum frameworks stress the centrality of voting as one of every individual's roles and responsibilities as an American citizen.

Although voting in elections is much discussed in history/social studies classrooms, other forms of democratic decision making and power sharing have been steadily emerging throughout American society. "Like a picture slowly developing in a photographer's darkroom," in political scientist Gar Alperovitz's (2013, p. 146) evocative phrase, these structures suggest that today's students will be asked to play roles as future members of these democratic organizations and communities that go beyond just voting. We consider three examples—cooperative organizations, the slow democracy movement, and workplace transformations—to underscore the importance of students and teachers collaborating to share power and make decisions, not only in school classrooms, but also outside of schools as engaged members of society's democratic organizations.

Cooperative Organizations

Cooperative organizations or more simply "cooperatives" are collections of people organized around goals of production and consumption. The National Cooperative Business Association (2011) lists five basic types of cooperatives: consumer, purchasing/shared services, worker, producer, and hybrid. For example, an electric cooperative is a consumer or purchasing organization because those who use the electricity own the co-op while a worker-owned business is a producer cooperative because those whose jobs it is to make a product also own the product-making business. It has been estimated that 40% of the nation's population—130 million people—are members of some form of cooperative organization (Alperovitz, 2013).

The International Year of Cooperatives (2012) estimated that there are 30,000 cooperative businesses in the United States, all committed to the following set of "Seven Cooperative Principles":

1. Voluntary and open membership,

2. Democratic member control,

3. Members' economic participation,

4. Autonomy and independence,

5. Education, training, and information,

6. Cooperation among cooperatives, and

7. Concern for community.

Wholesale and retail food co-ops perhaps are the most familiar of these organizations, ranging as they do from large-scale supermarkets to small specialty shops, but cooperatives extend to many different services and products, all built around the assumption that members exercise voice and control over organizational activities and goals.

Exploring the growth of cooperatively structured organizations and businesses in *America Beyond Capitalism*, Gar Alperovitz (2011) found that 11,000 businesses are fully or partially owned by their employees; there are 6 million more workers in these firms than in private-sector unions; more than 1,000 mutual insurance companies are owned by their policyholders; 30% of all farm products are marketed through cooperatives. Further evidence of what Alperovitz (2013, pp. 40, 41) calls the "quiet democratization and evolutionary reconstruction" of traditional capitalist social and economic systems can be found in the nation's 11,000 worker-owned companies that employ around 10.3 million people.

In Alperovitz's view, cooperative and employee-owned organizations challenge the dominant capitalist system's hierarchies of power and control. They provide workers/owners with voting rights and responsibilities, and those individuals respond with commitment and drive. Studies by multiple economists, Alperovitz (2011) notes, "demonstrate that greater participation leads to greater productivity and thus greater competitiveness in the marketplace" (pp. 86–87). For Alperovitz, such cooperative organizations depend on individual participation and democratic decision making for their viability and vitality.

Writing in *Yes! Magazine*, Marjorie Kelly (2013, p. 20) characterized worker and citizen-led cooperatives as "seeds of a different kind" of economic and political system in the United States. Cooperative organizations generate more than $500 billion in revenue and workers receive $75 billion in wages and benefits. Credit unions and other consumer cooperatives ("owned by the people who buy the goods or use the services") are by far the most common, comprising 92% of all cooperative organizations. There are also producer cooperatives ("farmers and others banding together to market their products"), purchasing cooperatives ("small businesses pooling resources to be competitive with large chains"), and worker cooperatives (organizations that are "owned and democratically governed by employees").

Cooperatives are generating new forms of ownership based on principles of local democratic control very different from the large-scale corporate structures that have dominated the American system since the beginnings of the Industrial era. In Kelly's analysis, the two great economic systems of the 20th century, capitalism (private ownership) and socialism/communism (public ownership) resulted in a "concentration of economic power in the hands of the few." Now in the second decade of the 21st century, a host of alternatives are emerging: "common ownership, municipal ownership, employee ownership . . . open source models like Wikipedia, owned by no one and managed collectively" (Kelly, 2013, p. 20).

The names of these cooperative organizations are familiar even if the underlying structures are not. Best Western hotels and Ace Hardware stores are examples of purchasing cooperatives; Organic Valley is a leading producer cooperative; Navy Federal is the largest credit union; Patagonia Corporation has as its formal mission to serve employees, the community and the environment as well as its stockholders. More cooperatives are on the way—federal funding under President Obama's Patient Protection and Affordable Care Act will spur the development of health care cooperatives while new wind and solar energy sources will lead to the development of new power cooperatives, even at a time when 78% of the nation's counties are served by electric cooperatives (Jarvis, 2013).

Democratic decision making is a central ingredient to the cooperative economy's ownership revolution. In organization after organization, members elect representatives, set policies directly, sit on boards of directors, and participate in the day-to-day operations of the business or the group. How will students in schools today best learn the attitudes and skills they need to be active members of cooperative organizations in the future? That is a question facing teachers in schools as they consider what should be the essential elements of history and social studies classes across the grade levels.

Slow Democracy Movement

The movement for slow democracy is another example of a shifting focus on democratic decision making in American society. As a concept, slow democracy seeks to distinguish between citizen-controlled local politics and a national system of "fast democracy" dominated by well-funded interest groups, corporate donors, and media advertising. Just as the slow food movement is "dedicated to the creation of a just, sustainable food system" through local farm markets, community gardens and ecologically friendly agricultural practices, slow democracy "encourages us to govern ourselves locally with processes that are inclusive, deliberative, and citizen-powered" (Clark & Teachout, 2012). Slow democracy honors local decision making and local accountability while emphasizing the need for everyone's thoughtful participation in building healthy, democratic communities.

Slow democracy promotes deliberative decision making over quick solutions and majority-rule politics. Although people often seek rapid solutions to pressing issues, "deliberation implies that, ideally, we will not only talk together, we'll decide together. And in an ideal deliberation, participants are not simply debating option A versus option B but co-creating C—inventing new solutions together" (Clark & Teachout, 2012, p. 146). As such, deliberation is a sharp contrast to both voting (done in silence by oneself) and debate (often done as a competitive encounter designed to produce a winner). Deliberation's goal is common ground rather than a single right answer. Deliberation is also a way for everyone to learn new information to sharpen and expand the discussion beyond initial impressions and conventional wisdom. Therein rests the lasting value of slow democracy where local involvement and deliberative decision making build a "virtuous cycle" of interactions that create new solutions, committed and empowered citizens, and transformative results for people and places (Clark & Teachout, 2012, p. 115).

Oregon's Citizens' Initiative Review Commission (CIRC) is one slow democracy example cited in Clark and Teachout's book. CIRC consists of a group of voters who examine statewide ballot measures, consider the merits of the proposals, and prepare and publish a "citizens' statement" highlighting their findings. The state publishes this review in an official voter information pamphlet that is mailed to every voting household before an election. In 2012, for example, the panel's 24 members split (17 opposed; 7 in favor) over a measure to amend the state's constitution to authorize the establishing of privately owned casinos with a percentage of revenues paid to a dedicated state fund. The measure would have created considerable competition for the state's Native American tribal casinos as well as the Oregon state lottery, but the measure failed to pass in the November 2012 general election.

The call for slow democracy is complemented by efforts of community members to preserve "the commons." The commons, explains author David Bollier (2014), represents the commitment of people to use and protect shared resources and spaces. Bollier cites the existence of "galaxies of commons" throughout society, including seed-exchange programs, open-access publishing by academics, local land use for hunting and recreation, organ and blood donations, and "time-banking" agreements where neighbors trade services, all developed democratically with a minimum of formal bureaucratic rules and regulations. Although such initiatives struggle to achieve sustainability within a capitalist market system, they offer concrete ways for people to actively participate in shaping the quality of their lives and communities.

Workers Transforming Workplaces

For many progressive reformers, democratic and collaborative practices are essential tools for transforming people's workplaces as well as the larger American economic system. Seeking a "cure" for the boom and bust cycles of a capitalist economy, economist Richard D. Wolff (2012) envisions the creation of workers' self-directed enterprises (WSDEs) throughout all sectors of the American system. The premise for these new organizational forms is rooted in connecting workers more closely to the product of their labor, for, as Wolff writes, "production works best when performed by a community that collectively and democratically designs and carries out shared labor" (pp. 1–2)

The emergence of WSDEs begins by replacing the powerful elites that control modern corporations with arrangements whereby the "surplus-producing workers themselves would make basic decisions about production and distribution" (Wolff, 2012, p. 12). These changes would be accompanied by further large-scale shifts in the relationships between producers and consumers. People in the communities affected by or connected to WSDEs would be engaged in ongoing democratic interactions with these new workers/producers, a process of "codetermination" of policy and practice that Wolff (2012) sees as a "new reality of social governance." This combination of reorganized workplaces and democratic codetermination "would effectively end capitalism" as the dominant economic system.

In *What Then Must We Do? Straight Talk about the Next American Revolution*, Alperovitz (2013) presents a vision of how democracy in workplaces can transform the American system. Citing the range of evidence of inequality in society—from the growing wealth of the top 1% to the economic hard times that persist for most Americans—Alperovitz (2013, p. xiii) sees a "systemic crisis—*something built into the way the political-economic world works.*" Such a system-based, society-wide cause demands not just new political or economic policies, but "the reconstitution of genuine democracy, step by step, from the ground up" (Alperovitz, 2013, p. xiv).

Although a people-centered, truly democratic system cannot happen all at once, Alperovitz (2013, pp. 132, 134) believes that the broad structure of such a system has been emerging over recent decades through a series of "wealth-democratizing, institution-building changes" that include "local cooperatives, worker-owned companies, neighborhood corporations, land trusts, municipalization of utilities and Internet services, sustainability planning and related public safety initiatives," to name a few. There is, however, no quick fix when "talking about developing *institutions*, not just trying to change policy." After all, those with wealth and power in contemporary society are not likely to relinquish the dominance of their positions without resistance.

Other commentators, while expressing commitment to the importance of workplace change, see democratic practices revitalizing rather than overturning modern capitalist organizations. Focusing on the future of work and careers, supporters of the movement for teaching "21st-century skills" emphasize the ability to communicate and collaborate with others as part of the essential knowledge that students need to succeed in a highly technological, information-based economy (Partnership for 21st Century Skills, 2008). Collaboration in the 21st-century skills framework means the ability to work with others in team-based settings where individuals make decisions and compromises to achieve common goals (National Council for the Social Studies, 2013). It envisions nonhierarchical workplaces where the contributions of every individual matter and the end results reflect the ideas and energies of everyone.

Beyond the pronouncements of commission reports and scholarly books, there are countless examples of people working together democratically in all sorts of settings throughout American society. Neighborhood groups, nonprofit organizations, small public libraries, and other groups are finding ways to build websites, raise funds, organize activities, and maintain infrastructures, all with democratic voice and participation from members and volunteers. As these examples suggest, preparing students for roles as democratic decision makers in evolving social, economic, and community organizations is one of the education system's current great challenges, and that preparation connects directly to how teachers and students go about making rules and managing classrooms together.

Voices of Teacher Candidates: Making Rules and Managing Classrooms

When asked about democratic decision making in schools, middle and high school history candidates focused mainly on how teachers and students make rules and manage classrooms. They did not directly address the different ways teachers and students might make collaborative decisions about the processes of curriculum and instruction. The candidates saw collaborative classroom management and joint rule making as a way for students to understand how democracy works in the larger society. As one high school candidate noted, "Collaborative classroom management is the foundation for any democratic classroom and is an essential building block for the entire school year." Another high school intern concluded "creating and maintaining a classroom environment from expectations and procedures that have been built collaboratively allow both students and teachers to feel more comfortable and secure."

Candidates recognized the importance of managing what happens in the classroom, from the rules governing student conduct to procedures dealing with homework, tests, and other administrative matters. They also recognized that as teaching interns, they were entering a system that had already been established by administrators and their cooperating mentor teachers. In these settings, the process of choosing and maintaining rules of conduct was seen as a balancing act involving the interests of multiple parties. Everyone agreed that the collaboration of students was essential. One candidate remarked that when he teaches, "instead of an authoritative approach, I try to include student input in my decisions pertaining to classroom management and class structure as much as possible." Another candidate reflected: "When students were instrumental in creating a consequence or a reward for behavior in our class their adherence to the rules was much more consistent. They were also more likely to police themselves since they all have a firmer grasp of the rules and expectations for behavior."

Rule setting with students was rarely a smooth, problem-free experience for the candidates. One candidate found it difficult to get a unanimous decision or to get students to understand the legitimacy of a majority vote. She recalled, "if they did not agree with the rule and did not vote for it, they feel antagonized and will not adhere to it."

One intern asked students to express in writing their thoughts about a list of behavioral and academic expectations she had proposed for the class. Those who responded "expressed one main concern: That I wouldn't discipline every person the same and that I would enforce the rules selectively." Taken aback, she came to realize that with "student input I can ensure that each person will be aware of the expectations that their classmates and I have set for everyone."

Candidates struggled with just how much they should direct students in making choices about rules, procedures, expectations and consequences. "There are times when I feel like I give the students the power to make their own decisions and they are often unwilling to do so," noted one intern. Yet, at the same time, "If I'm an influence in all decisions being made, then the democratic practice of collaborating no longer exists because in the end I get what I want the way I want it. That isn't democratic at all." The candidate concluded that as a teacher, he must find a "delicate balance between authority figure and concerned member of the class."

Given the importance of the topic in the minds of the candidates, many interns were already looking ahead to being full-time teachers in charge of students in classrooms. "Next year I plan on devoting the first two to three days of the school year to collaborative rule making," one candidate told us. "I will encourage discussion and debate on rules and try to have them come up with the rules themselves. I also want to make sure I schedule time once a month to assess how the system of class rules, consequences, and rewards is working so far." Another candidate, reflecting on students' lack of participation when he asked for input about school rules, concluded "I didn't phrase the questions in the right way and possibly didn't make students feel empowered to speak up." That will be a theme for changing his future teaching.

Collaborating Strategies for Building Democracy

In 1943, a series of now-iconic paintings by illustrator Norman Rockwell appeared as covers for *The Saturday Evening Post* magazine. The paintings later toured the country with the title, "Four Freedoms War Bond Exhibition." Inspired by President Franklin D. Roosevelt's January 6, 1941 "Four Freedoms" speech to Congress, Rockwell drew the scenes depicting freedom of speech, freedom of worship, freedom from want, and freedom from fear. In "Freedom of Speech," a man resembling a young Abraham Lincoln rises to his feet to speak at a New England town meeting. The assembled citizens, seated around the room, look up at the speaker with rapt attention as he expresses his ideas. The painting conveys an enduring image of citizen participation in public debate and decision making in a democratic society.

This chapter's "Building Democracy" activities present ways for students and teachers to explore the dynamics of making decisions democratically. The goal is for students and teachers to experience democratic decision making while expanding how they think about democratic practices in schools and society. We look areas where students and teachers can build democracy together around the theme of decision making and power sharing: collaborative rule making, different models of decision making, and approaches to sharing power equitably.

Strategy: Making Rules Collaboratively

Like history candidates in our program, classroom teachers, parents, and students have strong, sometimes opposing views about what school rules should be and what should be the consequences for those who break them. School rules cover a wide set of behaviors, starting from prohibiting bringing weapons to school, physically assaulting another individual, or engaging in persistent disobedience to less severe actions such as being tardy to class, using inappropriate language in the building, disrespecting teachers, or loitering in the halls. Given the attention being paid to such issues, rules and suspensions offer insights for a broader discussion of democratic decision making by teachers and students.

Many students come to school lacking images of how to make deci-sions democratically. On television, they see players and coaches verbally confronting referees before being ejected from the game or even engaging in fisticuffs to settle differences after a play on the field or the ice. In movies, they see heroes and villains alike resorting to violence to solve problems. In peer groups and in many families, they see the loudest voices domi-nating whatever decisions and choices get made. These students have not experienced processes where thoughtful deliberation about differences and disagreements result in peaceful and productive outcomes. Making class-room rules offers firsthand opportunities to see the results of democratic decision making.

Examining Inequalities in School Rules

As a first step in collaboratively making rules, students and teachers in his-tory/social studies classes can examine how rules are made at their school as well as at other schools in their community or state. Following categories outlined by the American Civil Liberties Union of Vermont (2014), this process can involve reading and analyzing a school's or district's codes of conduct and policies toward student speech, due process and discipline, equal protection and discrimination, search and seizure, students records and privacy, health, and other aspects of school life. Members of history/social studies classes can then examine the broader national context of rules and rule making. For students and teachers alike, understanding national trends provides important background knowledge for understanding local policies and practices.

Nationwide, although every school has rules, not every student experi-ences those rules in the same way. Using data from all 97,000 of the nation's public schools, the U.S. Department of Education' Office of Civil Rights (2014) found racial disparities in school discipline that begin in preschools and early elementary schools. Black students who make up less than 20% of the preschool population account for more than half of those suspended more than once during the school year. Racial disparities are found at older grade levels as well. Suspension or expulsion results in significant lost instructional time, a situation that academically disadvantages suspended students. It is difficult to learn academic material and develop intellectual skills when not in school. Policymakers find themselves in a quandary, need-ing rules to maintain order and safety but also needing consistent structures that create opportunities for learning success for all students.

Also at the national level, as concerns for order and safety have esca-lated in recent years following school shootings and drug problems, many schools have adopted so called "zero-tolerance" rules for students. Under zero tolerance, students who break rules are automatically suspended or expelled from school for a specified amount of time and such punishments are non-negotiable. In some schools, milder infractions also carry zero-tolerance requirements so students must be go detention centers or "time-out" rooms. Such practices have led to perplexing situations such as a kindergartner in Rhode Island suspended from school for bringing a plastic knife to a classroom cookie cutting party (Simpson, 2012).

In 2012, President Barack Obama joined the dialogue about rules and schools when he issued an executive order establishing a White House Initiative on Educational Excellence for African Americans. The Departments of Education and Justice subsequently followed the president's lead by issuing materials designed to guide schools in administering school discipline in nondiscriminatory ways (Lhamon & Samuels, 2014). The goal is to focus attention on the discouraging educational experiences of Black youngsters who, in his words, "lack equal access to highly effective teachers and principals, safe schools, and challenging college-preparatory classes," and who "disproportionately experience school discipline and referrals to special education" (Obama, 2012).

The discipline-related challenges facing racially diverse students in schools include:

- Despite some narrowing of the achievement gap, White students out performed Black students by some 26 points on national assessments in math and reading (Vanneman, Hamilton, Baldwin Anderson, & Rahman, 2009).

- More than 80% of Black and Latino children fail to reach a proficiency level in reading by fourth grade—an educational disadvantage that contributes to a downward spiral of loss of interest and motivation in academics and, for many, leaving school before graduation (Fiester, 2013).

- Nationwide, about 75% of students who enter high school graduate 4 years later, but the percentage is 15 or more percentage points lower among Blacks, Hispanics, and Native Americans as well as students attending urban schools (Chapman, Laird, Ifill, & Kewalramani, 2011).

School rule enforcement marks another area where educational outcomes are unequal based on race and disability. Students who break school rules face different punishments. As reported by The Center for Civil Rights Remedies (CCRR) at the University of California Los Angeles, more than 3 million youngsters were suspended from school in 2009–2010, about the number needed to fill every seat in every major league baseball and professional football stadium in the country (Losen & Gillespie, 2012). The consequences for suspended students are multifaceted—lost instructional time, reduced self-esteem, lowered teacher expectations, and increased risk for dropping out of school. Many youngsters who leave school before graduation find themselves on a "schoolhouse-to-jailhouse" track where lack of educational stability contributes to involvement with crime and the criminal justice system.

School suspensions fall unequally on Black students. In a study of 7,000 school districts nationwide, the CCRR found that 1 in 6 Black students (17%) were suspended compared with 1 in 13 (8%) Native Americans, 1 in 14 (7%) Latinos, 1 in 20 (5%) Whites, and 1 in 50 (2%) Asian Americans (Losen & Gillespie, 2012). In California, Black students were suspended at rates 20 percentage points higher than White students (Losen, Martinez, & Gillespie, 2012).

Students with disabilities face similar inequitable suspension patterns—1 in 7 special needs youngsters were suspended compared with 1 in 16 regular education students. Racial factors are present. One in four Black K–12 students with disabilities (25%) were suspended at least once in 2009–2010. Additonally, students with disabilities and Black students were more likely to be suspended more than once during a school year, whereas the reverse was true for nondisabled students and youngsters from all other racial groups (Losen & Gillespie, 2012). Gender also affects who gets suspended from school. Black males are more likely to be suspended and Black males with disabilities are the highest risk category. In California, 59% of Black males with disabilities in the San Bernardino City Unified School District were suspended in 2009–2010, whereas the figure in the Los Angeles Unified School District was 36% (Losen et al., 2012).

Reversing national trends is a huge undertaking. But classroom and school levels offer immediate opportunities for involving students and teachers in collectively understanding their rights and responsibilities as members of school communities and how they can work together to begin building jointly supported structures for rules and discipline. Change at the local level begins with a recognition of large-scale issues followed by concrete steps to keep students in school and out of trouble involving a combination of responses such as more culturally relevant curriculum, greater support from teachers and other adults and mentors, specific steps to reduce racial prejudice within school organizations and consistent messages to students about the importance of school success (Toloson, McGee, & Lemmons, 2013).

Involving Students in Making Rules

Racial inequities in school suspensions and the excesses of zero-tolerance discipline policies have given rise to calls for more student-centered, less punishment-based approaches to school rules and student discipline. The Advancement Project (2012), a Washington D.C.-based organization committed to ending the schoolhouse to jailhouse track, expressed this emerging consensus thusly: "The most successful discipline policies are those that take a non-punitive approach to addressing student misbehavior and promote the development of a positive school culture."

Ross W. Greene (2009), clinical professor at the Harvard Medical School and author of *Lost at School: Why Our Kids With Behavior Challenges are Falling Through the Cracks and How We Can Help Them* is a strong advocate of collaborative approaches to school discipline. Greene argues that students who present problems to teachers are often characterized as having "psychiatric" problems—it is the child who must be changed. Alternatively, teachers and schools blame parents and families as the cause of school discipline issues. The result is that discipline rates in schools are now double those of the 1970s and continuing to climb.

In Greene's view, the problem of school discipline needs to be fundamentally redefined. Students who seem challenging are really not challenging at all, except when "the demands being placed upon them outstrip their skills to respond to those demands" (Greene, 2009, p. 26). Schools need to focus less on disciplining students through detentions and suspensions and more on teaching students the skills they need to understand and solve problems. The core of Greene's (2011) approach is collaborative problem solving between adults and youths. Although he does not use the term *democratic decision making*, Greene urges adults to avoid imposing discipline unilaterally, opting instead to treat students as partners in setting rules and taking responsibility for personal actions and decisions.

There is an explicit connection between establishing school rules and building democratic classrooms. In most schools, argues lawyer and educator David Schimmel (2003), students experience classrooms as largely undemocratic places due to a "fundamental conflict between the formal curriculum of lectures, texts, and tests and the informal curriculum of rules, punishments, and norms" (p. 17). Adults, mainly without the input or participation of adolescents, write the rules for the schools. Those rules then are often selectively enforced, in largely authoritarian ways, where certain individuals or groups receive harsher treatment than others. The effect is "to unintentionally teach many students to be nonquestioning, nonparticipating, cynical citizens in their classrooms, schools, and communities" (p. 18).

Schimmel examined school conduct codes to assess their effects on student behavior. In theory, codes of conduct promote models for helpful behavior as well as the values that underlie those behaviors. Yet, in Schimmel's view, most school codes of conduct share common characteristics that tend to undermine their legitimacy in the eyes of students: They are negative in tone and unexplained in practice; written in authoritarian and legalistic language; and implemented in nonparticipatory ways that are perceived as unfair by students. As a result, "most schools teach their rules in a way that unintentionally contradicts the goals of citizenship education, encourages students to subvert or ignore school rules, and violates the norms of good teaching" (Schimmel, 2002, p. 11).

Schimmel advocates "collaborative rule making" by students and teachers as way to build democracy in schools. In his view, only when students are invited into the process of discussing and deciding the rules do they become invested in those codes of conduct. Rules must not be framed as just restrictions and limitations. Collaborative rule making means that students learn about their rights and responsibilities as citizens in a democratic society, including the right to "present petitions, complaints and grievances to school authorities," to "exercise the rights of free speech, assembly, press, and association," and to experience a safe school environment (Schimmel, 2003, p. 27). Although individual rights do not extend to the limiting of other people's rights, within a framework of what can be freely expressed are opportunities for students to learn the moral basis of laws in a democratic society.

Writing a Classroom Constitution

Collaborative rule making invites students to be active makers and shapers of their classroom community. As an affirmation of commitment to collaborative rule making, students and teachers can develop and decide their own classroom constitution. Such a document sets forth a collective vision of everyone's roles and responsibilities in a fair, respectful, and democratic classroom. History and global studies teacher Allison Evans and her students developed a constitution for their eighth grade civics class (Table 3.1).

The document was assembled collectively with everyone in the class participating. Individual students wrote the drafts of the preamble based on the constitution's original words and those drafts were brought together

Table 3.1. Student-Written Class Constitution

We the members of Civics G, to form a more perfect class, establish curiosity, ensure good listeners, provide for a great learning environment, promote good behavior, and secure the wishes of Ms. Evans to ourselves and our posterity, do ordain and establish this constitution for the civics class of Williston.

Article I
Treat people the way they want to be treated within reason.

Article II
Turn homework in on time unless there's a valid excuse.

Article III
Students and teachers will inform each other if they believe they're lacking in their studies. This means that teacher will inform the student if the student is falling behind and if the student needs help the student will ask questions for reassurance.

Article IV
All students should respect each other's ideas.

Article V
In this class one shall not interrupt when another student is talking. If someone has something to say let them say it without making fun of them.

Article VI
If your peers are being annoying and disruptive kindly suggest that they reevaluate their behavior.

Article VII
When working in groups, all students should cooperate with each other, listening to each other's ideas, explaining why or why not they're relevant, and including them if they are.

Article VIII
Have fun while maintaining respectable behavior.

Article IX
Come to class prepared and with an open mind.

Article X
Everyone will keep their hands/eyes off their Surface [handheld tablet computer] when someone else is speaking.

---

into one final version. All students proposed articles based on what they felt were the most important values and behaviors for the group. Small groups reviewed all the proposed student articles and chose their top three selections. Working from the small group–chosen list, each student was given a hypothetical $1 to spend to endorse articles for the document. Each student had to decide how much of their $1 to allocate in support of an article they thought should be part of the classroom's constitution.

The effect of the constitution-writing activity in Allison's classroom was striking. Students enjoyed composing possible articles and lively debates ensued about which ones to adopt as the consensus of the class. Yet, as important as the document's content was the process of creating it. Students felt invested in the community they envisioned on paper and were committed to making it happen every day through their actions at school.

Strategy: Examining Democratic Decision-Making Systems

Political scientist John Gastil (1993) has observed that democratic groups, large and small, mainly use one of three methods to make decisions—majority rule, consensus, and what he calls "proportional outcomes." Majority rule means that a decision needs the support of more than half of the members of a group. Consensus seeks to find common ground for agreement among differing points of view, whereas proportional outcomes give more influence to groups or proposals that have a larger number of supporters.

Students and teachers can explore the dynamics and complexities of these democratic decision-making models to guide thinking about how democratic groups might function well. Beginning with majority rule, a class can study milestone events in history of voting to see how the right to vote has been both regulated by ruling elites and contested by social movements using collective action and political struggle. Current debates about voting rights in the United States present a further opportunity to examine the implications of majority-rule decision making and its potential for creating disaffected and disenfranchised groups. After exploring historical examples of democratic participation, students engage in making decisions about important classroom or community topics using different decision-making systems and approaches.

Exploring the History of Voting in America

Making decisions by voting has been an enshrined practice in American history from colonial times to the present. Voting for the "president" of the colony was one of the first acts of the Jamestown settlers in 1607, although only 6 men of the original 105 colonists made the decision—an historical precedent for restricting those who can vote that has marked a several centuries–long struggle to broaden the numbers of men and women who can participate in making choices about public issues (Crews, 2007).

The first New England "town meeting" was held on October 8, 1633 in Dorchester, Massachusetts by a group of men who wanted to address issues that affected the "common good." Town meetings in New England gradually expanded participation from landowning males to all free men aged 21 years and older (Robinson, 2011). Alexis de Tocqueville greatly admired this development, writing that "town institutions are to liberty what primary schools are to science; they bring it within the people's reach, they teach men how to use and how to enjoy it" (p. 73). But women remained excluded from these decision-making bodies for much of American history; for example, women were not allowed to vote in town meetings in Vermont until 1917 (Coffin, 2009).

Today only a limited number of towns and school districts in the United States practice a town meeting form of direct democracy. Instead, representatives elected by voters make public policy decisions at local, state, and national levels. This information can be revelatory for students who know little of the history of democracy as an institution or why participating as a voter is an important civic responsibility. Examining current town meeting practices in his book *Real Democracy: The New England Town Meeting and How It Works*, University of Vermont professor Frank M. Bryan (2003) concluded that people will actively participate in direct democracy government when they think the issues are relevant to their lives and the decision-making arena is small enough that they believe their vote will make a difference.

The history of voting practices in America offer many topics to explore in the classroom: The Constitution did not explicitly set forth a right to vote; the expansion of voting qualifications between 1787 and 1820; the women's suffrage movement before the Civil War; the first opportunities for Blacks to vote in post-Civil War South; the adoption of the 13th, 14th and 15th Amendments to the Constitution; the Jim Crow-era poll tax for voters; the Chinese Exclusion Act of 1882 that denied voting rights to Chinese Americans; the 19th Amendment giving women the right to vote; the Indian Citizenship Act of 1924 giving Native Americans the right to vote; the Civil Rights Acts of 1957, 1960 and 1964; the 24th Amendment, the Voting Rights Act of 1965; the 26th Amendment; and the Military and Overseas Voter Empowerment Act of 2009. Steven Mintz's essay, "Winning the Vote: A History of Voting Rights," online at the Gilder Lehrman Institute of American History website, is a comprehensive summary of the topic. A useful timeline of "Women in Politics" as well as other resources can be found at the website of the International Women's Democracy Center.

Current efforts by state election officials and conservative political groups to restrict voting serves as another compelling topic for classroom study. One notable case was *Crawford v. Marion County Election Board* (2008) where by a 5 to 4 vote the Supreme Court upheld the constitutionality of a stringent Indiana voter-identification law, despite, as dissenting Justice David Souter noted: "The Judiciary is obliged to train a skeptical eye on any qualification of that right." Contrary to the majority of the Roberts Court conservative justices, Souter found that "Indiana's Voter ID Law thus threatens to impose serious burdens on the voting right," including the requirement that people without cars travel to a motor vehicle registry to secure voter identifications and its real economic burdens for the poor, elderly and disabled individuals. Tova Andrea Wang's (2012) book, *The Politics of Voter Suppression* provides an insightful overview of the continuous struggle to expand voting rights in American history.

Examining Majority Rule and Instant Run-Off Voting

Majority rule voting is a revealing way to begin exploring a range of democratic decision-making approaches with students. In majority-rule voting, a question or topic must be endorsed by at least 51% of the voters. The voters might be the students in a class or school—the teacher may or may not also be a voter. Such votes usually involve an either/or or yes/no decision and the majority viewpoint becomes the adopted policy or procedure for the group. To illustrate majority-rule voting, students might be asked to decide whether or not to have an open book/open note test format for next exam or whether or not to have different options for a required in-class presentation about an historical topic (in writing, using pictures and drawings, making a video, or constructing a Prezi or PowerPoint).

Making decisions by majority rule allows students to see the inherent complexities in these practices firsthand. In majority rule, advocates for a particular point of view or course of action seek to convince people to adopt their proposal. The format is argumentative in nature, as in a debate, as one side competes against the other side for votes. There is often little opportunity in such formats for participants to find common ground, develop compromise proposals, or come to understand more fully the ideas of those from the other point of view. Majority-rule voting can also result in a "disgruntled minority" among those who feel their voices were not heard or respected.

One alternative to majority rule would be to have students elect a small group of representatives to a classroom council that would make a series of decisions for the rest of the class. Students could then assess the differences between direct and representative democracy in terms of how open and responsive these systems are to the issues and concerns of individuals and groups. Everyone can ask whose interests do elected representatives actually represent: the entire class, those who voted for them, or themselves?

After examining winner-take-all decision making, students and teachers can explore alternative democratic models, specifically instant runoff voting (IRV). This method is also called ranked-choice voting. In IRV/ranked-choice voting, voters rank order candidates according to their preferences (first, second, third). When the votes are counted, the candidate with the lowest number of votes is eliminated and those votes are reassigned to the voter's next highest preference. This process continues until a candidate receives a majority of the votes. Ranked-choice voting systems are used in Burlington, Vermont; Berkeley and San Francisco, California; Memphis, Tennessee; and Springfield, Illinois as well as by numerous other state and municipal governments. Cambridge, Massachusetts uses a variation of IRV for its city council elections. The FairVote website from the Center for Voting and Democracy maintains a list of where IRV is being used in governmental and nongovernmental organizations around the world.

In theory, IRV gives voters a greater sense of meaningful choice because they can express support for more than one candidate. Advocates also see this as a way to encourage greater voter interest in participation, particularly among voters under the age of 30 whose rates of voting, although rising, still lag behind other age groups in the population. Young people, aged 18 to 29, constitute only 21% of the electorate. The Center for Information and Research on Civic Learning and Engagement (CIRCLE; 2010, 2012) at Tufts University estimates that 37% of young people voted in the 1996 presidential election, 41% in 2000, 48% in 2004, 52% in 2008, and 49% in 2012. Interestingly, 19% of non-college youth and 12% of college students believe that voting or not voting does not matter to the outcome of an election (CIRCLE, 2011). Students and teachers can discuss whether an IRV system might make young people more likely to vote in the future.

As part of a study of voting, teachers and students could decide an issue or question using IRV and then discuss its advantages and complexities as an electoral reform concept. Here again, members of the classroom community experience firsthand how this type of democratic decision-making approach might work in actual practice. Design an election based on an historical or contemporary question that can be decided by IRV. Ask everyone to vote, expressing preferences in a rank-order from first to last. Tabulate the results in an open forum so everyone can see how the choices evolve according to the preferences expressed by the community. More information and an online demonstration can be found at "Instant Runoff Voting and the Single Transferrable Vote Elections Online" at the OpenSTV software website. An engaging way to explore how different voting systems produce different outcomes is the "Whammy Awards," an online simulation from the National Library of Virtual Manipulatives at Utah State University.

As a further point of comparison, students and teachers can make decisions using a weighed point system model such as that adopted by the Baseball Writers' Association of America (2013) for choosing the MVP (Most Valuable Player), Cy Young (best pitcher), Jackie Robinson Rookie of the Year, and Manager of Year award-winner for each league. The baseball writers vote for up to 10 choices for MVP, 5 for Cy Young, and 3 for rookie and manager of the year. Points are assigned to each position on the ballot with first place receiving the most points, second place the next highest, and so on. In baseball, a first place vote for MVP is worth 14 points; the rest of the points are worth 9, 8, 7, 6, 5, 4, 3, 2, and 1 respectively. The highest score is the winner. Similar point distributions could be established for a classroom voting simulation and students could then analyze the strengths and drawbacks of this type of decision-making model.

Strategy: Making Decisions by Sharing Power

Compromise and consensus are frequently used terms in American politics; open conversation is a less-mentioned concept. All three approaches are important in how students and teachers go about exploring democratic decision making. The meaning of the term compromise was prominently in the news in early 2013 when a firestorm of controversy erupted over an essay written by Emory University President James Wagner in which he referenced the Three/Fifths Compromise to the United States Constitution. That compromise (found in Article 1, Section 2, Paragraph 3) stated that in determining state representation in Congress, the government was to count "the whole number of free persons, . . . and, excluding Indians not taxed, three fifths of all other persons." The term *all other persons* was code for enslaved Blacks, numbering some 700,000 people throughout the original 13 states.

President Wagner cited the Three/Fifths Compromise to show the importance of compromise in a government and society dedicated to democratic decision making. In highly divisive political times such as then and now, Wagner (2013) wrote, political and civic leaders must work to achieve "pragmatic half-victories." At the Constitutional Convention, "both sides found a way to temper ideology and continue working toward the highest aspiration they shared—the aspiration to form a more perfect union." The Three/Fifths Compromise was eventually ended by the ratification of the 13th Amendment that abolished slavery throughout the United States.

Faculty and students from the history and Black studies departments spoke out angrily against Wagner's comments, declaring that a compromise negotiated by 55 delegates to the Constitutional Convention could not be viewed as an occasion of democratically driven decision making (Roark, 2013). The controversy is an instructive example of the complexities of using compromise to make decisions in any democratic system. Compromise between competing viewpoints does not automatically ensure a fair and just outcome has been achieved. In every situation, it matters not only what decisions are made, but also the kinds of systems and processes that are used to arrive at those outcomes.

The delegates to the Constitutional Convention may have reached a democratic result among themselves in passing the Three/Fifths Compromise, but they did not advance the larger values and purposes of a democratic society in which all members are created equal. Instead, they institutionalized discrimination based on race and made possible an exaggerated southern influence on national politics known as "the slave power." As Leonard Richards (2000) noted, before the Civil War "the slave states always had one-third more seats in Congress than their free population warranted" (p. 56). Garry Wills (2005) has suggested that without the power dynamics created by the Three/Fifth Compromise, Thomas Jefferson would not have won the electoral vote in 1800, "slavery would have been excluded from Missouri, Jackson's Indian Removal policy would have failed, the 1840 gag rule would not have been imposed, the Wilmot Proviso would have banned slavery in territories won from Mexico, the Kansas-Nebraska bill would have failed" (p. 5).

The story of the Three/Fifth Compromise creates teachable moments in history/social studies classes where the day-to-day processes of organizing and conducting learning include multiple opportunities for teachers and students to make decisions democratically. Students and teachers can consider whether or not other important compromises in American history including the Constitutional Convention's Great Compromise that created two houses for the national legislature, the 1820 Missouri Compromise, the Compromise of 1850, or the Compromise of 1877 resolved competing interests in ways that preserved and extended democratic values.

At the classroom level, rules for conduct, types of learning activities, topics for study, homework assignments, test assessments, and ways of responding to peer writing are all possible issues where students and teachers might compromise together, but such compromises need to explore not only competing proposals, but whether the result of compromise promotes or blocks democratic collaboration and decision making. Finding common ground on any decision means ensuring that no one is left feeling disrespected and no viewpoint is left unheard.

Using Consensus and Open Conversation

Consensus is a form of democratic decision making used in many organizational settings. In this approach, individuals or groups who are facing different or opposing courses of action seek common ground or consensus so that everyone feels as though their views have been heard and their interests fairly represented. Proposals are discussed, revised, and reassessed until all members of the group are satisfied with the final outcome. At this point, the consensus proposal or policy is enacted. Instead of one side getting a complete victory and the other side a total defeat, in a consensus model, everyone can feel as though they achieved important goals, at least partially.

Consensus means that solution or decision is "consented" to by the members of a group. Not everyone has to support all aspects of the decision, but "at least no participant believes the solution is so far outside of the group's best interest that it is necessary to block it" (Clark & Teachout, 2012, p. 159). Consensus can take time, it allows many ideas to be advanced for consideration, and it focuses on solutions rather than just problems. But groups must have a strategy for what to do when consensus cannot be reached—maintain the status quo, resolve the issue by majority vote, or use some other decision-making approach.

One effective consensus-building activity is a "Human Spectrum" where instead of taking a simple opposed-to or in favor-of position, students place themselves along a spectrum of agreement as they discuss an issue. An example might be a class study of Supreme Court cases involving student rights in school such as *Tinker v. Des Moines*, *Wallace v. Jaffree*, or *New Jersey v. T.L.O.* Students line up across the classroom with those most strongly agreeing with the one side at one end and those agreeing with the other side at the other end. Those who are not firmly for one side or the other, stand somewhere in the middle. The teacher then asks students along the spectrum to explain their position. As students hear the ideas of classmates, they are free to move themselves along the spectrum when a speaker prompts a shift in viewpoint. Often by the end of the discussion, the class has moved toward a more unified consensus.

In practice, consensus approaches can produce some of the same complexities as majority-rule voting. Some members of a group or organization may agree with a decision without having any real commitment to the proposed plan of action. There may even be lingering resentment or alienation among those who feel as though they had to compromise more of their goals than did other members of the group.

For this reason, some democratically inclined decision makers prefer to think in terms of having extended discussions that result in more complete support among all members of a group. Management consultant Peggy Holman (1997) called this "open conversation" to achieve "alignment" of beliefs. When facing a decision, group members continue talking about different ideas and proposals, exploring what they agree on, where the tensions or disagreements reside, and what are the various alternative courses of action that are open to them in this situation. The goal is for everyone "to be personally committed to actively implementing the decision" (Holman, 1997, p. 11).

Slow democracy advocates Susan Clark and Woden Teachout (2012) prefer the term *dynamic facilitation* to describe processes where group members spend the intensive time needed to develop support for a specific course of action. Dynamic facilitation "invites the assembled group to define (or redefine) the problem statement, helps underlying and previously unrecognized issues to emerge, allows multiple (potentially conflicting) solutions to be considered, and continually seeks additional options" (p. 160). Clark and Teachout acknowledge that a well-trained facilitator or leader is needed to guide the group through the choice creating process to a solution or new direction. Students and teachers using open conversation/dynamic facilitation will be in a position to experience these dynamics firsthand.

Following Martha's Rules of Order

Martha's Rules of Order offer another way to use discussion-based open communication as a classroom decision-making approach. *Martha's Rules* were developed in the 1970s at a residential housing cooperative in Madison, Wisconsin by co-op members dissatisfied with the length of time and complex procedures involved in making consensus-based decisions using

Robert's Rules of Order (Earth Conclave, nd. Minahan, 1986). The members of Martha's Co-Op wanted a simplified system that was responsive to and honored everyone's points of view and that gave the group a means to determine what issues were important enough to spend the time needed to develop a working consensus.

In making shared decisions about school and classroom matters, students and teachers can follow *Martha's Rules* as an alternative to *Robert's Rules of Order*. *Robert Rules* govern parliamentary procedures, such as how motions for voting can be raised for consideration by a group. They were created by Brigadier General Henry Robert of the Army Corps of Engineers just after the Civil War as a way standardize majority-rule decision making while allowing opportunities for the respectful presentation of minority viewpoints. Although the procedures may seem complex and arcane in a middle or high school classroom setting, using them as part of a lesson on voting procedures can be a useful introduction for students.

Following *Martha's Rules*, members of a group discuss an issue and generate a series of proposals for future action. Then, rather than a binding "yes/no" vote, the group takes a "sense" vote to determine who "likes" each proposal, who can "live with" that proposal (even if they do not agree with all aspects of the idea), and who is "uncomfortable" with that proposed course of action (Gastil, 1993, p. 60). After repeating this process for all proposals about an issue, the group has a much clearer idea of where everyone stands and what proposals merit consideration as items for final vote.

A variation of the "sense vote" in *Martha's Rules of Order* happens when students indicate their preference by putting their thumbs up (approval), thumbs sideways (they can live with a decision), thumbs down (disapproval). Any vote where students indicate a thumbs-down position requires further discussion with attention to those students who disapprove. This model allows for the minority voices to be heard even when a clear majority position exists.

Conclusion

Winston Churchill once remarked that "democracy is the worst form of government, except for all other forms that have been tried from time to time" (Langworth, 2008, p. 574). In theory, democracy enables a majority of decision makers to express their preferences while allowing minority decision makers the right to dissent and the opportunity to build new majorities around their viewpoints in the future. In practice, issues of power, information, access, and finances disturb and disrupt democratic outcomes, as the growing role of money in elections has amply demonstrated. Moreover, the way a decision-making system operates has a profound effect on how and what decisions are made. A winner-take-all voting system, for example, where a candidate can be elected or a resolution can be passed with a simple majority of votes can restrict the issues being decided to either/or decisions.

In this chapter, we have proposed ways for students and teachers to make decisions and share power collaboratively. Establishing classroom rules and handling discipline, building learning-oriented mindsets, and analyzing different decision-making models all serve to teach students about democracy in schools and society. Such collaborative decision-making and power-sharing practices connect students to the key issues and complexities in America's larger democratic system in two important ways.

Students and teachers, used to longstanding adult-centered approaches to classroom control, tend to think narrowly about the topics and practices they might decide collectively. Democratic decision making shows them how it is possible, indeed, desirable to collaborate together on many more aspects of classroom and instructional activity than they may have first imagined. Making decisions democratically builds a participatory classroom culture where students feel invested in the both the process and the outcome. Rules, regulations, and routines ranging from when homework is due to how discussions and presentations will happen can be decided in democratic fashion rather than by teacher-stated procedures.

As they conduct multiple decision-making activities in the classroom, students and teachers experience a variety of power sharing practices first-hand, thus giving them intellectual and experiential frameworks for analyzing the "democratic nature" of each approach. Decision-making practices and power sharing can be done at younger and older grade levels. What is needed are authentic issues or questions around which students and teachers can express their ideas, opinions, and proposals for change.

Influenced by America's dominant political culture, students and teachers tend to think first of making decisions by majority-rule voting where the winner takes all and everyone accepts the outcome. But majority-rule voting is not the only approach and there are important benefits to be realized when other models are introduced and discussed. Cooperative organizations and workplaces as well as slow democracy practices illustrate the value of deliberative ways of deciding issues and conducting business democratically. Classrooms provide students and teachers with living laboratories where they can try different approaches to democratic decision making and assess them in terms of their advantages and drawbacks for all participants.

Chapter 4

Conversing

Conversations, Discussions, and Student Voice

> As educators, we cannot simply teach through discussion but need to teach for discussion. I think we forget that having a meaningful, organized discussion is not necessarily easy, especially when students are not accustomed to it. Taking the time to have students figure out how this is to be accomplished is well worth it.
>
> —Middle School Teacher Candidate

More than 50 years ago, sociologist Philip Jackson began conducting the observations of elementary school classrooms that would become the basis of his classic book, *Life in Classrooms* (1990). Determined to document the everyday realities of schools, Jackson quickly found "the task of looking at the commonplace quite challenging." School classrooms, places seemingly familiar to all of us since our days as students, "have a way of lulling the visitor into a comfortable state of inattention that can easily lead to drowsiness" (p. xiii).

Unsure how to fulfill his research goals and "wishing to stay as awake and attentive as possible" during the long school day, Jackson started counting and timing the physical movements and interpersonal communications he saw in classrooms. As he made the "familiar feel strange," he found that communications between teachers and students were "surprisingly high . . . not only higher than I would have predicted but also higher than any of the teachers guessed it to be when I questioned them about it later" (p. xiii). In Jackson's view, those seemingly commonplace events constituted the reality of education for many students.

Jackson's observations made apparent how teachers engage in hundreds of verbal and nonverbal communications with students every teaching day.

The effect of these interactions accumulate to more than 900 to 1,000 hours that children and adolescents spend in school each year as ideas and information flow back and forth from adults to students and from students to adults through spoken and written language, facial expressions, and meaningful gestures. Teacher and student conversation also happens throughout the school building—in offices, hallways, and lunchrooms as well as on playing fields and auditorium stages. Conversations are so central to the collective K–12 education experience that we could hardly imagine school without them.

Conversing, the next of democratic teaching's 7 Cs, advances the idea that democracy is fostered in the ways that teachers and students communicate with one another in school classrooms and corridors. Conversing includes how teachers "communicate with students so students will participate and participate with students so students will communicate," to paraphrase the title of Adele Faber and Elaine Mazlish's (1999) popular book on adult–child communication strategies. Conversing also includes students believing in themselves as individuals who have important ideas to share and who are learning how to express their voices publicly through classroom discussions and activities.

In democratic classrooms, communication must be genuine, respectful, and inclusive so students feel their ideas matter and adults are willing to listen, even when adults disagree with what is being said. Substantive and respectful patterns of communication make possible the active engagement of multiple individual voices, creating a foundation for engaging and stimulating teaching and learning in the history/social studies classroom.

Communication in Classrooms

Ideally, members of a democratic society are constantly communicating with one another through voting, discussing issues, joining political parties, participating in protests, writing letters to politicians, blogging about politics, and sharing personal viewpoints at family gatherings, recreational events, and social functions. Free communication is the essence of the democratic experience. A long intellectual tradition extending from John Stuart Mill to John Dewey to modern theorists has held that "in a democracy, leaders should therefore give reasons for their decisions, and respond to the reasons that citizens give in return" (Gutmann & Thompson, 2004, p. 3).

In a "deliberative democracy," open and honest discussion is essential for political governance where "leaders give reasons for their decisions and respond to the reasons that citizens give." As political scientists Amy Gutmann and Dennis Thompson (2004, p. 4) note, such deliberations must be conducted in public arenas where everyone has access to what is being considered: "To justify imposing their will on you, your fellow citizens must give reasons that are comprehensible to you. If you seek to impose your will on them, you owe them no less."

Classrooms are laboratories for democracy, generating experiences that help form how students will think about and participate in democratic institutions and practices in their lives and careers. To build informed understandings about the issues they will face in their future lives, students need experiences where they share their ideas with other individuals who may or may not agree with them. As workers, voters, and community members, students face a lifetime of situations where multiple viewpoints may not coincide and in which they must decide how to make sense of what to do.

In theory, democratic communication happens through the frameworks that teachers create for students for discussing history/social studies topics and for interacting with one another as members of classroom communities. "Good discussions in the social studies," observed teacher Nora Flynn (2009), "are essential for both tackling content and practicing an essential democratic and human process. . . ." (p. 2023). Democratic communication in classrooms means students are learning to discuss ideas and issues in open-minded, thoughtful ways—a key to building the thinking skills needed for active, engaged citizenship in our modern, fast-paced, highly complex technological society.

Teacher-led presentations and lectures are not the equivalent to student-led discussions and conversations, and the differences between the experiences convey distinctly different messages for both adolescents and adults. After a year of teaching in an urban high school, one history teacher candidate concluded: "Students have more meaningful experiences when interacting with one another, rather than me being the focal point of the conversation or learning experience."

Teachers and students do not regularly converse in ways that promote active participation or communication by everyone in the classroom. In the 1980s, as part of a large-scale study of hundreds of schools across the country, John Goodlad (1984) found that in most classrooms at most grade levels, teachers talked and students listened. The percentages of how time was spent in school classrooms were staggering—as much as 90% of the time, students listen to teacher lectures, do worksheets, or otherwise experience school in ways that do not promote active learning or critical thinking. As Goodlad (1984) observed:

From the beginning, students experience school and classroom environments that condition them in precisely opposite behaviors—seeking "right" answers, conforming, and reproducing the known. These behaviors are reinforced daily by the physical restraints of the group and classroom, by the kinds of questions teachers ask, by the nature of the seatwork exercises assigned, and by the format of tests and quizzes. (p. 241)

Recitation versus Authentic Discussion

"*Recitation*, rather than *authentic discussion*, is the common mode of discourse in most classrooms," concluded educator Thomas M. McCann and his colleagues (McCann, Johannessen, Kahn, & Flanagan, 2006, p. 2). In McCann's view, many teachers tightly control discussion time in classrooms, if they allow discussion to happen at all. There is little actual discussion (meaning an in-depth exchange of ideas and information) in typical middle or high school classes. What happens instead is a predictable form of classroom communication where teachers ask questions, wait for one or two students to offer answers, and then provide commentary as to whether the student responses met the teacher's criteria for correctness.

These "initiation–response–evaluation" patterns of communication, noted a group of English educators, "places a premium on transmission of information, providing very little room for the exploration of ideas, which is necessary for the development of deeper understanding" (Applebee, Langer, Nystrand, & Gamoran, 2003, p. 689). Far less often do teachers ask open-ended questions where students consider alternative ideas or explanations and then respond thoughtfully from their own points of view.

Through conversation and talk, students get to explore ideas, engage in critical analysis, hear differing perspectives, and make personal judgments. Education reformer Deborah Meier contends that a meaningful discussion not only promotes learning academic material, but also "fosters an environment of tolerance, critical thinking, and democratic spirit" (cited in McCann et al., 2006, p. 5). Other educators note the lasting importance of teachers engaging in authentic conversation with students. If teachers pose authentic questions, invite multiple responses, and encourage wide participation while challenging students to support their ideas, "then, over time, students internalize the process, imitate the behaviors of the teacher, and expect discussions to be a dynamic exchange and exploration of ideas" (McCann et al., 2006, p. 6). In short, students learn to act and think in more democratic ways.

The growing cultural and linguistic diversity of today's classes are causing increasing numbers of educators to focus on the importance of discussion and conversation as tools for learning the academic language of schools. Students speaking English as a new language and students from lower socioeconomic backgrounds come to schools with a rich linguistic background, but that background does not always prepare them for the speaking, reading, and writing challenges presented by teachers, textbooks, and other students.

Language in school classrooms is academic, featuring particular English grammatical constructions and advanced subject-specific vocabulary. Students must develop the literacy skills needed to understand and use academic languages of math, science, history, and English/language arts. As language educator Pauline Gibbons (2009, p. 5) remarked, "the development of literacy within *any* subject in the school curriculum involves learning to control new language." How conversation happens in classrooms is vital to the process of students learning the languages needed in different academic and educational contexts.

Class Discussion and Student Performance

Research in high school physics classrooms offers evidence of how the structure of class discussion can affect the academic performance of students, providing insights for history/social studies teachers using debate and dialog with their classes. In one widely cited study, the use of debate-oriented discussion formats was linked to the fact the number of girls pursuing physics in high school continues to lag well behind boys—despite test results showing young women just as capable as men at learning and mastering science concepts. Reviewing research on gender participation in science classrooms, Laura Ann Robertson (2006, p. 178) found that many women "feel a social pressure to hide their intellect in a public or school setting." This pressure includes a strong reluctance to express ideas in class, in effect, choosing to remain silent during discussions and not volunteering ideas or hypotheses when asked by teachers.

Women face multiple pressures in science classrooms, including a longstanding assumption that men are more gifted in math and science and should be in control of science experiments. One teacher recalled that she "had very few females take over the experiments" (Robertson, 2006, p. 178). Teachers also contribute to student attitudes by favoring or appearing to favor males over females in classroom discussions and activities. As Robertson (2006, p. 178) noted, "If females even think that they perceive discrimination in their classroom, they will be less likely to apply themselves to their studies." Many girls in science classrooms simply do not believe that they have the ability to be successful in physics or other hard science areas.

"Refutational discussion" is a common teaching approach in the science classroom, much like debates among students are a popular instructional method in the history/social studies classroom. In refutational discussion, students argue with one other, sometimes defending or responding to an incorrect opinion that the teacher has inserted into the discussion. Many girls are unwilling to enter into the clash of ideas or theories with boys or with other girls. A similar dynamic happens when history/social studies teachers implement debates in class. A percentage of girls and boys are unlikely or unwilling to argue verbally in class, preferring to remain disengaged from the activity.

Robertson (2006, p. 179) recommends the use of writing as a way for students in general and girls in particular to express their ideas without the interpersonal confrontations that can emerge in refutational or debate-oriented discussions. She also sees great benefits in "circle talk," a discussion format "where students sit in a circle and discuss concepts, ideas, and questions they have with the materials." Both approaches promote dialogue rather than debate and can be used in the history/social studies classroom as well. In each case, students become active participants rather than passive observers whose voices matter, skills that are central to future participation in democratically run organizations and society. They also enable students to build mindsets of themselves as capable thinkers and problem solvers whose voices and values matter in the school and the community.

Voices of Teacher Candidates:
Democratic Discussion as an Instructional Method

The history and social studies teacher candidates in our program expressed a strong commitment to using discussion as a primary instructional method for learning history. Even candidates paired with cooperating teachers who emphasized lectures, worksheets, and minimal teacher–student interactions still imagined themselves using discussions regularly when they became full-time lead teachers. As one high school history candidate stated:

> I have found that all students respond well and learn through discussion-based instruction. I teach one class in particular that most would not characterize as "the best and brightest," but those students engage in some of the highest learning discussions

I have facilitated in class. They have strong and well thought out opinions about government, economics, and the law. Discussions provide a way for them to express those thoughts in way that works better for them than testing or other traditional assessments.

Generally, teacher candidates also endorsed the idea of student-led discussions. One middle school teacher intern noted: "I really appreciate the focus on having students effectively communicate with each other face to face and that it emphasizes active listening." Another intern said: "I think getting students to think about the role they play in discussions is a good way to make them realize the different aspects of a discussion." A high school intern, although recognizing that as a teacher he is comfortable in a leadership role, agreed that for students "there is no more powerful learning tool than being asked to lead a discussion."

In one high school, candidates from our university program used the "Harkness Model" for class discussions. Developed originally at Phillips Exeter Academy, an independent school in Massachusetts, the Harkness model promotes student-led discussion with a minimum of teacher guidance or control (Mullgardt, 2008; Phillips Exeter Academy, nd). To begin the conversation, an open-ended guiding question is posed for a class to consider; for example: "Are the powers of the federal government balanced and appropriately distributed throughout the executive, legislative and judicial branches?" Students, who have done the homework and had a chance to think about the question in advance, begin a discussion in which everyone is expected to participate. The students direct the discussion, listening respectfully to each other's ideas and following the flow of the conversation through different aspects of the question.

Group motivation and direction are keys to a successful Harkness discussion. The entire class receives the same grade—A, B, C, or D—depending on how successfully everyone engages with the question and encourages everyone to participate as equally as possible. It is the responsibility of the group to generate a full and thoughtful process. To receive the highest grade, the students encourage less vocal classmates to share their ideas, they maintain a respectful conversational tone, and they support their statements with historical evidence from the textbook, other readings, and primary source materials. The teacher intervenes only to redirect the conversation or to ask students how they can respond differently to improve the depth and substance of the conversation.

After conducting his first Harkness discussion, one candidate admitted, "I had never thought about allowing students to drive the entire conversation without teacher input. Allowing students this freedom seems to be a great way to get them to express ideas over just regurgitating facts." The process is not without challenges. This history candidate noted that "the lack of direction seems to perplex some of the more rule-oriented students," whereas usually quiet students sometimes struggle to find the confidence to express their ideas. Over time, the candidate concluded, this format promotes the "building of teamwork skills, trust between students, and a commitment to studying in order to be prepared and not let your classmates down."

Each year, some candidates are uncomfortable allowing students to lead discussions. One high school candidate wrote a lesson in which students gathered information to assess Napoleon's historical legacy and to judge whether he should be remembered as "Napoleon the Great" or "Napoleon the Terrible." When all information was collected, students discussed their findings with classmates. Observing interactions between students, the candidate concluded, "even though the student-driven sharing was constructive and helpful, I constantly felt an urge to lead the discussion."

Teacher candidates cited the pressures of adhering to curriculum frameworks and respecting the attitudes of mentor teachers as major obstacles to the use of student-led discussions in the classroom. Noted one: "Most teachers who I have worked with extol the importance of covering the frameworks at all costs; regardless of the fact that covering the standards often leaves half the class unconscious." A middle school candidate observed: "In general, most people want to see a teacher who can control a class like a lion tamer controls lions in a circus. Supervisors do not seem to care if students are trained to participate in a democracy." A third concluded, "the brisk pace of the curriculum leaves these discussions entirely teacher facilitated and not long enough for all students to actively participate and engage with the material."

Additional concerns about student-led discussions focused on the demands of classroom management. One candidate commented: "In the past, the class has quickly devolved into loud, disrespectful arguments—often including students who have impulse control issues. So I've decided to make a list of those who raise their hands to keep one person talking at a time, but that keeps me in a controlling role." Another candidate suggested that truly student-centered discussions might not be possible because "no matter what, the teacher is always going to have a hand in the discussion, whether it's by choosing the topic or the activity. Students may be given the chance to make choices as often as possible, but the teacher will always play a role."

Conversing Strategies for Building Democracy

In *Democracy in Small Groups*, John Gastil (1993, pp. 3, 6) observed that "group decision making can proceed according to democratic or undemocratic principles." Family gatherings, community meetings, governmental chambers, and public school classrooms can be places for small group democracy when members have "equal and adequate opportunities to speak, neither withhold information nor verbally manipulate one another, and are able and willing to listen."

This chapter's "Building Democracy" activities provide students and teachers with ways to converse democratically in school classrooms. The goal is for them to build patterns of communication and establish norms of discussion that make schools democratically based places for both students and teachers to learn from each other. Without multiple voices expressing and sharing ideas and perspectives in classes, history/social studies education remains top–down, nonparticipatory, teacher-centered time.

The following activities are intended to support open exchanges of ideas in democratic classrooms. Each is more student-centered than teacher-centered, and each emphasizes the importance of thoughtful questions, respectful interactions, and insightful interpretations. The first focuses on how teachers can support students in building positive, growth-oriented mindsets for learning; the second looks at how teachers and students can sustain writing as a form of creative communication and self-expression; the third explores how students can lead productive classroom discussions.

Strategy: Affirming Students' Beliefs in Themselves as Learners

In a now classic book, *Developing Talent in Young People*, Benjamin Bloom (1985) explored the early learning experiences of world-class athletes, musicians, scientists, and mathematicians. Individual talent is not enough to produce exceptional performance, said Bloom; a highly successful person's abilities and interests have been nurtured and expanded through support from family members, teachers, coaches, and other adults. Rejecting the idea that anyone is naturally predisposed to success, Bloom (1985) concluded: "What any person in the world can learn, *almost* all persons can learn *if* provided with appropriate prior and current conditions of learning" (p. 4).

To build favorable learning conditions for all students, other researchers call for teachers to affirm everyone's belief in her or himself as a learner.

Students need to believe that they are smart, capable, worthwhile individuals whose contributions matter to the classroom community just as citizens need to believe their roles matter as members of a democratic society. In this sense, students possess what the early 20th-century sociologist Charles Horton Cooley called a "looking glass self": They are what they think others think they are. When students are told they are smart, they strive to perform well academically. Teachers can dramatically influence students' conceptions of themselves by how they support student mindsets, acknowledge student effort, and mentor student writing.

Developing Growth Mindsets

Seeking ways to help students to succeed in school, Stanford University psychologist Carol Dweck has been researching the effect of "mindsets" on individuals' academic performance. A mindset is a group of taken-for-granted assumptions and beliefs that each individual develops about her or his skills and capabilities. These assumptions influence how students and teachers face challenges and opportunities by embracing or avoiding them.

In her book, *Mindset: The New Psychology of Success* (2006), Dweck observes that each person, through interactions and conversations with others, develops beliefs about his or her abilities that form either a "fixed" or a "growth" mindset. A person with a fixed mindset sees his or her talents, abilities, and intelligence as determined at birth by genetics, and not subject to change. Accordingly, for a fixed-mindset individual, the goal is to go through life avoiding challenges that might lead to failure. A person with a growth mindset, by contrast, sees her or his talents, abilities, and intelligence as fluid, always in a state of change based on experience and practice. Therefore, for someone operating from a growth mindset, life is a series of new challenges to be met and refined.

Mindsets powerfully affect learning school performance. Encountering a difficult or unfamiliar math problem, youngsters with a fixed mindset might say "I have never been good at math" or "Math is not my thing," signifying an inherent belief that no matter how hard they may try, they basically lack the intuitive intellectual capacity to understand the concepts, or worse, to successfully learn math. By contrast, youngsters who view intelligence in more open, malleable terms through a growth mindset believe that they can learn just about anything they put their minds to. Facing the same math problem, these students might say "I can do it if you show me how" or "With a little (or a lot) of effort and practice, I will learn how to figure it out." They are confident in their abilities because they continually see themselves as able to learn what they want or need to learn.

The use of praise in classrooms is a key to developing or inhibiting growth mindsets. Praise is a crucial variable in how students think about themselves and their abilities (Dweck, 2006; Kohn, 1999; Tough, 2013). In one of Dweck's well-known praise experiments, two groups of students were given a nonverbal IQ test based on solving fairly easy puzzles. They were told their score and given a single statement of feedback about their performance. One group was praised for their intelligence: "You must be smart at this." The other group was praised for their effort: "You must have worked really hard" (Bronson & Merryman, 2009, p 14).

On a subsequent test, the children could choose whether to see harder puzzles or take another test with fairly easy puzzles. Students who were praised for their intelligence chose to see the easier puzzles; 90% of those praised for their effort chose to see the harder ones. Dweck concluded that praising someone's intelligence made the so-called "smart" students risk averse to failure; they were reluctant to risk their perceived status as smart by doing poorly on a harder task. Dweck repeated her experiments with students of different ages and from different socioeconomic groups, but the dynamic remained consistent—praising individual effort had a different effect on learners than praising personal intelligence.

For Dweck, praise, as a much-used form of teacher–student and student–student communication, should be carefully and selectively directed. It must be specific, sincere, and focused on a person's real efforts and determination, rather than on innate or "natural" skills or abilities. Students are perceptive, able to identify insincere forms of praise. They may assume insincere praise means that they did poorly and that the adults are simply trying to cover up the lack of performance with statements of encouragement (Bronson & Merryman, 2009, p. 20). This does not mean that criticism rather than praise is the best way to demonstrate support for someone's performance. Rather, students develop growth mindsets from genuine communications about their work that identify strengths as well as areas for improvement, all within a context that explains how strong academic performance in school is enhanced by thoughtful work and sustained commitment.

Acknowledging Student Effort

We have all heard the statements "good job," "way to go," "nicely done," or "do it again just like that" uttered by adults when students have done something that the adults wanted to see happen. Adults assume broad compliments will motivate and inspire students to continue what it was they were being praised for doing. Education reformer Alfie Kohn (2001) summarized the case against such broad use of praise in his article, "Five Reasons To Stop Saying Good Job." Kohn asserts that teachers and other adults who offer praise by telling students "good job!" after they finish an assignment or activity are in fact perpetuating a set of teacher-dominated power relationships that block students' meaningful engagement with learning.

In Kohn's (2001, 2014) view, "good job" not only fails to convey adult support for student learning, but also unambiguously asserts adult control over students in the classroom. Spoken by teachers to students, "good job" declares, "I'm happy you did the activity the way I want or expect." It is a hierarchical statement that gives all the authority to teachers and none to students—after all, students never say "good job" to teachers. Students learn to look to adults for approval of their work rather than see adults as learning partners who can assist in acquiring new skills and understandings.

The word "good" is often delivered as a single declarative statement without additional information or clarification. Pressed for time in a busy classroom, a teacher gives a student's work a quick look, declares "good job," and moves on to the next student. "Good job" in this context implies a brief judgment or evaluation, in the sense that something is complete and finished. Students, Kohn believes, are not looking for such judgments or evaluations of goodness from their teachers. Instead, they want substantive feedback about their work that might include both what is learned and what needs improvement. They want a communicative conversation about their work, including ideas for how to change, improve, or broaden thinking rather than a simply stated positive evaluation.

Hidden in these communications are subtle definitions of the role of teaching as understood by many teachers and experienced by many students. When teaching is seen primarily as transmitting academic content and students learn that material as it has been presented, then teachers can be perfectly comfortable saying "good job," meaning "you did what I wanted you to do." But, when teaching is defined as multimodal, differentiated instruction that uses different activities to reach all learners, then the praise should go the other way—from student to teacher. In this context, students should be comfortable saying to adults: "good job, you have succeeded in helping us all to learn."

Kohn's approach begins to recast the ground rules of teacher–student conversation about academic work in the classroom. Instead of "good job" praise, Kohn recommends the following alternative types of responses:

- Teachers "say nothing"—just smile or give a thumbs up sign.
- Teachers say what they observed and then "provide feedback not judgment."

- Teachers ask more questions such as: "What do you like best about what you wrote?"

- Teachers appreciate and honor genuine effort and work: "you did it" or "you put in the time and accomplished this project," or "I see the improvement you've made."

In this context of building growth mindsets, any single response is insufficient; what students need are ongoing conversations with adults that lets them explore ideas and issues. Teacher responses, presented in a complimentary tone of voice, can open conversations with students while simultaneously affecting how those students think about themselves as learners. Statements such as "That's very interesting; how did you come up with that idea?" or "I would like to hear that story again" set the stage for further discussions about the substance of what students are thinking.

Growth mindsets and thoughtfully delivered praise of student effort create foundations for democratic communications by empowering students to express thoughts, contrast positions, and explore questions. No one is a "natural" at discussing ideas publicly. All of us, students and teachers alike, must learn how to effectively participate in class conversations and discussions. Communicating democratically requires that students develop beliefs in themselves as capable, confident learners and competent communicators who can present well-developed arguments and easily understood explanations.

Teachers are instrumental in creating these beliefs; oral and written responses influence how students perceive their abilities, skills, and potentials as learners. In the framework of mindset research, teacher comments are key to promoting a growth mindset where students see themselves as capable of greater learning; in the framework of democratic teaching, teacher comments can reduce what students see as a hierarchy of adult control in favor of more equal learning communities.

Responding to Young Writers

Many students lack confidence in their writing. Generating ideas from their imagination and expressing them in written language has not been a regular part of their school experience. They need mentors, not evaluators of writing performance—mentors who support writing within a social and conversational process that affirms the belief that every student is a writer, right now. Every student has ideas, information, perspectives, and opinions they can express using multiple genres of written language in both print and digital mediums.

We have called this approach a "writing process fit for young writers" (Edwards, Maloy, & Verock-O'Loughlin, 2003; Maloy, Verock-O'Loughlin, Edwards, & Woolf, 2014). This approach builds on the widely used model of a "writing process" where ideas unfold in written language through a non-linear combination of brainstorming, drafting, revising/editing, and publishing (Calkins, 1986). A writing-process approach expands the definition of school writing from only formal essays and research papers to include all forms of written and artistic expression by students.

Every part of the writing process has a participatory conversational focus that teachers can use to communicate with young writers:

- Brainstorming = Opening

- Drafting = Supporting

- Revising/Editing = Responding

- Publishing = Celebrating

Teachers unlock hidden realms of creative possibilities by carefully crafting what to say and when to say it as they communicate with students about writing. Here are some statements that teachers might use, orally or in written language, as they respond to what students have written. They are general in nature so they can be used with both nonfiction and fiction writing. The statements are arranged by the stages of the writing process.

Opening. Opening sets writing in motion by activating students' powers of imagination and self-expression. Teachers create openings by reading aloud the work of other writers, showing how students have used a writer's approach or genre, or reading their own writing to the class. All these strategies will inspire young writers to put pencil to paper and begin sharing their ideas. During openings, a teacher's conversation focuses broadly on what the student is writing. A teacher might say:

- "Are you writing a new idea or something you have been thinking about for a while?"

- "You sound really excited about this idea. Tell me more about it."

Supporting. Supporting includes whatever helps students express their ideas, orally or in written language: Writing student dictation, sharing the pencil or computer keyboard as co-writers with students and teachers both writing parts of an essay or story, answering questions about word meaning or spelling, or recording an oral draft so young writers can listen to the draft of ideas in their own voice. The goal here is supporting students to continue writing so initial efforts are revised to completed drafts. Teacher communications include:

- "This section really surprised me? Did it surprise you?"

- "Would you read this section aloud? Let's both hear your ideas."

- "This character reminds me of [insert favorite character and/ or author] who is always getting into complex situations like [insert other example]."

Responding. Responding serves as a supportive first audience for a student's writing while providing positive feedback and useful comments about how the writing might convey ideas more effectively to readers. In responding, a teacher might say:

- "These words create a picture in my mind. I can see what you are describing here. This [sentence, paragraph, dialogue] is less clear. What is on your mind here?"

- I do not yet understand what is happening here. Tell me more about your ideas so we can figure out what it is you want the reader to know."

- The punctuation is less clear here. Let's read it aloud and I will put a tiny dot wherever your voice stops. Then let's decide if you want a period, a comma, a dash, an exclamation point, or a question mark."

Celebrating. Celebrating finds different ways to showcase and share students' writing, bringing the writing process full circle from initial ideas and first drafts to a completed text that can be shared with readers. Celebrating, a teacher might say:

- "I enjoy reading what you have written; it always surprises me and that is why it is so interesting."

- "Your writing makes me think about my own writing." "I will go back and revise mine after reading yours."

Opening, supporting, responding, and celebrating are powerful communication opportunities for teachers. They let students know that a writer does not have to work alone, but can develop ideas in dynamic conversations with adults who offer perspectives, comments, and support. From such communicative partnerships, students' confidence and talent as writers and citizens begin to emerge.

Strategy: Expanding Student Voice Using Social Media

Students in history/social studies classes regularly share ideas and information using oral and written language—often in response to teacher-directed assignments—while teachers routinely provide comments and evaluations of student work. This instructional pattern has profound implications for how students think about themselves as communicators of ideas who can express viewpoints and exert influence on organizations and communities.

When communication is largely based on students responding to teacher prompts and questions, and used to assign a letter grade, students often conclude that their ideas only matter as a way to pass a class. But when teachers and students converse with each other in less formal ways, then students start to see communication, both oral and written, as important ways to carry one's ideas into the public arena. They find new ways to express their voice through conversation and writing.

Social media is the way students increasingly converse with one another outside of school. Texting, Facebook, Twitter, Instagram, Snapchat, and other formats combine the informality of oral speech among friends with the use of written text to create authentic communications that are not evaluated or graded by adults. Yet, these very formats open new ways for students and teachers to converse about academic topics. Low-tech instant messaging (IM) and microblogging backchannels are two strategies in which student-centered conversations can be used to support democratic communication in the history/social studies classroom.

Sharing Ideas through Low-Tech IM

Low-tech IM is an instructional approach that uses middle and high school students' sophistication with text messaging to generate word and picture exchanges of ideas and information about curriculum topics. Displaying writing on paper or whiteboards, low-tech IM offers a way to use a writing process fit for young writers to promote student-led communication in the history/social studies classroom.

In recent years, text messaging has emerged as perhaps the most popular form of digital communication among teenagers, allowing for private real-time exchanges between two or more individuals using text instead of voice. For many years, SMS (short message service) texts on computers, phones, and other mobile devices were the most widely used form of text-based communications. In 2013, instant messaging using chat apps surged ahead in usage. It has been estimated that 50 billion messages a day using chat apps will be sent this year.

To begin a low-tech IM conversation, a teacher or a student posts a thread on the classroom whiteboard or on one of the sheets of large newsprint paper hung around the room. For example, studying the home front during World War II, a teacher might post a comment along with some questions about Japanese internment and the accompanying Supreme Court decisions that defended these incursions on civil liberties of Japanese Americans. Students then go to the board or papers to offer their own comments, first in response to the initial post and subsequently in response to other students' comments. This creates multiple threads in the conversation. Alternatively, students in a class can be broken into groups and reply to a comment on each other's thread response.

This conversation functions like an online blog or discussion board, except that it is on paper in the classroom where everyone can easily read all the preceding comments before posting their own thoughts about the topic. Text-messaging language is allowed so abbreviations, shorthand statements, and made-up symbols are frequently used. Students like the approach because they feel as though they are using a familiar outside-of-school tool during academic time. Students who are reluctant or unwilling to speak aloud in class have the option of using written language instead. Teachers appreciate the activity for its capacity to keep students thinking analytically about the causes and consequences of key historical events.

Low-tech IM connects to democracy and democratic teaching in multiple ways. First, the discussion is written and sustained by students. The teacher can be a contributor, but not a director of the conversation. Second, teachers and students have a ready-made opportunity to discuss the implications of writers offering signed or unsigned comments in response to a post.

Third, low-tech IM involves students expressing their own ideas in writing and responding to other students' writing as well—both important aspects of democratic citizenship. Exploring this idea, one teacher candidate gave each student in her high school class a small piece of paper and asked them to write keywords they remembered from the previous day's lesson. "Then they switched [papers] and another person had to respond to what they wrote in terms of what they thought [the keywords] meant, or remembered about it. They returned the paper back to the original person and that person got to grade the other on what they wrote. The students really took it seriously because their peers were grading them." The teacher saw great value in students responding to other students: "They have to completely understand the material before they can judge someone else's understanding of it." The grade was less important to the students than the idea that peers were paying close attention so everyone's writing needed to be thoughtful and clear.

Opening Microblogging Backchannels

Microblogging using Twitter offers another way to use student writing to promote democratically based communications in the history/social studies classrooms. Twitter has already dramatically transformed how people communicate. In 2013, Twitter claimed 200 million active accounts. On Twitter, one can follow news stories, athletic events, or celebrity happenings as news reporters and citizen journalists tweet about what they are observing at a scene in near-to-real time. Additionally, politicians, commentators, and spokespeople instantly react to daily developments. Friends, too, regularly share information and updates by tweeting back and forth. All of these digital interactions have led to interesting experiments with how to use microblogging tools in school classrooms.

There are numerous creative ways for students and teachers to use Twitter, including linking in-class Prezi presentations to the teacher's Twitter account so students can view and review material on a computer or mobile device at any time. With class material available anytime online, students can concentrate fully on activities during class and later go to the Prezi for note-taking and test review. Teachers can also tweet information and links about daily lesson topics. Joe Emery, a high school history candidate and already a daily Twitter user remarked:

> One of my favorite activities is to find answers to students' questions that I do not have during class. By posting information on Twitter, I am responding to students' passions and interests and allowing them to more fully investigate questions they have.

Teacher-generated tweets are one-way communications from adults to students. TodaysMeet, a Twitter-like microblogging system, enables students to use smartphones or laptops to post comments about learning activities as they happen during class time. The use of TodaysMeet accesses and makes explicit a communication backchannel that exists in every classroom—the conversations and commentaries not generated by a teacher. It includes thoughts and questions that students think to themselves or share with friends. TodaysMeet invites students to display on a classroom smartboard their backchannel thoughts so everyone can learn from these ideas and questions. Joe viewed TodaysMeet as "a space where students could connect with me and with their peers, and I really liked the idea of having only 140 characters so students focus their thoughts and are selective about their word choice."

While studying the use of the atomic bomb in World War II with a high school class, Joe asked students to use TodaysMeet to rank five end-the-war scenarios that American policymakers had available in 1945 after the development of the bomb technology by the Manhattan Project. The bomb could be: (a) kept secret; (b) detonated in the desert so Japan could hear about the new weapon; (c) detonated in the desert with a Japanese delegation present to observe the weapon in action; (d) used in military demonstration in a deserted part of Japan; or (e) dropped immediately on a Japanese city. After posting their policy choices, the class compared their results with the recommendations of American scientists at the time. In this format, students' own writing enabled them to simulate the actual role of historians, evaluating decisions and critiquing policy choices.

In a different class, Joe asked groups of students to post on TodaysMeet their recommendations to President McKinley about what to do with the Philippines following the Spanish-American War in 1898. Should the United States annex the islands, maintain only a portion of the archipelago, leave Spain in control of the area, or pursue another policy? The class divided into five groups, each representing a different perspective for or against annexation, including: business interests (*Chicago Inter-Ocean* and *Railway Road* magazines), religious representatives (Reverend Wallace Radcliffe), military leaders (General Wesley Merritt), Republicans (Henry Cabot Lodge and Albert Beveridge), and Democrats (William Jennings Bryan). After consulting primary sources, each group sent recommendations, recreating in the classroom the national debate of that time.

With these interactive conversations, Joe made microblogging a regular feature of classroom communication and instruction. The technology encouraged students' historical thinking as they went about analyzing primary sources, reading multiple accounts of events, understanding historical context, and weighing evidence to support claims about what happened. The short responses on TodaysMeet gave students valuable practice in formulating viewpoints and cogently expressing them online. Finally, by asking clarifying questions during presentations, posting comments for later discussion, and expressing reactions to primary source documents and historically themed videos, students' voices and viewpoints were featured and respected in the classroom.

Strategy: Implementing Student-Centered Discussions

Anyone who has taught at any grade level remembers moments when students spontaneously talked to each other about the topic of the day. Back and forth the comments flow—substantive, informative, respectful, greatly enhancing the process of learning. Most of the time, a teacher does not know when such student–student exchanges will happen. They emerge unexpectedly, often while the teacher is attempting to orchestrate a whole-class discussion. The teacher poses a question, one or two students hesitatingly answer, but the discussion seems forced and destined to fail. Then suddenly, the right combination of questions and comments create interest in the class, and the students begin talking and listening to one another, and each interaction builds on the previous one, adding to the group's understanding.

With teacher willingness to relinquish some classroom control to students and strategic planning, student–student discussions can be a regular feature of democratic classroom communication. As one of the candidates in our program commented:

> I appreciate the distinction between student-centered and student-led discussions. I feel the two concepts are used interchangeably, but there are clear differences. Too often, teachers feel like they are planning classroom discussions that are student led when in fact, the discussions still rely on the teacher as an authority figure or the facilitator.

Student-led discussions fundamentally change the dynamics of the history/social studies classroom for students and teachers. When students assume leadership roles in discussion, teachers must step out of a familiar "sage-on-the-stage" posture featuring "stand-and-deliver" lecture methodologies. Students, at the same time, must abandon longstanding roles as passive receivers of information and more actively take responsibility for the pace and success of classroom lessons. As Nora Flynn (2009, p. 2025) observes: "Student-led discussions have a different agent in charge . . . students should talk to one another, not to the teacher." The shift is fundamental: "The movement from discussion which is facilitated by a teacher to student-*led* discussion allows students to take control of how they learn, while directing, debating, and reconsidering ideas" (p. 2024).

How can teachers orchestrate student–student exchanges regularly in the history/social studies classroom? They can step out of the role of discussion director and into the role of discussion bystander, after students have been taught to conduct discussions with appropriate sources and structures in place to guide the process. As Flynn (2009, pp. 2049–2050) found studying ninth graders in Chicago, teachers need to adopt the following elements:

- Communicate to students the teacher's appreciation of different forms of active participation including questioning, clarifying, and summarizing what has been discussed.

- Give students roles to play and vocabulary to use when participating in thought-provoking conversations.

- Provide students with primary sources and other materials so discussions can include interpretation and analysis of historical evidence.

- Create multiple forums for discussion such as role plays, online discussion boards, "graffiti boards," simulations, fishbowls, conferences, and salon conversations.

- Suggest opportunities for meaningful action to follow thoughtful discussions so individuals can proceed from ideas and issues to actions and solutions.

Letting students lead discussions might be likened to trying to steer an automobile from the back seat. The teacher is not the driver, but is still responsible for the overall direction of the vehicle. The teacher's role is to set the discussion activity in motion, maintain a calm disposition, and offer guidance to students, while allowing them to direct the discussion.

Initially unfamiliar, leading discussions is a potentially disconcerting experience for students who may not know what to say or when to interject comments. With instruction and practice, these initial ambiguities and uncertainties fade away, replaced by the confidence to offer substantive comments about topics of interest.

Organizing Fishbowls and Resonating Threads

Fishbowls are discussion formats where students play leadership roles in organizing, conducting, and assessing what happens when members of a class talk together with minimal teacher involvement and intervention. Many of the candidates in our program are drawn to this method, for as one middle school intern noted: "I feel this strategy gives students the chance to get their options heard, while not having to worry about being interrupted by another classmate." A high school candidate agreed:

> I have been a fan of the fishbowl technique since I saw it in one of the classrooms in school. I think it propels students to think for themselves and to take initiative. I am only concerned about students being afraid to speak or refusing to speak, but that happens in any discussion activity. The fishbowl provides a format that inclines students toward speaking.

A fishbowl format has half the students placed in chairs in an inner circle while the other half forms an outer circle around them. Students are paired; each student in the outer circle has a partner in the inner circle, someone she or he observes and evaluates during the ensuing discussion. Only students in the inner circle are allowed to speak. After 10 to 20 minutes, the student pairs switch positions with the student from the inner circle moving to the outer circle and the outer circle student moving to the inner position. Evaluation is based on participation in discussion, respectful responses to others' viewpoints, originality of thought, and clarity of argument.

In a version of the fishbowl, the student in the outer circle may enter the inner circle to make a comment by tapping the shoulder of his or her inner circle partner, indicating a temporary switch of seats. In this format, students can move back and forth from inner to outer circles several times during the discussion in order to offer comments as a part of the inner circle.

A related method, resonating threads, gives students a supportive process for preparing their ideas and for sharing them so all voices are heard. The activity begins with the teacher posing an open-ended question, for example, "Is America a land of opportunity?" Students engage in a 10- to 15-minute silent free write in response to the question before the discussion begins. They take turns responding to the question by reading a part of their writing or using it to structure their verbal remarks.

Listening to each other, students compare what the speakers are sharing with what they themselves wrote. They listen for threads in the conversations that they can link to, either a similar idea they share with the speaker, or something the speaker says that is in opposition to what they want to say. As one speaker finishes, another picks up the thread, identifies the linking theme, and shares their ideas. The threads of conversation continue until everyone in the group has had a chance to share. Students do not raise hands, but yield politely to each other when more than one student attempts to join in the conversation at the same time. The teacher takes notes during the discussion and is also a participant. When the conversation ends, the teacher asks students to identify themes in the discussion and shares his or her notes to provide a summary of the points.

Student-centered discussion formats like fishbowls and resonating threads encourage democratic participation. First, everyone is evaluating personal levels of respectful participation. This focuses individual accountability for one's actions and words. Second, the format's structure indicates how and when someone can speak, inhibiting loud or opinion-laden voices from dominating the discussion or intimidating other speakers. Third, students act as facilitators of the discussions. "This peer mediation," said one candidate, "allows students to take control of the conversation, encourages respect of others' opinions, and promotes debate and critical thinking."

Students Teaching Students

In a triad teaching method, groups of three students teach each other about a curriculum topic from three distinct sets of reading materials. Students might begin in three large groups with others who have the same reading. In these large groups, students read and process with each other, identifying key points and questions to discuss in the smaller triad groups. Once each large group is ready, members break off to form groups of three with students who had different readings to analyze. Each student in the triad is responsible for teaching the others about his or her reading and leading a discussion about key questions. The triad group summarizes by making connections between the different readings and sharing them with the whole class orally or in writing.

In another version often called a jigsaw, teachers place topically related materials in different parts of the classroom, creating three stations or centers. One station might have primary source materials, another interactive digital or video sources, whereas the third has secondary materials such as newspaper articles, trade books, or textbooks. The members of the triad visit an assigned station, gaining a collage of information to analyze to formulate their own interpretations of events and bring that knowledge back to their small group to engage in triad teaching.

Conversation stations are another student-led discussion format stemming from student reactions to class readings. Students work with a partner, or individually, to identify a meaningful quote or passage from a class reading. The quotes or questions are posted on large poster paper and hung in different stations around the room. Students pair up with a partner to visit each conversation station and use the prompt on the poster as a conversation starter. The teacher circulates, listening to conversations and acting as timekeeper. Every few minutes or so, the conversation ends and a new one begins at the next station with either a new pairing or the same pairing of students.

Students and teachers express favorable impressions of triad teaching and conversation stations as a format for discussion. One candidate recalled using "conversation stations as a group work activity and many students loved it. They felt that conversation stations allowed them to talk about something meaningful with different students." Both formats require participatory listening by teachers to focus student attention on conveying information clearly and succinctly. These methods shift the classroom focus from the teacher as dispenser of knowledge to students and teachers acting as knowledgeable individuals with insightful ideas and information to share.

Engaging in Dialogue and Dialogic Teaching

Debate is popular teaching method in history/social studies classrooms where individual students or small groups engage in a competitive, argumentative forum intended to reveal different sides of a historical or contemporary issue. Many debate formats have as their major goal proving the other side wrong; the design typically features a judge (often the teacher) who determines winners and losers among the debating sides.

From a democratic teaching perspective, debates may not be the most inclusive way to engage all members of the class with academic material. Less competitive students tend to tune out during the back-and-forth exchanges of a debate, whereas multifaceted historical situations can be reduced to a simplified one-side-versus-the-other-side perspective. Also there are complexities of managing a debate format with excited students who are not used to formulating arguments and discussing issues. One teaching candidate recalled how in one classroom debate, the class "quickly degenerated into a shouting match between the groups; the students forgot my explanation of how to debate and what the format would be. I struggled for the rest of the time to just keep the class under control and make sure only one person spoke at a time."

Dialogue, by contrast, is "a conversation in which people who have different beliefs and perspectives seek to develop mutual understanding" as participants purposefully "set aside persuasion" in favor of seeing issues from multiple perspectives and viewpoints (Herzig & Chasin, 2006). Writing for the Australia-based Conflict Resolution Network, Keith Suter (nd) explains the differences between debate and dialog in terms of both style and substance. Debates are conducted in a "threatening" atmosphere where the goal is to defeat the other side at all costs by winning the discussion. Dialogues are intentionally less-tense situations where "the participants listen to, understand, and gain insight from others."

In politics, debates rarely produce new information as candidates recite well-rehearsed talking points designed to elevate their plans and proposals relative to those of their opponent. In dialogue, participants might still disagree, but the approach is one of learning from each other's ideas and more clearly understanding alternative ways to solve problems and resolve differences.

To promote more dialogue-focused discussions, Montclair State University (New Jersey) professor Alina Reznitskaya (2012) suggests students and teachers purposefully discuss texts that have "contestability," and focus on topics for question and debate. Such discussions become occasions of "dialogic teaching" where members of a class share "authority over the content and form of discourse," explore open-ended or "divergent" questions that do not have ready-made or widely accepted answers, receive "meaningful and specific feedback" about their ideas, engage in self-reflection, offer "lengthy, elaborate explanations of their ways of thinking," and co-construct knowledge as they "listen to and react to each other's positions and justifications" (Reznitskaya, 2012, pp. 447–448).

To illustrate dialogic teaching, Reznitskaya has teachers view and evaluate the language use found in videotaped segments of classroom conversations and interactions. The language use of teachers in classrooms can be plotted along a continuum from monologic to dialogic. In a "monologic classroom," the teacher is the sole authority, controlling the form and content of discussions. The teacher dictates student interactions, gives minimal feedback, and permits little collaboration. Students give short responses without much explanation or comment. In a "dialogic classroom," ideas flow back and forth among the members of the class as students take responsibility for managing the discussion while taking turns when speaking. Students explain their thinking in detail and the teacher asks questions that help clarify student thinking.

Dialogic teaching supports democratic practices in history/social studies classes. It encourages thoughtful explanations and clear reasoning. It put the focus on ideas, not individual personalities. It encourages the expressing of multiple points of view, and it reinforces the idea that everyone in the classroom community is a teacher and a learner whose contributions matter. And, as students engage in thoughtful discussions where they explain their thinking while listening to and learning from each other, their knowledge of history content and their readiness to be engaged citizens will grow.

Conclusion

Communication and conversation between teachers and students is a constant feature of every classroom. For a democratic society to flourish, communication must be free flowing and broadly based, allowing diverse viewpoints to be heard and giving every individual a feeling that their unique voice matters. In school classrooms, the ways that adults and students share ideas and information establishes a climate, sets a tone, and conveys a feeling of openness or closeness. When students sense that teachers are not listening, issuing false praise, or exercising authority arbitrarily, those students see school as undemocratic and themselves as powerless to make change.

If voice and participation by students is a hallmark of democratic teaching, and communication and conversation are prime instructional methods for generating engagement and interest, then the dynamics of discussions among teachers and students are a focal point for how to teach democratically in the history/social studies classroom. As Flynn (2009) noted: "Because civic education is an enterprise of the social studies, viewing discussion as a democratic act must be a primary perspective and practice of teachers" (p. 2023). Flynn cites John Dewey's classic 1916 statement that "democracy is more than a form of government; it is primarily a mode of associated living, of conjoint communicated experience" (p. 2023). Genuine discussion builds democratic values and practices.

Widely practiced teacher–student communication patterns currently stress "recitation" and "praise" rather than "authentic discussion" and mentoring conversations. In many classroom lessons, teachers ask questions and students are expected to provide right answers or brief synopsis instead of engaging in more open-ended explorations of ideas and issues. In response, teachers offer short statements of praise—the often used phrase "good job"—instead of probing more deeply into student thoughts by distinguishing what has been accomplished and what is next to learn. Recitation supported by broad praise is not likely to prepare students for future situations as democratic decision makers when they will have to develop effective responses to ill-structured social and economic problems that have many competing solutions.

The ways that teachers converse with students about writing is another form of teacher–student communication that has long-lasting implications for democratic teaching. Ideally, through writing, students learn to express their ideas, develop their voice, and gain self-confidence and agency. For students to develop their potential to become confident writers, teacher responses ideally support a "writing process fit for young writers," where each facet of the writing process is sustained by thoughtful communications between adults and young writers.

Student-led rather than teacher-led discussions present a more open and democratic way to conduct history/social studies lessons. Students can express their ideas, orally or in writing, while teachers guide the flow of the discussion toward key concepts and understandings. In many classrooms, teachers tightly control the flow of discussions, often citing classroom management and student misbehavior as the reasons for doing so. Yet, student-led discussions in formats they learn to direct offer the promise of students teaching each other while learning how to regulate their behavior, listen to other speakers, and formulate cogent responses to questions or comments—qualities imperative when participating as future members of organizations and communities confronting political, social, and economic issues.

Chapter 5

Conferring

Student Feedback to Guide Teaching Practice

"It's amazing what I hear when I stop to listen."

"When I listen to what students have to say about my courses I make changes based on their suggestions."

—High School Teacher Candidates

It's a Monday morning in mid-April and Jessica and Adam, three-fourths of the way through a yearlong master's degree internship as history teachers in an urban school, are about to begin an unfamiliar instructional activity with high school students. At the beginning of class, Jessica and Adam explain that during the forthcoming 5-day curriculum unit investigating the Great Depression and the New Deal, they, the teachers, will be asking each student for ideas and suggestions on how to improve their teaching methods. "We want to know how we can help you succeed in this class," they tell the students. Having commented on students' performance throughout the year, Jessica and Adam now are requesting students do the same for them.

Receiving feedback about academic performance and instructional methodologies is not new to Jessica or Adam. In their university history/social studies teacher preparation program, both receive continual feedback from different sources—college faculty, public school teachers, student teaching supervisors, and program administrators. Throughout 7 months of classroom teaching, Jessica and Adam also have had many opportunities to assess their own effectiveness in promoting student learning through results of tests, papers, quizzes, and daily class participation.

Yet, as Jessica indicates in a reflection paper for one of her college classes, "although these assessments quickly measure the effectiveness of teaching, they lack student input on *why* student comprehension is or is not at a certain level." Jessica and Adam desire to learn how students evaluate their own educational experiences, which includes the interns' work as teachers.

The story of Jessica and Adam introduces *Conferring*, our next C of democratic teaching. Conferring refers to teachers seeking and using student feedback to assess and change instructional and educational classroom practices. Student feedback about learning is a powerful way for teachers to gauge the impact and effectiveness of teaching methods and curriculum content. Leaving at the end of a class period or a school week, a teacher knows only what she or he has attempted to teach, but not whether, or to what extent, students have learned. The act of teaching remains incomplete: Words have been spoken, but what did students hear? Ideas were presented, but what did students understand? Instructional methods have been tried, but what did students gain from those experiences? Asking students for ideas and input about teaching practice offers a unique way to answer these questions.

Evaluating Teacher Performance

Teacher evaluation is a contested topic in education today. Both progressive and conservative groups alike assume greater teacher effectiveness will improve educational outcomes, but there are sharp differences of viewpoints about how to achieve better teaching and increased student learning. Conservative reformers favor stricter teacher accountability measures based on student performance on standardized tests. Progressive reformers stress the importance of ongoing teacher professional development as a way for educators to improve their knowledge of how to support today's increasingly diverse student populations. Mostly omitted from these conflicting approaches is whether concentrating on teacher evaluation is the best way to generate better schools, smarter students, and more engaged democratic citizens.

The main sides in teacher evaluation debates are well known. For conservative-minded reformers, increasing teacher accountability means removing (firing) "ineffective" teachers while advancing (promoting and rewarding) "effective" teachers, with student scores on standardized achievement tests serving as the primary measure of teacher performance. These reformers urge use of an approach called "value-added modeling" (VAM) to measure teacher performance in the classroom. After adjusting for student or school characteristics, VAM uses test scores to plot student achievement gains from the beginning to the end of a school year. Rising or declining test scores show the effect of an individual teacher on learning. VAM advocates believe that effective teachers consistently improve student test scores, and they should be rewarded with higher pay, internal promotions, and other rewards for excellence in teaching.

VAM-type evaluations serve another important function for conservative reformers, that of breaking the hold of teacher unions and liberal groups on substantive change in educational systems. In this view, seniority and tenure rules, as well as contractually lengthy teacher removal procedures, keep less effective teachers in jobs, regardless of student performance on learning measures. Moreover, current school system teacher evaluation methods are inadequate; in district after district most teachers receive rankings of "satisfactory" or higher. By failing to distinguish between effective and ineffective teachers, critics point out, the system remains locked in an outdated and dysfunctional approach to improving teaching.

In response, critics of teacher accountability measures based on student tests scores contend that a broad body of research shows how VAM methods do not identify more or less effective teachers. The measures themselves are inexact; beginning with the idea that effectiveness is a stable quality that can be quantified over time. In a study conducted in an urban district, many of the teachers who were rated in the top 20% of effectiveness in the first year moved down the effectiveness scale in subsequent years (Rothstein et al., 2010).

Furthermore, progressive and liberal reformers assert, there are just too many variables in addition to teachers' actions in the classroom that influence how students perform on tests. Poverty, institutional racism, test bias, student health, and other factors influence students' readiness to achieve academically on high-stakes tests. Smaller class sizes, roles of other teachers and tutors, and presence of high-quality curriculum materials have been shown to positively affect the learning gains of students (Baker et al., 2010). As the National Council of Teachers of English (2012) noted in its Position Statement on Teacher Evaluation, increased teacher professional development represents a fair and effective "means to support teachers as they develop skills and learn more about students in order to meet their needs."

Missing from all these teacher-driven evaluations are ways for students to be actively and democratically involved in any assessment process. Adding student feedback to the teaching and learning process would give teachers dynamic new sources of information about the effect of their teaching and make students active partners in assessment and evaluation processes.

When asked to give feedback to teachers, students play at least three new roles, each of which changes their view of themselves as learners while establishing school classrooms as more democratic spaces and places. First, students can collaborate with teachers in the design and implementation of the assessments being used to measure school performance. Second, students can engage in self-assessment of their own learning. Third, students can enlarge the assessment process by giving information about the effectiveness of teaching methods and academic content.

Inviting students to regularly help establish and evaluate the learning activities happening in classrooms can produce heightened levels of democratic engagement with history and social studies education. As one history candidate told us: "When students realize that they are genuinely being asked for their opinions, they really seem to be engaged with the lesson. At first they are skeptical, as if the teacher is only asking them as an exercise, but when they see that the teacher is truly interested in the feedback and plan on using it, they [students] are open with their ideas and opinions."

Ironically, although debates over teacher evaluation center on improving learning outcomes for students—what they know and are able to do as a result of going to school—in most schools, students themselves are given hardly any role to play in the teaching and learning evaluation process. Reformers are wrestling with how to conceptualize the most useful roles for students to play in evaluating teaching and learning at the classroom level.

Student Perceptions of Teachers and Classrooms

The Measures of Effective Teaching (MET) project (2010, 2012a, 2012b, 2012c, 2013) was a large-scale effort to identify what constitutes effective teaching in K–12 schools. In addition to examining student achievement gains on standardized tests, conducting classroom observation studies of teachers in action, and collecting teacher perceptions about the work of teaching, MET surveyed 100,000 students about how they were experiencing teachers and schools. Under the leadership of Harvard University economist Thomas Kane, project researchers collected data during the 2009–2010 and 2010–2011 school years in six large school systems: Charlotte-Mecklenburg School District, Dallas Independent School District, Denver Public Schools, Hillsborough County Public Schools, Memphis City Schools, and the New York City Department of Education.

MET researchers have announced the following dramatic findings:

1. Effective teaching can be measured using a variety of measures including classroom observations, test scores, and student perception surveys.

2. Students will give honest and compelling feedback about teaching practice.

3. Student perceptions of classrooms and teachers differ greatly, not only between schools, but within schools.

4. Classrooms where students rate their teachers higher on a series of seven teaching behaviors tended to produce greater student achievement gains (Measures of Effective Teaching Project, 2010, 2013).

MET's (2010) initial report of findings concluded: "The average student knows effective teaching when he or she experiences it" (p. 4).

MET used student questionnaires developed by the Tripod Project, an initiative begun by Harvard University Professor Ronald F. Ferguson as a way to close academic achievement gaps among students from different racial, ethnic, and economic class backgrounds in schools. More than 1 million elementary, middle, and high school students nationwide have been Tripod participants over the past 10 years (Ferguson, 2012). Through survey questionnaire statements, students were asked how effectively their teachers created favorable conditions for learning in the following seven areas of teaching practice:

1. Caring: Students feel encouraged and supported in class.

2. Captivating: Students feel learning is interesting and engaging.

3. Conferring: Students feel their ideas are heard and respected.

4. Controlling: Students feel there is an atmosphere of order and cooperation.

5. Clarifying: Students feel their questions are answered clearly.

6. Challenging: Students feel encouraged to work hard and perform well.

7. Consolidating: Students feel ideas and information are explained fully (Ferguson & Ramsdell, 2011).

Ferguson and his co-researchers discovered that students were happier, worked harder, and felt more satisfied academically in classes where teachers ranked higher on each of the seven areas of teaching practices. In these classrooms, students also performed better on high-stakes achievement tests. The researchers concluded that educators should view student success in school as dependent on achievement gains as measured by tests, as well as on additional factors such as positive student attitudes about educational ambition and the belief by students that they belong to a community valuing each individual as a worthwhile and contributing member.

The data contained surprises too. First, there were no significant differences based on student race or income. Second, thinking effective teachers would most likely be found in schools with smaller class sizes and greater instructional resources, researchers found a greater "variation within schools—from one classroom to another—than between them, from one school to another" (Ferguson & Ramsdell, 2011, pp. 8, 11). They concluded that students have widely varying educational experiences in different classrooms in the same school. Third, a student's rank in class standing did not significantly alter the teacher rankings—students earning A grades rated their teachers merely 10% higher than students earning grades of D.

From the complete data, high rankings on six specific statements from the MET student surveys connected most closely to high student learning gains:

1. Students in this class treat the teacher with respect.

2. My classmates behave the way the teacher wants them to.

3. Our class stays busy and doesn't waste time.

4. In this class, we learn a lot almost every day.

5. In this class, we learn to correct our mistakes.

6. The teacher explains difficult things clearly (Ferguson, 2012, p. 27).

These results suggest that students want academic learning situations where teachers maintain order, challenge them intellectually and academically, and clearly explain important concepts. Such information from students can be invaluable to educators. After many years surveying students about their classroom experiences, Sarah Brown Wessling (2012), the 2010 national teacher of the year, remarked: "what really drives my reflection is the comments they offer. It is the comments that in the end—nine times out of 10—will change my instruction, or solidify my instruction" (p. 1).

The pattern of students rating teaching more effective in some classrooms than in others was found across elementary and secondary schools, among academic subjects (math, English, science, and social studies), and between urban and rural districts. In Memphis, for example, 79% of the students in classes scoring in the 75th percentile on tests agreed with the statement "My teacher explains difficult things clearly" but only 50% of the students in the 25th percentile agreed with the same statement (Crow, 2011). The pattern is found on statewide exams as well. Students in classes where teachers scored highly showed a 4.8-month gain on state math assessments and a 2.3-month gain on state English/language arts assessments (Ferguson & Ramsdell, 2011).

The Tripod Project initiated new ways for thinking about how student feedback supports teacher improvement. The "tripod" represents the center of a teacher professional learning triangle whose three points are "content knowledge," "pedagogic skill," and "relationship building" with students. Effective teachers know the academic content they are teaching; use teaching methods that successfully convey that content to students; and construct strong, trusting relationships that convince students that they are cared about as individuals and learners. Success in the classroom depends on all points of the tripod being strong and lasting; otherwise, the teaching and learning process is severely weakened in the minds of the students and will not be sustained.

Student Feedback and Teacher Improvement

There is a growing movement to use student perception surveys as part of the ongoing professional development and/or evaluation of students. In spring 2014, Kentucky began piloting the use of online "Student Voice Surveys" in which students in grades 3 to 12 provide feedback about seven aspects of school experience based on the acronym "STUDENT": support, transparency, understanding, discipline, engagement, nurturing and trust (Kentucky Department of Education, 2014). The Gates Foundation reported that by December 2013, five states (Georgia, Hawaii, Massachusetts, South Dakota, and Utah) began requiring student perception data be included in teacher evaluations, whereas 29 other states were allowing schools to use student survey information in locally developed evaluation systems (EducationCounsel, 2013).

School systems too are expanding their use of student feedback in teacher professional development. In Memphis, student survey results account for 5% of a teacher's yearly performance evaluation; in 2013 Chicago began using student feedback as 10% of teacher evaluation. Additionally, the New York City public schools and schools in Rhode Island are using surveys from students to assess how students are experiencing instruction in class, school safety and discipline, and teacher expectations (Crow, 2011).

As school systems implement the use of student feedback, MET approach has faced strong criticism. Two National Education Policy Center analysts found issues with MET's experimental protocol where certain students changed teachers or did not participate at all (Rothstein & Mathis, 2013). The analysts also disagreed with using test scores, class observations, and student surveys to produce a single measure of effectiveness. Each type of data reflects separate and distinct aspects of classroom reality, they contend, and should be not used to generate broad conclusions about which teachers are most successful with student achievement.

Other researchers questioned the connections that can be drawn between classroom observations and test score information; it is difficult for an observation measurement rubric to accurately assess the effect of highly individualized teacher actions such as asking questions clearly or challenging students intellectually (Guarino & Stacy, 2012). Other critics say that a claimed correlation between student evaluations and test score performance is overstated and overrated as an education reform strategy (Camburn, 2012).

Beyond these criticisms, many educators are reluctant to use the results the MET studies as evidence that student evaluations should be given direct roles in decisions about teacher retention and promotion. They believe that students should not be asked to "grade" teachers by giving feedback that is then used to influence hiring and firing of school personnel, because student feedback by itself does not take into account the multiple factors affecting how teachers teach and students learn in school.

It is important to note that student feedback does not have to be connected to formal teacher evaluation efforts by schools or districts nor does it have to be shared with school administrators or outside groups. Feedback can be a low-stakes, classroom-centered form of communication between students and teachers, intended to improve the day-to-day instruction in the classroom while promoting a sense of ownership and involvement in education among students. As one teacher noted: "When anything is part of formal evaluation I think it has to be coupled with real professional growth opportunities and in a climate that's supportive, not punitive" (Wessling, 2012, p. 2).

Voices of Teacher Candidates:
Asking for Student Feedback About Teaching

Unlike the broad support expressed for collaborative rule making and contrasting content (two Cs of democratic teaching discussed in earlier chapters), most teacher candidates in our program found the prospect of asking students for opinions about instructional practices and classroom learning activities to be unfamiliar, and mostly unnerving.

As public school and college students, few history teacher candidates had been asked by teachers to offer reactions to lessons as they were being taught. Student comments about teacher performance always happened when a course finished, usually as part of the last meeting of the class. Such evaluations involved fill-in-the-blank sheets that were then scanned into a computer database to produce a statistical report to be viewed by the teacher and administrative supervisors. As students, these teacher candidates said, they never saw the results of the surveys nor did they know about changes that teachers made in the courses based on student feedback.

Candidates remembered end-of-the-college-course evaluations as an uninspired activity, with students eager to make their way out the door quickly after completing the forms. Some recalled occasionally hearing remarks from angry classmates about their intentions to slam a teacher they did not like by rating her or him low on the evaluation forms. Only two candidates recalled efforts of a public school teacher to get student feedback about a class, usually at the end of a marking period or the end of the school year; another recalled a high school teacher who paused for informal student feedback during a teaching unit, but the information collection process was haphazard and follow-up on student concerns was unclear. No candidate had an experience where a public school teacher implemented a process of regular student feedback in her or his classes.

A general uneasiness about the idea of asking students for feedback originated from strong misgivings about the idea itself. "I was apprehensive at first about seeking student feedback," said one middle school intern. "I thought it might undermine my authority in the classroom by reminding my students that I'm still a student myself. I also thought that the students wouldn't take seriously answering the feedback questions." Other candidates also felt that class members would see inviting student comments—and then having to act on them—as a sign of weakness on the teacher's part. In this view, teachers are the prime classroom authority, responsible for managing an orderly learning environment. Any change in that power relationship would undermine authority, emboldening students to act disrespectfully, avoid doing assignments, and cause disruptions of learning for everyone else.

The assumption that teachers need to maintain authority and control in classrooms was well documented by Linda McNeil (1988) in her book, *Contradictions of Control*. McNeil examined history/social studies teacher practices as well as administrative policies designed to improve high schools in the 1980s at the beginning of the accountability-based era of education reform. In control-centered school environments, argued McNeil, history and social studies teachers resort to "defensive teaching," deliberately omitting or avoiding controversial topics or material that students would have wanted to discuss. Instead, teachers rely on a consistent pattern of fact-based lectures, fill-in-the-blank worksheets, and get-the-right-answer style tests. Teachers maintain they "needed to control the students, both to avoid discipline problems and even more to avoid inefficient exchanges which might alter the pace of the lesson or provide the opportunity to question the teacher's interpretation of history" (McNeil, 1988, p. xx).

In response, the students resist, some by becoming passively disengaged with the content, others by acting out in defiance of classroom and school rules. As McNeil succinctly noted: "When students see minimal teaching, they respond with minimal classroom effort" (pp. 160–161). Resisting behaviors lead to greater teacher-control efforts that serve to deepen student apathy and discontent. McNeil (1988) called this pattern the "contradiction of control," where the more teachers try to control students, the more students seemed to need to be controlled, concluding, "When the school's organization becomes centered on managing and controlling, teachers and students take school less seriously" (p. xviii).

Related to the idea of maintaining teacher authority, another aspect of student feedback where teacher candidates were unsure how to proceed was whether students should provide feedback anonymously. Most candidates insisted on anonymity: "I think student feedback should be anonymous because it provides the students with a more comfortable feeling of being honest on the [comment] sheets." Another said that unless feedback was anonymous, students would "tell me what they think I want to hear rather than telling me the truth." Some candidates disagreed, saying students should sign their names to the feedback sheets: "I am going to explain to them that I really need to know what methods are the most helpful. I will also let them know that I will not be offended if they don't like the lesson and it will help me be a better teacher." One candidate concluded that giving students the choice to include names or not is a reasonable compromise, especially when teachers usually recognize everyone's handwriting.

Interestingly, the candidates drew a clear distinction between the viability of asking students for feedback about teaching methods versus asking students for feedback about curriculum topics. It was harder for them to envision how students might usefully comment about academic topics. As one high school candidate remarked, "many students may not be familiar with what a curriculum is or exactly how it fits into the class." A middle school candidate in an expeditionary learning school explained her belief that "sixth graders need training and scaffolding in order to give effective feedback," and they "may not be prepared to give feedback on the curriculum," including what types of learning excursions a class would take outside school.

One high school candidate cited the "standards factor," noting that although he had a "good amount of latitude in how much class time to devote to subtopics within the standards," academic content choices were made "with my supervisor reminding me of the school curriculum maps, which limits latitude." But he felt there was "room to explore topics of the students' choosing, or expand the amount of time I would usually dedicate to a part of the unit if student interest is high for that topic." A teacher candidate from another high school was less ready to ask students about academic topics, stating that because curriculum topics are already set and teachers must follow them, feedback from students "would not accomplish change of any kind." At the same time, this candidate believed that "student feedback about teaching methods has the possibility of propelling positive change in the classroom if the teaching methods being used are not working for them."

Two themes stand out in the comments of the candidates, each somewhat opposing the other. First, giving students meaningful roles in deciding what happens educationally in the classroom makes sense conceptually. Students always have ideas about school, "an endless supply of suggestions," as one middle school teacher candidate recalled. Moreover, the candidates remembered wishing to have voice and agency in teaching and learning as students in middle and high school. It is important, said one high school student teacher, for students to "feel that their voices are being heard and that what they say may really make a difference."

Second, candidates did not eagerly embrace the idea of asking students for opinions and suggestions about their teaching practices. All expressed concerns about challenges to their authority, image, and control as teachers. The ideas of being "evaluated" by students and allowing expression of potentially negative comments seemed in conflict with widely held assumptions that it is important for teachers to be seen as authority figures respected by students. Then, even when student feedback was accepted as an element of democratic teaching, candidates were unsure how to conduct such activities without losing perceived authority status.

Conferring Strategies for Building Democracy

The rationale for teachers conferring with students as part of teaching became clearer when, in an effort to present a visual model of how teachers construct daily lesson plans, we drew a Venn diagram of three interconnected circles on a whiteboard. Labeling one circle "Curriculum standards," the second "NCSS themes," and the third "Teacher knowledge," we explained that teachers incorporate elements from all three circles into every instructional design or classroom lesson plan as follows:

- Curriculum standards refer to state and local requirements for what academic content to teach.

- NCSS themes highlight the 10 themes for social studies instruction set forth by the NCSS.

- Teacher knowledge emphasizes the decisions that teachers make about what academic content to include and what instructional methods to use every time they teach a lesson.

State and local curriculum standards as well as the NCSS themes refer to the "prescribed" and the "tested" curriculum, whereas "teacher knowledge" is part of the "hidden" curriculum of the classroom (Stitzlen, 2011). In our initial formulation, every teaching lesson emerges in the space where the three circles intersect.

At this point, one of the history candidates asked, "What about the students in classes? They need a place in the circles."

The "What about the students?" question dramatically shifted the direction of our discussion. It was apparent that our framework had omitted middle and high school learners, and in so doing, neglected an essential element of lesson development in democratic classrooms. Students bring a wealth of knowledge and experience to every academic class, the so-called "external" curriculum, what students have learned outside of school, that effects what they will learn inside school (Stitzlein, 2011). Teachers need to incorporate the ideas and perceptions of students in the process of deciding what to teach and how to teach it. Listening to students builds student engagement and investment in school and makes the classroom into a laboratory for ongoing democratic thinking and acting.

This chapter's "Building Democracy" activities focus on ways that students and teachers can confer with one another about how teaching and learning is occurring in classes. Students know effective teaching when they experience it, and teachers can learn to improve their techniques by listening and responding to what students have to say. The key is to establish ongoing, nonthreatening ways for students to voice their ideas along with positive ways for teachers to respond to what students have to say about curriculum and instruction in the classroom.

To institute ways for students and teachers to confer together about teaching and learning, we first discuss the importance of feedback as an ingredient for successful learning, both in terms of how teachers give feedback to students and how students might give feedback to teachers. Next, we share the procedures and results of our own student feedback efforts. Over the past 5 years, hundreds of middle and high school students have provided new history/social studies teachers with ideas and suggestions for improving classroom instruction.

Strategy: Building Frameworks for Student Feedback

Assuming that most individuals learn new ideas or improve skills through regular practice with supportive feedback from mentors or coaches who both assess and improve performance, most educators consider feedback to be an essential element for successful learning. Rapid, self-correcting feedback from an instructor to a learner guides the student's future activity, in terms of what is being accomplished successfully and what needs to be changed to achieve better results.

Think of a new skill, talent, or activity you are learning—using a new smartphone or tablet, performing a recreational activity like golf or swing dancing, or managing the information needed for federal and state tax returns. These activities may be self-taught, learned in a class, or acquired in an informal small-group setting. Feedback tells you if you are proceeding in a positive direction or moving off track. Feedback encourages learning from mistakes as well as successes.

Feedback also can be a democratic practice, depending on how it is conducted by teachers and perceived by students. When students perceive they are being given guidance and support in school, they invest in the learning process. In such situations, they see themselves as individuals whose voice, participation, and future direction matters. Research reflects students wanting adult feedback that conveys high expectations for success accompanied by reasonable structures for self-discipline and personal accountability (Ferguson, 2008; Wilson & Corbett, 2001). They want teachers who create orderly classrooms, explain academic material patiently and clearly, and assign schoolwork that is relevant to their daily lives and future aspirations. In short, students want teachers who will listen and respond to what they have to say and lead them to aspire highly.

Establishing the Importance of Feedback

Creating democratic frameworks in the classroom begins with understanding the kind of feedback that best supports student learning. Control-oriented and authoritarian feedback will not produce lasting learning, but it will increase student resentment and resistance. Rapid, supportive feedback will promote student learning in history/social studies classes, especially if historical inquiry and social problems propel the content of the curriculum.

Immediate self-correcting feedback was, and remains today, a fundamental element of Maria Montessori's pioneering educational work in the early years of the 20th century. Her designs of original educational materials (cut-out continent map puzzles that have correct sizes of land masses color keyed to a globe with the same shapes and colors; proportional-length wooden blocks that build a staircase; beads that can be strung on strings by tens and then hundreds to form a cube of 1,000; and all her other materials and manipulatives) embody three commanding features that attract the inner attention of learners:

1. A point of interest that draws children to the materials;

2. Open-ended exploration that invite children to learn each time they use the materials; and

3. A self-correcting feedback feature that teaches in a nonjudgmental way (Montessori, 1964).

These characteristics in combination capture a student's curiosity and desire to learn independently of constant adult attention and supervision. Regardless of age or grade level, immediate self-correcting feedback provides students the experience and motivation to become self-directed learners.

Feedback is a key variable to maximize the impact of teachers on student learning outcomes, states University of Melbourne professor John Hattie (2009, 2011), who has spent more than 15 years examining the research on what factors influence student achievement in schools. His 2009 book, *Visible Learning*, synthesized 800 meta-analyses of 50,000 research articles with 150,000 effect sizes involving 240 million students. He has continued adding to his database since, and in 2011, published a second book, *Visible Learning for Teachers*.

Examining the "practice" of teaching, Hattie (2011) recommends teachers center their practice around the following two ideas: "I see learning through the eyes of my students" and "I help students become their own teachers." These statements form the framework for a changed conception of what it means to be an effective teacher. Hattie urges teachers to use multiple forms of feedback to determine what each student already knows and what each needs to learn academically. Knowing that information, teachers can create clear and focused learning goals for individuals and utilize instructional and assessment practices designed to help students realize those goals.

There are multiple opportunities for democratic participation within Hattie's framework of increased and focused adult feedback to students. By establishing known-in-advance learning goals and assessment procedures, teachers and students become invested in working together. Students can be given voice and choice in the process by providing feedback about what types of instruction and assessment best supports their learning. Throughout, Hattie (2009, p. 4) stresses the importance of a two-way process: "It is feedback to the teacher about what students can and cannot do that is more powerful than feedback to the student." As teachers gather information about students from the students themselves, successful learning experiences emerge.

Gathering Feedback From Students

There are varied ways that teachers get feedback from students. Many use informal verbal or written feedback systems during the school day or week, including "Do Nows" (to see how clearly students understand a topic), "Exit Tickets" (focusing on what students have learned that day), and "Write-Arounds" (collaboratively written responses to an assessment-like question). They also assess with quizzes, tests, and homework assignments to ascertain what students learn in class or understand about a topic. Some teachers ask for written feedback at the beginning, during, and at the end of a lesson, unit, or school marking period. They may request feedback about how students would like to take tests, write papers, or present research. All of these approaches convey a sense of democratic participation by showing that not all academic or class matters have been decided in advance without student input.

Jeremy Greene, teaching high school history in eastern Massachusetts, collects student feedback every 3 weeks (the length of an instructional unit) throughout the school year (Table 5.1). His questionnaire asks questions specific to student learning needs and also open-ended questions. The first sentence of the student feedback questionnaire is always: "This is a survey for me to know how I am doing."

There are more examples of student feedback questions from the MET project website. MET questions focus less on whether students like or dislike a learning activity or instructional method and more on how teachers can create and sustain a positive learning climate for every student.

Table 5.1. Student Feedback Survey Questions

1. In this class, do you have the opportunity to do your best every day?

Yes, every day	Most days	Not enough	Rarely	Other

2. There are students in my class who help me learn.

Yes	I think so	No	Other	

3. The purpose of this class makes me feel that my role as a student is important.

Always	Most of the time	I don't think so	Never	Other

4. The teacher communicates with me about my progress.

Too much	Enough	Not enough	Never	Other

5. This class gives me opportunities to learn and grow.

Always	More than most classes	About the same as others	Less than others	Other

6. Tell me about the lesson you learned the most and why.

7. What else can I (as a teacher) do better as a teacher/person during class?

8. What question do you think I should ask in the next survey?

Strategy: Students and Teachers Conferring Together

In the MET project, as in many teacher-generated questionnaires, feedback flows from students to teachers without indicating how much information then flows from teachers to students. Feedback becomes part of a more democratic process when adults and students are able to hear from each other, consider different or competing ideas, and arrive at shared understandings.

We use *Conferring* as a term for describing the process of teachers and students providing each other with sincere and supportive statements about what is and is not working academically, instructionally, and interpersonally in a classroom. Conferring suggests a conversation between interested parties, each talking to the other in ways that promote greater understanding and improved relationships.

Conducting a "Conferring with Students" feedback activity each year in our history/social studies teaching methods class is a compelling experience for the candidates, and a unique one for the middle and high school students. This activity asks teacher candidates and students to participate in democratically based information sharing where all members of a classroom community have opportunities to express opinions and generate ideas about instructional methods and individual learning preferences. The following strategies outline how "Conferring with Students" has been done with history/social studies candidates in our teacher preparation program. We encourage teachers and students to modify or vary the structure to fit their own situations and interests.

Asking Questions That Generate Responses

Student feedback can generate new insights important for teachers. After reading aloud a fictional story to seventh graders in a unit on Mesopotamia, one teacher candidate received comments from two students about the vocabulary of the story and the way the teacher read it aloud (Table 5.2).

Reflecting on the students' feedback, the teacher saw areas for immediate change and improvement. In terms of her read-aloud style, she noted "I thought I emphasized the story really well when I was reading it to the class. I assumed the students did not want the story to be read in an overly dramatic way, but clearly they enjoy when I do." As for the unknown vocabulary, she decided that in the future, "I would encourage students to raise their hands when they do not understand a word. I think it would be most helpful if I had stopped after each paragraph to define

Table 5.2. Comparison of Student Comments

	Student A	Student B
Ideas	*"I learned about the city of Babylon."*	*"Reading about Hammurabi helped me learn about how he ruled his world and tried to keep everything in order."*
Issues	*"You could have stopped right when there was word we didn't understand and explain it."*	*"What was difficult was the new vocabulary."*
Insights	*"Maybe we could try to act it out."*	*"I suggest putting us into groups and she can read it with more expression."*

words and clarify the meaning of the passage upcoming." In this example, student feedback was instrumental to changing and improving that teacher's instructional practice.

Importantly, the first time students participate in a conferring activity, not everyone provides detailed and informative feedback. Many offer sparse comments or simply say that "It was fine," causing teachers to assume the students are not interested in providing feedback. Our research shows one reason students give minimal comments is the wording teachers use to phrase the questions. Table 5.3 presents examples of candidate-written questions from two different seventh-grade social studies classes learning about ancient civilizations in the Middle East. Both candidates taught a lesson that included student group work for part of the class period, but the purpose of each set of feedback questions was different, producing very different responses.

The questions for class A in the left-hand column of the Table were general in nature, asking mainly what students liked or didn't like about group-work activities. Many students wrote that they liked talking with classmates during group work: "You get to think over many ideas," said one student, who also remarked that working in groups "helps me learn because we learn how to agree. It also helps because we learn how other people think and see." Those who did not like the activity emphasized that they "don't get as much done" in a group setting and prefer working alone.

By contrast, the specific questions asked by teacher of class B in the right-hand column of the Table produced detailed responses from the stu-

Table 5.3. Survey Questions from Two Seventh-Grade Classes

Class A *Student Feedback Survey*	*Class B* *Student Feedback Survey*
Please answer the following questions about working in groups:	Please answer the following questions about the student activity you began yesterday in class and finished for homework. Use complete sentences and provide detail.
1. What do you like about working in groups while doing class work?	
2. What don't you like about working in groups while doing class work?	1. How did it help you learn about the Dead Sea Scrolls?
3. How does working in a group help you to learn?	2. What could have been changed to help you learn more about the Dead Sea Scrolls?
	3. Would you enjoy doing a similar activity in the future? Why or why not?

dents. One student noted: "We could express imagination . . . this helps us learn about the Dead Sea Scrolls because we get to show that we know the information." Another wrote, "It helped because while I was writing I was learning—and I could do it however I want it to be." One student objected to the activity, citing it was "boring because I don't like newspapers that are very dull." Another commented that a video would have helped him to learn more about the topic. The wording of questions and what the questions ask influenced how students responded.

To generate more concrete responses, we suggest asking students for feedback using an Ideas, Issues, and Insights framework based on the model described in the chapter on conducting (Table 5.4).

Although our Ideas, Issues, and Insights template provides questions more specific than those composed by most teacher candidates, student responses to them vary in length and substance. Occasionally, students struggle to identify the methods a teacher is implementing during class. For instance, in classes where the teacher candidate used primary source analysis as a teaching method, some students were confused about the differences between primary and secondary sources and were unsure how to comment about whether or not the method helped them learn.

Student confusion about identifying teaching methods illustrates a need for guidance and practice in completing feedback forms. Teachers

Table 5.4. Ideas, Issues, and Insights Feedback Questions

Ideas: How did this method help you learn? What did you find useful in how [teacher's name] used this method?

Issues: What was difficult for you in using this method? How would you suggest [teacher's name] improve the way she/he teaches with this method?

Insights: What other ways would you like to see this method used? What other topics would you like to see this method used for?

---

can facilitate understanding by talking in advance about what they hope to learn from students' feedback. A particular area of instruction might be the focus of a feedback activity; for example, a teacher asks students if the introduction to a new unit was clear, whether an adapted version of a primary source was easier to understand, how a video segment did or did not increase their understanding of an historical event. At first, feedback activities may not produce lengthy responses from all members of a class, but as students see teachers taking their comments seriously, they become more invested in the process and usually provide more detailed information.

Exploring Comfort and Reach Methods

As part of conferring, we ask teacher candidates to develop student feedback questions for two different types of instructional practices—"comfort methods" (methods they as teachers feel confident using) and "reach methods" (methods they as teachers feel less confident using). Students give feedback about both—when the candidate uses a comfort method and when a candidate tries a reach method. The candidate chooses at what point to collect information from the students during instruction.

   To guide planning, we present a list of student-centered instructional methods, emphasizing those practices we have addressed in history/social studies teaching methods classes: group work/cooperative learning, multicultural his-stories and her-stories, primary sources, student writing, children/adolescent/adult literature, dialogue and debate, civic ideals and practices, role play/simulation/drama, and technology-integrated learning.

   Candidates teach lessons, one using a comfort method and the other a reach method, collecting student feedback on each lesson. Based on candidates' experiences, here are key points to consider when collecting student feedback about comfort and reach teaching methods:

- Talk in advance with students about the importance of their ideas and input to your teaching and how you will use it. Let students know that you are asking for their participation because it is valued. Inform them that their responses will be shared (without names or any identifying feature) with members of your teaching methods class as a way for new teachers to better meet the needs of students.

- Model the kind of content and level of specificity that will be helpful to you as a teacher. Talk with students about listing reasons why they felt as they did. Give students enough time to complete the questions and emphasize the value of the feedback to you as a teacher.

- Consider making student feedback forms anonymous to encourage honest feedback or give students the choice of whether or not to sign their names.

- After the lesson, complete the feedback form yourself. The goal is for you to record your immediate reactions to the lesson you taught in a reflective way.

- After you collect student forms, read them more than once to identify themes and main ideas. Compare your own responses and comments to theirs. Then discuss your analysis with students so they know you are thinking about what they had to say and ask if they have insights about or different ideas from your analysis.

- Use the following writing and thinking prompts to reflect on the meaning of student feedback experience for you as a teacher, drawing on specific comments from student forms and your own experience in the classroom. Answer each question separately for the comfort and reach methods.

  - What surprises you about students' comments and suggestions?

  - Describe areas where you agree with the students about the use of the method.

  - Describe areas where your reactions differ from those of the students.

- What did you learn about individual students that will help you to meet their needs in the future?

- Based on student comments and suggestions, what would you change about how you teach using this method in the future?

- Does conferring with students make you more or less inclined to use a particular teaching method in the future? Why?

- What was helpful and what was challenging about the process of conferring with students? What will you do differently next time?

- After completing this activity, what are your reactions to including student feedback about teaching methods as part of your instructional practice?

Strategy: Responding to Students' Comments and Concerns

Once feedback surveys have been completed, teacher candidates read and respond to what students have to say. At first, many candidates approached reading feedback surveys with trepidation—"It was terrifying," said one student teacher—yet student comments were relevant and almost always thoughtful and supportive. Several hundred middle and high school students have completed feedback surveys since 2009. Few students wrote a nasty or sarcastic comment, and only a handful made a flippant remark like "I got off task because of Eric." Although in every class, some students gave very brief comments or chose not to comment on some questions, this was more than offset by the great majority of students who wrote statements about the ways that different instructional methods helped them educationally and offered useful suggestions for improvements in class activities.

Using student feedback surveys, we ask teacher candidates to complete two assignments, both key strategies for ensuring that feedback has been read and understood by students and teachers:

1. Write a reflection paper about the experience of receiving feedback from students, including how—if at all—student comments influenced your plans for using different instructional methods in future classes.

2. Share with students a summary of the questionnaires, including what you as the teacher intend to do instructionally based on their feedback.

Learning From What Students Say

Every year candidates adjust their responses from skepticism about the value of asking students for feedback to focused consideration of a new arena of information for their practice as teachers. "It was a great learning experience for me," said one high school candidate, "as well as groundbreaking in many relationships with students. I think it opened their eyes to the fact that I am evaluated and graded for what I'm doing in and outside the classroom, and I think they really enjoyed being part of that process." For that teacher, there were unexpected results: "Some students gave a level of feedback I was not expecting. Some were much wiser about their learning abilities than I gave them credit for."

In many instances, student comments reaffirm for candidates that a lesson has worked effectively for a class. Table 5.5 presents a selection of ninth-grade student comments about the use of multicultural literature in a U.S. history lesson on the Trail of Tears. During class, the students read and discussed *The Journal of Jesse Smoke, A Cherokee Boy*, Native American author Joseph Bruchac's historical fiction story. The teacher asked students how reading these fictional journal entries helped them learn about this period in American history.

Other candidates expressed wonder that students responded to a teaching method and offered concrete ideas for how to use that method in the future. After using writing as her "reach" method, a high school candidate noted she was "surprised at how well writing went for this lesson; it seemed to give students a new outlook on the chapter notes. Looking ahead to the next time she uses writing with students, the candidate said, "I need to be more clear when giving instructions and make sure everyone includes the pertinent information in their writing." The teacher concluded, "I think I would use more writing in my classroom now that I see how engaged my students are with this type of activity."

Other candidates found student feedback was a new way to assess what students knew and did not know about historical topics. After a lesson asking students to use the Code of Hammurabi to make inferences about the role of women, the importance of property, and the treatment of lower-class citizens in Babylonian society, one middle school candidate realized most of the class had great difficulty reading the primary source text

Table 5.5. Students' Comments on Multicultural Literature

"The journal entries did help me learn because everyone did their own part and we added them together so it made sense."

"Reading the journal really helped teach us how much worse it really was leaving their homes to go to some unknown place."

"The ways that helped me learn from reading journal entries from *Jesse Smoke, A Cherokee Boy*, was that when we drew a picture about part of an entry and read the entry over, it made more sense."

"What helped me learn was we didn't have to read all of the journal entries, we just had to read a 'small section'."

"Reading the book helped us learn by getting to understand how life was at that time."

"I thought that reading the journal entries were helpful and making a book and having her read the book to us was helpful for us to learn."

"Drawing the pictures and writing words and having it read made it sink into my head a little more."

"It helped me learn because people moved from one area to another by being forced to."

"I found it useful because she didn't have us read all of them on our own. She gave each one of us one, and when they were all read together in the book, it made a lot of sense."

---

of the laws. "The most helpful insight I gained: Don't assume students have the skills to paraphrase," the teacher wrote. "Based on student feedback in the future, I would take more time to teach paraphrasing skills. I will also stop periodically to check for class understanding."

After reading feedback about role playing part of the Boston Massacre, a key event in the timeline of the American Revolution, a high school candidate commented: "The role play was helpful for students because it was so engaging." Their comments showed that the students "were so nervous about it being their turn to speak, they had empathy for one another so they remained focused." After the role play, the class reviewed the different aspects of the event together. Thinking ahead to when he would again teach this topic, the candidate noted: "I think social simulations—with appropriate introductions and debriefing—are an excellent way to learn. I absolutely will be using simulations in the future."

Another candidate, teaching about the same period before the America Revolution, focused on Paul Revere's engraving of "The Boston Massacre" and how it was used as a device to influence Colonial thinking against England. He asked students to create their own propaganda posters for an event during the time leading up to the Revolutionary War. Reading feedback from students, he noted that "many students enjoyed the method but may have found it difficult to show their point or argument." He concluded that he needed to "model how they were supposed to create their posters and what a persuasive poster might look like."

Talking With Students About Their Feedback

As part of the conferring with students activity in our history/social studies teaching methods class, we asked candidates to read what the surveys had to say, envision possible changes in teaching methods and instructional approaches, and share their thoughts and plans with their classes. Students need to know what the teacher has learned from the feedback and what she or he intends to do because of it. We wanted teachers and students to confer about the questions, responses, and next steps that might happen based on the feedback.

A few teacher candidates showed reluctance to confer with students about feedback received, asking, "What if the comments are negative?" Other candidates' worries were how to confer negative or unhappy comments. Their view of themselves as authority figures in the classroom seemed to stymie readiness to discuss all details of feedback with students. One skeptical candidate reflected that "in some classes, it could lead to a good class discussion, while in others, it could create tension and animosity between groups." A small group of candidates openly welcomed the idea of conferring with students about feedback, reasoning that members of a class would show more respect than disrespect to someone sincerely asking for ideas about how to be a more effective teacher.

When conferring began, many candidates informed students that feedback prompted immediate changes to the planning of classroom structures and instructional methods. For example, a high school candidate intended to use primary source letters written during the development of Utopian communities in Massachusetts in the 1830s and 1840s. Then she wanted to have students compose their own letters based on their visions of what a perfect community might be like. The students struggled with the activity and told her why on their feedback forms. "That was the biggest thing I learned," the intern noted. "I didn't think about the lack of engagement or the difficulty of the this assignment before planning my lesson."

Another high school candidate, using art to teach a lesson about the Trail of Tears, reflected on receiving glowing responses from students: "Having such positive feedback from the students makes me much more inclined to use this method in the future. . . . I was surprised by the amount and variety of ideas students had for other events they would like to learn using art." A middle school candidate concluded: "I will definitely use student feedback as my student teaching progresses. I want to help the students learn. Having student input into the effectiveness of the lessons will enable me to improve my craft and hopefully inspire the students to actively participate in their education as well."

At the end of the school year, despite their initial reservations, the majority of teaching candidates strongly supported the idea of conferring with students about feedback survey results, even when the comments are not all glowing or positive. One middle school candidate stated, "I think students should feel that their voices are being heard and what they say may really make a difference." Another middle school intern echoed a similar theme: "I believe in transparency in the classroom. I like students to know the impact of their contributions to, or inversely, their disruptions to their own learning. It happens to be a major part of the way I support classroom community."

Additionally, middle and high school candidates endorsed how back-and-forth communication between teachers and students supported democratic values and behaviors. One noted, "I like the idea of students taking their opinions and weighing them against the broader class perspective. This is an important concept of popular rule that they should have experience with." Another remarked that without conferring about feedback, "some students may realize that there has been a change due to their feedback but others may not." Student–teacher discussions about feedback create a balanced learning context, making it "more likely that the students will respond honestly and earnestly in hopes that their suggestions will also be implemented." A third candidate framed conferring about feedback surveys as a way to build greater participation among members of the classroom community: "Otherwise students will not feel that their voices have been heard, which could undermine further attempts at implementing democratic methods."

Conclusion

This chapter explored students and teachers "conferring" together about how instructional practices and curriculum materials build democratic practices and understandings in history/social studies classrooms. In conferring, teachers invite students to give them feedback about their teaching—including what they appreciate about the lessons and what they would like to happen differently. After collecting student feedback, teachers evaluate what has been said and then discuss the results with students, identifying changes they intend to make based on student ideas and inputs. Teachers also continue in their longstanding practice of giving feedback to students.

Most students come to school hoping to participate in meaningful and relevant academic schoolwork, guided by teachers who care about them and inspire them as learners. Student feedback can form the basis of democratic dialogs between teachers and students about what is working well and what might be changed in a classroom. In this approach, student feedback becomes the foundation for enriched conversations between teachers and students about educational activities and outcomes, the essence of "conferring" as a democratic teaching practice.

Once initiated, there are many opportunities for teachers to confer with students. Feedback is a central element of teaching and learning at every grade level and it can flow from students to teachers as well as from teachers to students. Before, during, and after lessons are taught are times when history/social studies teachers can request, respond to, and learn from the ideas and views of students. We have seen teacher candidates consistently gather student feedback throughout the school year. Rather than neglecting what students have to say thinking it is immaturely biased or easily manipulated by how much work a teacher assigns in class, they see ways that students can assist them to become more effective teachers.

Gathering the views and perspectives of students prompts history/social studies teachers to be reflective about the choices they make about curriculum content and instructional methods. Discussing with students the effects of curriculum and instruction expands the extent of everyone's teaching and learning experiences. As they listen to and learn from students, teachers further their own development as educators while simultaneously building more democratic spaces where everyone's voices are integral to the educational experience.

Chapter 6

Co-Constructing

Digital Technologies and Student Inquiry

As individuals, we are constantly searching for the best videos, the latest games, the most enjoyable apps. If we know our students are interested in these, why not incorporate them into the classroom? This is the digital age and our schools should reflect that.

—High School Teacher Candidate

More than a century ago in Paris, Auguste and Louis Lumiere screened what is believed to be the first publicly shown motion picture. Members of the 1895 audience reportedly screamed in fear and ducked for cover at the image of a moving train pulling out of a station. Because those viewers had no experience with moving visual replications of real life, they could not distinguish between the "virtual" and the "actual." Afterward, the Lumieres were quoted as saying they did not believe motion pictures would have much lasting appeal to the public. Why, they reasoned, would people choose to watch moving pictures when they were living the real?

One hundred years later, many teachers, administrators, and parents greeted the arrival of computers in schools with similar skepticism. "What can you do with technology that you cannot do just as well, if not better, without it?" was a question posed to one of our colleagues, an elementary school teacher who was an early adopter of computers in the classroom. Since then, computers, what economist and Noble laureate Herbert Simon (1983) called a "once in several centuries innovation," have transformed every aspect of American society, culture, and economy even while many schools lag far behind the pace of technological change.

When fully implemented in the classroom, computers can act as "disruptive innovations," fundamentally changing how teachers teach and students learn (Christensen, Horn, & Johnson, 2008). When used only as a curriculum add-on or a reward for student behavior, computer technology fails to effect teaching and learning in meaningful ways. As learning tools in schools, many technologies serve to maintain existing relationships and practices as teachers continue lecturing, only adding technology peripherally as PowerPoint presentations. Disruptive innovations, by contrast, often happen at the margins and may not initially seem as useful for learning as existing practices. But as students and teachers adopt them, these innovations supplant older methods.

Computer technology makes possible *Co-constructing* ideas and information—the sixth of our 7 Cs of democratic teaching. Computers possess the potential to disrupt traditional practices and present students and teachers with opportunities to foster democratic classrooms. No longer does schooling have to rely on a one-way, teacher-as-expert, transmission-based model. With technology, everyone can learn to *access* and to *assess* online information—skills necessary for every member of a democratic community.

In democratic settings, students not only view information in class and online, but *construct* original presentations for themselves and their peers. They learn to use computer programs and databases to *design, create,* and *evaluate* information. In other words, teachers and students forge new digital age relationships as co-creators, co-designers, and co-evaluators of schooling, practicing and refining the attitudes and skills needed in a digitally driven democratic society. As one teacher told us, now that computers have arrived in most classrooms, the still being answered question is: "Will students and teachers be active in the development, implementation, and evaluation of technology or will they be primarily just users and consumers of what others have done?"

Constructing Knowledge for Democratic Learnng

We derived the term *co-constructing* from the educational learning theory known as "constructivism" (Ambrose, Bridges, DiPietro, & Lovett, 2010; Dean, Hubbell, Pitlier, & Stone, 2012). A constructivist view of learning, noted the editors of the influential *How People Learn* series (Donovan & Bransford, 2000, 2005), examines ways "people construct new knowledge and understandings based on what they already know and believe" (Donovan & Bransford, 2000, p. 10). It emphasizes how students construct knowledge through active engagement with meaningful puzzles and authentic-to-their-own-life problems. Co-constructing means teachers not only teach students, but students teach each other and adults as well.

From a constructivist perspective, co-constructing knowledge happens as teachers challenge students' taken-for-granted assumptions, presenting them with issues to resolve through inquiry-based learning and problem-solving activities. For example, studying the Civil War, high school students might assess Abraham Lincoln's views on slavery in light of his issuing the Emancipation Proclamation, a seminal document of American freedom. Students evaluate primary and secondary sources to build a nuanced picture of Lincoln's motivations. In so doing, simple or straightforward accounts of Lincoln's actions are replaced by more complete explanations of his views toward Blacks as well as the importance of the Proclamation to the Union war effort. The students themselves construct their own understandings, point by point, through the study of historical evidence as they evaluate the decisions people make within the social context of the times.

However, constructivist approaches are not the norm in history/social studies classrooms. Instead, teachers using textbooks, state curriculum frameworks, reading lists, and local lesson plans assemble knowledge, and then present it to students. Such "school-sponsored knowledge" reflects what is "produced or endorsed by the dominant culture" while silencing the "voices of those outside the dominant culture, particularly people of color, women, and, of course, the young" (Apple & Beane, 2007, pp. 14–15).

By contrast, when teachers and students co-create the curriculum together, young people learn to be "critical readers" of their society, so when confronted with some knowledge or viewpoint, they feel encouraged to ask: "Who said this? Why did they say it? Why should we believe this? And who benefits if we believe this and act upon it?" (Apple & Beane, 2007, p. 15) The result is that "young people shred the passive role of knowledge consumers and assume the active role of 'meaning makers'" (p. 17).

As constructivist perspectives suggest, making history/social studies education a place for creating and receiving knowledge can be vitally important as preparation for students' roles in a democratic society. As citizens, voters, workers, and members of social organizations and multiple communities, today's students are tomorrow's history-makers who, constantly facing uncertain situations and making independent choices and decisions. When teachers unilaterally transmit the curriculum, students are not afforded opportunities to ask substantive questions, collect data and analyze evidence, and draw informed conclusions based on thoughtful analysis.

History Learning and a Digital Generation

Summarizing a wide body of research on how students learn history, Keith C. Barton (2004) found that "many students know a great deal about history, think of themselves as historically knowledgeable and aware individuals, and are motivated to learn more about the subject." Young people's history learning comes from multiple sources: historically themed discussions with parents or relatives (often involving family history), trips to museums, parks and historic sites, historical movies and television programs, and books and magazines about historic figures. Their knowledge is incomplete, contains misconceptions and misinformation, and reflects social life more than political, legal, or diplomatic topics. Nevertheless, students come to schools with interest in and questions about history on which teachers can build productive learning experiences.

Looking deeper into the dynamics of how students think about history, Barton (2004) identified three prime challenges for teachers.

1. Students tend to interpret historical change as the result of the "actions and intentions of individuals rather than societal structures or collective action." They overemphasize the role of key historic figures while showing "little regard for institutional contexts."

2. Students tend to "overnarrativize" history, seeing the past as a relatively straightforward march of progress in which a few main characters overcome major obstacles as they resolve a historical problem. For example, students think that since Martin Luther King Jr. marched in the South and delivered the "I Have a Dream" speech, civil rights were achieved for Blacks. Students do not understand that historical problems are not resolved in a single way by a single individual, but evolve over time, generating new versions and permutations of longstanding patterns.

3. Students do not understand how historians make use of sources and evidence. On the one hand, most students have developed specific ideas about what constitutes a reliable source, having found themselves deceived or scammed by product ads and claims at one time or another. These experiences generate a sense of cynicism in which they tend to dismiss all sources as just someone's opinion. They have not learned to look at sources from a critical perspective to analyze what is being said based on certain assumptions and perspective. So, they view sources as information not to be questioned.

The implications of the research, Barton believes, is that in order to make history/social studies relevant, teachers must build on what students know and care about in their own lives. In this way, teachers fulfill the goal of teaching tomorrow's citizens to understand "how people lived in the past" and identifying the decisions all of us must make to build the present and the future. Barton's comments were published in 2004. Since then, computers, the Internet, video games, smartphones, and handheld digital devices have become the 24/7 companions of many children and adolescents, raising new questions about how a digital generation learns about history.

Students Using Technologies

The presence of computer technologies in the lives of students is staggering. By the beginning of the 21st century's second decade, American teens and tweens were averaging, on a typical day, 7 hours and 18 minutes using entertainment media (computers, video games, music players, and other forms of screen media) (Rideout, Foehr, & Roberts, 2010). Media multitasking (experiencing more than one media at a time) meant 8- to 18-year-olds experience 10 hours and 45 minutes of media time during a day. Whereas the children of the baby-boom generation grew up with television, children of the new millennium are growing up immersed in multiple computer and media-based environments (Fox & Rainie, 2014).

Young people use a wide collection of communication and information technologies. Virtually all adolescents play video games on computers or cell phones. Three of four teenagers send text messages, half use social websites, about two of five blog or journal online. Large numbers download video and music to personal digital devices. Learning in school, as traditionally defined by teacher-led learning activities that feature print books, cursive writing, and deliberate study, seems increasingly remote for today's youngsters.

In a digital world where people use multiple interconnected electronic devices, researchers Lee Rainie and Barry Wellman (2012, pp. 6, 11–18) see the emergence of historically new forms of social interactions, what they characterize as "networked individualism." Tied together digitally, "it is the person who is the focus: not the family, not the work unit, not the neighborhood, and not the social group." These changes are products of a triple revolution made up of the Internet, social networks, and mobile technologies. The Web, mobile phones, and social networks while giving students and teachers enormous access to information, also generate uncertainty about what information is reliable and trustworthy.

Commentators and researchers are vigorously debating the effects of computer technology on young people's learning. Critics see technology as a negative force, minimizing children's opportunities for exploratory play and physical activity. Long hours in front of screens leads to social isolation, physical sedateness, and intellectual stagnation. In most schools, computers have been, to use historian Larry Cuban's (2003) memorable phrase, "oversold and underused" while making little difference in how teachers teach or students learn.

Technology advocates see immense potentials for computers to allow young learners to explore, problem solve, and innovate within electronic environments. Nearly three decades ago, the computer visionary Seymour Papert (1994, p. 5) foresaw that many students would regard traditional teaching as "slow, boring, and frankly out of touch" while computers will generate new collaborative learning environments where students exercise democratic choice and "intellectual self-determination" over what they are learning in school.

For students, the ways computers are used in school generates a "digital disconnect" where technology-inclined students want more digital learning than less technology-comfortable teachers provide (Project Tomorrow, 2008, 2013). Drawing on data from national surveys of K–12 students (with an emphasis on third, sixth, ninth, and twelfth graders), the Speak Up national research project found increasing numbers of students have personal smartphones, digital readers, tablets, and laptops, all with Internet access. Yet only 21% of middle and high school students were assigned homework where they accessed the Internet. In high schools, only 18% of seniors reported being allowed to use their personal laptops in class (Project Tomorrow, 2013).

When teachers do use technology, it often is for routine drill and practice-learning assignments, administrative record-keeping, or electronic monitoring of students' online activities. The digital disconnect takes on particular significance in the history classroom where many students struggle to recall people and events that happened far away and long ago (Lesh, 2011). Students who do not see the connections between historical material and their personal lives are distanced from essential ingredients of historical study, including one's own past and one's role as a history-making individual whose choices and decisions matter in a democratic society.

Technology's slow integration into schools, and history teaching in particular, is not solely tied to a preference for traditional teaching methods among teachers. Many schools have outdated, poorly functioning equipment, making it difficult to infuse technology into daily lessons. In schools where computers are located in labs, there are scheduling issues as well as the time needed to get an entire class moved from classroom to computer lab and back again, all in a 50-minute teaching period. And, although many families now have computers with Internet access at home, teachers are reluctant to give computer-based assignments and homework that might disadvantage those youngsters who lack home technology learning resources. In a rapidly evolving digital world, schools remain slow-to-change institutions where, in Seymour Sarason's (1982, 1996) memorable phrase, "the more things change, the more they stay the same."

Voices of Teacher Candidates: Constructing Knowledge With Students

To explore the idea of teachers and students co-constructing knowledge, we asked teacher candidates how they thought about the concept first, as a general teaching and learning strategy in the history/social studies classroom, and second, as a way for teachers and students to integrate technology into classroom instruction.

In broad terms, most candidates acknowledged the value of teachers and students co-constructing knowledge, mainly by having students engage in the teaching of academic material to other students. One history candidate recalled that in high school she had to teach a math concept to her peers in trigonometry class: "It was the first time I realized how much you really grasp the material when asked to teach it." This year, as part of her student teaching practicum, she has students "create our class notes for the standards or chapter we are studying."

Another candidate asked students in an economics class to "teach the substance of the chapter to other students in this class or in a different class." Looking back, he recalled the "lessons were very well done and interesting for the students," and the presenters did a professional job in the teaching role. Acknowledging that the approach has risks (students may not construct meaningful teaching lessons), all drawbacks are "outweighed by students learning the very valuable and transferable skills of being able to effectively deliver ideas, information and content to others."

Using this same approach, a third high school candidate had small groups of students teach the names and functions of different New Deal-era agencies and programs to the class. For him, the most important part "was that it required students to research, analyze, and then come up with how to present information to their classmates." Some students were the presenters, others the visual designers. This method "empowers students and allows them to control the learning that takes place in the classroom." Additionally, "it is a democratic way of teaching because in some ways this models

Congress in that the work is divided up into many different subgroups before being presented before the Senate or the House of Representatives."

Several candidates raised co-constructing knowledge in connection with history research assignments for students. One candidate admitted, "the idea of allowing students to take full responsibility for their learning was a scary idea for both me and the students." At first, "they appeared hesitant and frustrated while researching. The one question I heard most frequently during the first times I tried this method was 'What if we don't get it right?'"

Over time, students' reluctance to research history lessened and they became actively involved in teaching themselves: "I have found that once students become more familiar with researching information on their own without me giving knowledge that they are expected to learn, they interact democratically with each other when recognizing that each individual has learned something that is unique and special." She concluded: "Giving students the opportunity to teach each other and me about various topics in history this year has been one of my best learning experiences as a new teacher."

Some candidates found that a students-teaching-students approach as they designed it did not work well in their classes. Following a lesson where student groups were asked to create presentations based on primary source documents and speeches from the American Civil War, one candidate was disappointed with the results. There was a "lack of analysis of the material" by the student groups. In the future, he concluded, "I need to be more involved with the students, to give more ways to think about the sources so they are fully confident in their statements. I can give the students some freedom, but it must be monitored to make sure that they are giving their best effort rather than just their minimum effort."

A middle school candidate found that "issues arise when trying to let go of the reins and hoping that students take them up seriously" because what students need is clarity. He found that "in middle school it is difficult to have to take the time to make information available to students in a clear-enough manner that they could teach themselves the material." Nevertheless, one system worked well for him; that of "having a student lead a part of the class once or twice a week . . . it can include everything from leading an activity or reading with the class and leading a brief discussion on what they read." The student leader comes to school early and the teacher provides notes and strategies for the teaching time. Over many weeks, all students in the class take on the teaching/leadership role.

Asked about using technology to co-construct knowledge with students, history teacher candidates acknowledge the powerful roles of the

Internet, social media, and other technologies in everyone's daily lives. They constantly reference how there is no escaping technology's complicated presence during the school day. Multiple competing interests surround technology: Students want to use their smartphones and mobile devices to communicate with friends; teachers want to use videos and games to enliven daily instruction; and schools want to appropriately regulate use of online and social media materials. Most candidates favored trying to achieve a balance between what they think would be too much or too little use by students. Still, at this early stage in their careers, these history candidates have few concrete ideas about how students and teachers together best co-construct knowledge with technology.

Co-Constructing Strategies for Building Democracy

Effectively engaging today's students with online information is an enormous challenge. Youngsters who grow up reading, writing, and communicating with screen media expect the interactivity provided by computers, smartphones, and other technologies. For them, learning through slow-paced analysis of textbooks, primary sources, and teacher-made notes is neither engaging nor memorable, no matter how interesting the academic content. At the same time, these Internet-engaged students are learning the skills needed to thoughtfully navigate online informational claims and counterclaims.

This chapter's "Building Democracy" activities focus on ways for students and teachers to use digital technologies for co-constructing history/ social studies learning through researching and creating information. Computer technology invites collaborative learning and collective action. There are reasons for adults and younger learners to work together—students know a lot about how to use some of the latest tools while teachers have a plan for what students will learn from the curriculum. Students want engaging formats for learning, while most teachers want students to understand key ideas and information. Digital technologies provide a common ground on which the democratic classroom learning communities can be built.

Strategy: Developing Technological and Media Literacies

In the digital world, how do computers and the Internet support the development and operation of democracy? During the Arab Spring uprisings in spring 2011, protestors used social networking sites to coordinate demonstrations that led to the toppling of dictators in Egypt and other Middle Eastern countries. That same year, Frank LaRue, the United Nations Special Rapporteur on the Promotion and Protection of the Right to Opinion and Expression (2011), declared that the Internet is a fundamental human right and governments must "ensure that Internet access is maintained at all times, including times of political unrest." The Special Rapporteur cited the "unique and transformative nature of the Internet" as a place where people exercise their human rights, resist inequality, and promote human progress. Governments are expressly forbidden to censor or filter online information, disconnect people from Internet access, or invade rights to privacy and data protection.

Expanding Ed Tech to IT

"In the modern world, print literacy is not enough," said computer researcher James Paul Gee (2007, p. 20). Students need to develop the skills and dispositions necessary for living and learning in a digital world. To do so involves, first and foremost, a shift from an educational technology (Ed Tech) to an information technology (IT) perspective on the part of students and teachers. As an approach to learning about technology, Ed Tech was grounded in the idea that teachers and students need to be computer literate—broadly defined as knowing how to use computer hardware and digital tools such as word processing, databases, spreadsheets, email, Web browsers, print/graphic utilities, multimedia presentations, and assistive devices as well as the ethical and social issues surrounding privacy, copyright and plagiarism.

In today's information society, hardware-based computer literacy is only a first step. Many teachers and students know the basic operating functions of computers and other digital devices. They can operate most of the latest software. But, facing the pace and scope of technological change, what teachers and students also need are new and expanded technology "life skills." An information technology or IT perspective means teachers prepare, deliver, and assess lessons differently while students think critically and creatively about the learning they do and the technologies they use. Here is one example:

- Ed Tech approach: Teachers use websites constructed by others as an instructional tool to transfer knowledge from sources to students. Students visit the sites, access information, and report their understandings and beliefs in the form of written papers and oral reports.

- IT perspective: Teachers and students co-construct knowledge by comparing, contrasting, and critically evaluating existing online materials, examining the assumptions that underlie how information is presented, and constructing information presentations for others to read.

Changing perspective and emphasis means teachers and students no longer primarily consume what technology offers them. They actively participate in the development, implementation, and evaluation of technology as tools for facilitating learning at all grade levels and in every history/social studies field.

Identifying Bias and Misinformation

In surveys conducted by the Pew Internet & American Life Project, most teachers noted that students struggle in assessing the quality and accuracy of online material, recognizing bias, and exercising patience and determination when searching for hard to locate information (Purcell et al., 2012, p. 6). A well-known study conducted by Donald Leu and his colleagues at the New Literacies Research Laboratory at the University of Connecticut offers a revealing example of student struggles with online research (Krane, 2006). The researchers asked students from schools in South Carolina and Connecticut to locate online information about an endangered animal species called the "Pacific Northwest tree octopus." The students were not told a tree octopus is a completely fictional creature created by the researchers.

The students (determined by a test to be among the best online readers in the school) easily located the assigned website, "Help Save the Endangered Pacific Northwest Tree Octopus from Extinction." The site featured an attractive color scheme, purported to be actual rare photographs, and an extensive amount of academic-looking text—all of it false and made up. The students overwhelmingly accepted the site at face value, believing the tree octopus and the movement to save it were real. Even when told the truth afterward, many students refused to believe that the website was a hoax.

Leu and his colleagues were surprised by the students' willing acceptance of the site's online information. None of the students took steps to evaluate the material by asking about the site's author or where and when the site was created. No one checked information for reliability. The site looked like what students thought a credible academic site might look like.

Because there was a large volume of information, written in long sentences with numerous scientific-sounding words, the students believed it to be accurate and reliable. Design and appearance created more of an impression than content. Leu concluded that schools must teach students to become "healthy skeptics" who think critically and do not immediately accept whatever they locate online as true.

As a fake website, "Help Save the Endangered Northwest Tree Octopus" can be viewed humorously, as can other hoax sites such as "Whale Watching on the Great Lakes" and "Dihydrogen Monoxide Research Division." There are few serious consequences from someone believing that there are whales in the Great Lakes or that dihydrogen monoxide is a threatening chemical agent. However, the Web includes enormous amounts of inaccurate, harmful, and hateful information that can be easily accessed and believed by students and adults.

In an older but still useful Web-information analytical framework, Nicholas C. Burbules and Thomas A. Callister Jr., (2000, pp. 96–100) categorized such "troublesome" Internet content under four terms, all beginning with the letter M:

1. *Misinformation* is content that is "false, out of date, or incomplete in a misleading way." Such information is everywhere on the Internet, but sometimes hard to identify. "Disinformation" is a particular type of misinformation where "knowingly false or malicious" material is posted online, often from unknown or unidentified authors, in an attempt to discredit individuals or organizations.

2. *Malinformation* is what reasonable people might consider "bad" or harmful information and includes "sexual images or material, potentially dangerous or damaging information, political views from militant fringe groups, and so on."

3. *Messed-up information* is "poorly organized and presented" material such as long lists of data without synthesis or context, Web pages marked by "gratuitous logos or other graphics that distract or clutter," or discussion boards and blogs that feature text rambling on without a clear focus or topic. There may be so much messed-up information about a topic that a reader is overwhelmed by the data and unable to make sense of it.

4. *Mostly useless information* focuses on trivial, mundane, or eccentric topics and interests.

Using these four Ms as a starting point for thoughtful analysis, students and teachers can become critical evaluators of Web content where they learn to recognize bias and misinformation in its many online dimensions. One effective classroom activity involves examining the Google search results for a history/social studies topic to show how seemingly straightforward websites can contain hidden information designed to influence readers and viewers. We cite the Great Seal of the United States, used to authenticate government documents and passports and taught in schools as an important symbol of American democracy, as an example.

On the first page of search results for the Great Seal, students will find, in addition to Wikipedia as the top entry, resources from credible government sites (including "Our Documents" from the National Archives, "Ben's Guide to the U.S. Government for Kids" from the U.S. Government Printing Office, and a history of the Great Seal from the U.S. Department of State Bureau of Public Affairs) intermixed with material from for-profit websites including the History Channel, GreatSeal.com, Asis.com, and StateSymbols USA.

These for-profit sites appear informative for students until readers look more closely at the page content and follow the links to learn more about the authors and sponsoring organizations. Each site is filled with advertisements running down the sides of the page, blurring the lines between where factual information ends and product sales begin. GreatSeal.com repeats information published by the U.S. Department of State's Bureau of Public Affairs, disclosing that fact only in very fine print at the bottom of the main Web page. Another site includes a link called "Come Home" that sends readers to an evangelical Christian site called "Straight Talk about God." A third site, in addition to discussing Medal of Honor recipients and related military topics, includes patriotic overviews of America's role in war.

Learning how to unpack the content of Internet search results to locate credible, historically accurate sources requires time, effort, and new skills for students and teachers. Doing an online search using the phrase "evaluating websites" will identify multiple sets of criteria and tools posted by college and university libraries to guide people in using the Web. The American Library Association offers online strategies for evaluating primary source websites. The American Association of School Librarians publishes a yearly list of the best websites for teaching and learning. These resources offer ways to expand students' and teachers' knowledge of the Internet and its resources.

Strategy: Redefining Research and Inquiry

At one time or another during the school year, most teachers ask students to do a history/social studies research paper or presentation. These assignments range from biographies of historical figures to reports on the causes and consequences of important events. Ideally, history research activities offer students opportunities to co-construct knowledge as they draw on sources and evidence to form and defend their own judgments about the past. Research, in this view, means to re-search or to search again. Students engage in building new conceptions and formulations that propel future learning.

In reality, many students resent and resist research activities for at least two reasons. First, they recognize that, in most cases, they are not being asked to do real investigations of the past, merely locating what others have already said about a topic. As novice researchers, these students realize they cannot match the efforts of professional historians and other experts. Teachers respond that students need research assignments to practice the skills of historical inquiry.

Second, school computers, which would seemingly energize history research by making primary and secondary source material readily available to readers and viewers, often do not. Many machines are old, slow, and marred by filters that block access to relevant sites. One high school student described the scene in the computer lab at her school: "Wait for access because the Internet is down or a slow-loading computer needs to be rebooted or face a delay from the slow-responding word processing program and a constantly breaking printer." For this student, "hearing the words 'We are going to the computer lab today' is one of the most dreaded of them all" (Fox, 2013). Yet, it is not technology, just old technology that students dislike. Three of four high school students surveyed by Project Tomorrow (2013) reported they wanted to use smartphones and tablets to find information online, but fewer than half were allowed to use these devices in class for academic purposes.

The result has been a standoff—teachers wanting students to research; students practicing wrong methodologies, some putting in minimal effort, others resorting to unintentional or deliberate plagiarism to finish assignments speedily. The length and depth of history research papers has steadily declined, replaced by short essays, summaries of assigned readings, and personal opinion papers. High school students are rarely asked to write a paper longer than three or four pages (National Commission on Writing in America's Families, Schools, and Colleges, 2006). History research papers of 2,000 words or fewer happen at least one or twice in a marking period, but extended length papers are far fewer. Less than one in five classes ask students to write a history research paper of more than 5,000 words (Center for Survey Research & Analysis, 2002).

Searching for Information Online

Online resources are capable of transforming history/social studies teaching and learning; never before has so much information been available so easily. Online primary source material present firsthand accounts of the past as it was lived by famous figures and ordinary people. Maps, timelines, and charts make learning compelling as do photographs, artwork, and pictures posted by museums, historical organizations, and libraries. Interactive learning games, tablet computer and smartphone apps, and real-world simulations put students in the roles of historical decision makers who face the choices and consequences of different courses of action. Blogs, wikis, and discussion groups offer ongoing commentary on historical topics and their present-day extensions. Streaming videos bring multimedia to the history classroom. Online databases provide immediate access to countless scholarly journals, newspaper articles, and other previously inaccessible print media. The instructional possibilities of digital technology are limited only by the imagination of teachers and students.

To students today, researching a topic means Googling it. A national survey of AP and National Writing Project teachers found that students were more likely to use the Google search engine ahead of any other information source (Purcell et al., 2012, pp. 2, 4). The next most popular information sources were Wikipedia or another online encyclopedia (used by 75% of students), YouTube or other social media sites (52%), other students, (42%), and cliff notes or other paper study guides (41%). Electronic books (18%) were consulted for research purposes more often than any books other than textbooks (10%) and 16% of students asked the school librarian for resources.

There are problems with the objectivity and reliability of even basic Google searches. Reviewing recent commentary about the effect of the Internet on people's thinking, Sue Halpern (2011) noted that most of us broadly misunderstand how Google's search engine actually works. The company uses a complex mathematical algorithm called PageRank "composed of 500 million variables and 2 billion terms" to locate Internet sites related to keywords. In this system, "popularity (the number of links)" serves as a "proxy for importance, so that the more a particular link is clicked on, the higher its PageRank, and the more likely it is to appear near the top of the search results" (Halpern, 2011, p. 33). The process, seemingly objectively scientific, is anything but. Profit-seeking companies and individuals, over Google's objections, have successfully engaged in "search engine optimization" that adjusts code and content so that sites move up the rankings in ways that do not necessarily reflect their actual popularity.

As Eli Pariser has shown in *The Filter Bubble: What the Internet is Hiding from You* (2011), complex technological processes are at work here. Google's technology enables "every search to fit the profile of the person making a query" (Halpern, 2011, p. 34). After several searches that establish a baseline of a person's interests and patterns, Google's technology predicts what search results someone will find most useful. Such personalized searches mean that even with the same keywords as search terms, different people will get different results. For instance, searching climate change will produce different results for an environmental activist and an oil company executive. In Pariser's terms, "there is no standard Google anymore."

Personalized searches enable people to get information quickly and efficiently. One does not have to wade through less relevant sites because the computer has done the work for you, identifying products and services to best fit your needs. But critics worry that personalization technology distorts democracy's need for citizens who are able to access a wide range of information before making thoughtful decisions. If searches yield only information derived primarily on previous searches and preferences, then search engines may be directing people to sources that will mainly reinforce rather than call into question already established views and perspectives. In this scenario, Republicans will listen only to like-minded Republicans while Democrats will hear only from Democrats who share similar perspectives, creating a political echo chamber of self-reinforcing beliefs. As Halpern (2011) concludes, "the Internet, which isn't the press, but often functions like the press by disseminating news and information, begins to cut us off from dissenting opinion and conflicting points of view, all the while seeming to be neutral and objective and unencumbered by . . . bias" (p. 34).

Given students' reliance on the Web, the act of research, what most teachers believe should be a "relatively slow process of intellectual curiosity and discovery," has become a "fast-paced, short-term exercise aimed at locating just enough information to complete an assignment" (Purcell et al., 2012, pp. 3–4). Teachers share some of the responsibility for students' get-it-done-quickly behaviors. When teachers assign fill-in-the-blank worksheets that ask for already known information about a topic, students have little reason to do more than finish the activity without high engagement. Recognizing this, more and more teachers now design online research assignments that either send students to teacher-chosen resources or require students to use a variety of information sources, both online and offline.

Finding High-Quality Web Resources

Researching online, students encounter materials of varying quality and reliability. At or near the top of the first page of Google search results, there is nearly always a Wikipedia entry, fact-based and text-heavy, composed in a dense writing style. That first page of search results will also include text-based summaries from other encyclopedia-style sites whose pages are filled with advertisements for products and services that have nothing to do with the search for historical information. Students may also find politically inspired sites presenting ideologically slanted information fitting the agenda of the site's authors. Intermixed within these materials are high-quality resources from historical associations, libraries, governmental agencies, and academic institutions. Students need to be taught how to discern relevant from less useful or clearly bias information.

Primary source materials are a crucial foundation for student research, presenting history as it was lived and understood by those who lived it. The Library of Congress has a wide-ranging collection of primary source information available for use by student and teacher researchers. The "American Memory" section has collections of written and spoken word materials, sound recordings, still and moving images, maps and sheet music from throughout American history. Students and teachers can access tools to use in interpreting these sources from the Library's Teacher Guides and Analysis Tools website. There are specific tools for primary sources, oral histories, books, photographs, maps, sheet music, and motion pictures.

"America's Story" (biographical information for figures in American history), "African American Mosaic" (materials for the study of Black history and culture), "National Jukebox" (sound recordings and sheet music from the past), and "88 Books That Shaped America" (an exhibition of some of the most significant fiction and nonfiction writing in American history) are resources for students and teachers. The National Archives also has impressive collections of online materials, including "DocsTeach" that lets students and teachers create interactive activities using more than 3,000 primary source documents and "Today's Document," an app that sends an historic document to a smartphone or tablet computer every day.

In addition to the Library of Congress and the National Archives, students and teachers can develop their own collections of online Web resources for student inquiry-based research. Collections of online materials addressing the presidency; courts and the law; economics; women's history; learning games and simulations; and lesbian, gay, bisexual, and transgender (LGBT) history are located in the "Web Resources" section of the *resourcesforhistoryteachers* website.

Introducing students to Web resources that provide information while also teaching them ways to analyze that information expands thinking about the accuracy and reliability of sources. FactCheck.org, a website developed by the Annenberg Policy Center at the University of Pennsylvania, seeks to be an online advocate for citizens by exposing factual inaccuracies and deception in politics. The site critically assesses all forms of political communications, including speeches, policy statements, news releases, interviews, television ads, and election materials from candidates. FactCheck.org also has a guide of recommended tweets for students and teachers to access on Twitter. Other notable websites devoted to uncovering misinformation in politics include the "Fact Checker" from the *Washington Post*, "PolitiFact" from the *Tampa Bay Times*, and "PoliticalCorrection.org" from the Media Matters Action Network.

Political conservatives have criticized these fact-checking sites for having a liberal and/or democratic party bias, citing studies by the University of Minnesota School of Public Affairs and George Mason University that found Politifact attributed false statements to Republicans more often than to Democrats (Cassidy, 2012). Conservative organizations have responded by establishing their own sites to counter information from sites they deem too progressive in approach. "NewsBusters" from the Virginia-based Media Research Center is one example.

One possible ongoing activity would be for students and teachers to review what has been posted on fact-checking sites and then offer their own analysis and interpretations of those issues and questions. As fact-checking commentators, students practice formulating responses using specific evidence to support their statements—skills they will carry with them after graduation as members of a democratic society.

Strategy: Using Social Media for Participatory Learning

Social media, a term for ways people connect with one another using computers, tablets, smartphones, and other digital devices, includes such well-known tools as Twitter, Facebook, LinkedIn, YouTube, and Flickr as well as blogs and wikis. Social media "form a new online layer through which people organize their lives," said digital culture scholar Jose van Dijck (2013, p. 4). At the outset of the computer revolution, social media offered the promise of networked communications between people, but huge for-profit organizations have come to dominate the ways people interact online, giving rise to a "platformed sociality" that shapes people's everyday activities. Today, van Dijck wonders if authentic communications are still possible within worldwide, connected media environments.

Media scholar Henry Jenkins believes we must create structures where everyone can participate fully and democratically in a digital world, shaping our uses of technology to build what he calls "participatory culture." Seen from the standpoint of schools, participatory culture allows students and teachers engagement, supports individuals sharing with others, encourages experienced individuals to mentor novices, sustains a belief that individual contributions matter, and promotes the belief that people are connected to one another (Jenkins, Purushotma, Weigel, & Clinton, 2009). Jenkins and Wyn Kelley (2013) argue that in such a culture "more and more people have the capacity to take media into their own hands, creating and sharing what they know and how they see the world beyond their immediate friends and families" (p. 8).

Curating Wikis

Wikis, websites that are collaboratively edited and maintained, have emerged as an important way for students and teachers to create and learn together (Koopman, 2010; Richardson, 2010; Watters, 2011). Wikis encourage students to work collaboratively in teams, to question processes, to make mistakes, and to monitor each other's reasoning—important features of democratic classrooms. The teacher's role shifts from expert-in-charge to that of supporter and facilitator of peer–peer interaction, social learning, and technology use. As one educator concluded after reviewing recent research on instructional uses of computer-based tools, "wikis are seen as capable of providing more possibilities of open learning environments than many other traditional uses of instructional technology" (Lee, 2012, p. 90).

Wiki (the Hawaiian word meaning "quick" or "rapid") is a term most people associate with the massive online encyclopedia, Wikipedia, a "go-to" source of information for many students and teachers. Wikipedia seeks to be a compendium of all information, continually being created and updated by a worldwide collection of authors and editors. But, Wikipedia is not the only model for how to create and use wikis. This interactive technology can be tailored to fit the needs and interests of students and teachers in a variety of fields, including history, and for different teaching and learning purposes.

A site developed at the University of Massachusetts Amherst, *resourcesforhistoryteachers*, is one example of students and teachers co-constructing knowledge using technology (Maloy, Poirier, Smith, & Edwards, 2010). The site has separate pages for each of the learning standards in the Massachusetts History & Social Science Curriculum Framework as well as the AP standards for world and U.S. history. Each page displays links to primary sources, multimedia materials, multicultural and women's history, historical biographies, maps, timelines, and other resources. When the wiki first began in 2006–2007, only college students preparing to become public school history teachers read and contributed to building the pages. Now, teachers and students from throughout the United States and around the world use and suggest materials for the site. One in four visitors come from countries other than the United States).

Wikis are a genre of digital textbooks with resources to cover, uncover, and discover curriculum topics. The mix of material on each wiki page enables users to encounter diverse resources for learning about historical events. One teacher described how high school students are using the history wiki: "Students access the site and explore the key concepts from every unit. Our AP World History textbook can be too dense for our student population and the site helps our students better comprehend history. They enjoy the organization and structure, along with many multimodal resources." One of the candidates from the UMass program planned to have students use iPads for multicultural history research, noting, "the students have told me that they are interested in the idea of untold stories, and they are pretty enthusiastic about finding some of their own."

Table 6.1 presents examples of cover, uncover, and discover resources for an American Revolution unit, drawn from the *resourcesforhistoryteachers* wiki.

Once assembled, a history/social studies wiki invites students and teachers to engage in wikiquests. A wikiquest, like a webquest, allows students to review material from a class-made wiki rather than the wider Internet. A wikiquest promotes focused topic investigations without Web distractions or loss of resources during the online search process. Middle school teacher Allison Evans constructed a Vietnam-era wikiquest using pages from *resourcesforhistoryteachers* wiki where students would view the following audio and video resources, primary sources, first-person interviews, and historical photographs:

Table 6.1. Cover, Uncover, and Discover Resources for an American Revolution Unit

Cover	"Teaching the Revolution," an overview essay by Baruch College and City University of New York historian Carol Berkin from the *History By Era* series of the Gilder Lehrman Institute of American History.
Cover and discover	The Coming of Independence, a video with transcript from *A Biography of America* from Annenberg Learner.
Uncover	Women in the American Revolution: Working with Primary Sources from the New Jersey Women's History Project highlighting the activities of women during the time.
Uncover and discover	The History of the American Revolution by David Ramsey, the first American national history written by an American revolutionary and printed in America in 1789, is now available as an e-text.
Cover	Timeline of British taxes and acts and American reactions until 1775 offers a chronological overview from the Library of Congress.
Discover	Battling for Liberty: Tecumseh's and Patrick Henry's Language of Resistance is a lesson plan about connections between Native American tribes in colonial North America from the professional resource site, *Thinkfinity*.
Uncover and discover	A Common American Soldier lesson plan from Colonial Williamsburg detailing the everyday experiences of members of the Revolutionary Army.

- *Historical Perspectives on the History of Vietnam* from Michigan State University's Windows on Asia website.

- *Battlefield Vietnam: A Brief History* from PBS.

- *Transcripts and Audio Recordings from the Presidential Recordings Program* at University of Virginia.

- *The War in Vietnam: A Story in Photographs* from the National Archives with documentary pictures of the war shot by military photographers between 1962 and 1975.

- *Vietnam War Causalities by Home of Record* from the Virtual Wall at the Vietnam Veterans Memorial.

- President Lyndon B. Johnson's 1968 speech "Peace in Vietnam and Southeast Asia" in which he announced he would not seek re-election to the presidency.

- Reverend Martin Luther King Jr.'s 1967 speech, "Beyond Vietnam: A Time to Break the Silence" in which he declared opposition to the war.

- *Clay v. United States* 1971 Supreme Court case arising from Muhammad Ali's (Cassius Clay) appeal of his conviction in 1967 for refusing to report for military induction.

- First-person interview selections from *Patriots: The Vietnam War Remembered From All Sides*, edited by historian Christian Appy, available from Amazon.com.

- *Women: The Unknown Soldiers* essay posted on the De Anza College website, "The Vietnam Conflict."

- *Women and the Vietnam War* from the Wellesley College Department of Political Science.

- *Teaching the "American War": Looking at the War in Vietnam through Vietnamese Eyes* from the website "Primary Source."

- Text of the Vietnamese Declaration of Independence, 1945.

The wikiquest asked students to explore two (three for honors credits) different sources from the list and respond to the following questions:

1. Who produced the source? When was it produced? Is the source trustworthy?

2. What is the perspective of the source? Is there more than one perspective?

3. What are the main points of the source?

4. How does the source relate to class notes, discussions, and readings?

5. Using facts, observations, and background knowledge, what is the essential question answered by the source?

Allison concluded that students' choices in the wikiquest promoted engagement and knowledge acquisition and supported the co-constructing of knowledge democratically. Class discussions featured students teaching each other as they cited the research they specifically learned which other students might have not viewed. The range of conversations widened beyond discussions in which research centered on one or two primary or secondary source readings. Students displayed newly gained confidence from using interactive technology, accessing multiple resources, and assessing the accuracy and credibility of different online sources.

Developing a wiki in history/social studies classes mirror ways that knowledge is created and shared in today's highly networked information world. In society, no single community member or organizational leader can know enough to completely address every pressing social, economic, and political problem. People must work together to develop solutions that make sense and then share those ideas collectively. Collaborating to develop a wiki gives students and teachers firsthand knowledge of the processes by which resources can be collectively identified, evaluated, and revised.

Building Tag Bundles, Playlists, and Education Boards

Social bookmarking is a type of social media with multiple uses for students and teachers who are building democratic and participatory cultures in schools. Broadly defined, *social bookmarking* is a Web-based information management process. People save and share Web links in a free public Web space. Using well-known social bookmarking sites like Delicious, Diigo, and Pinterest, students and teachers create collections of digital information about individuals, groups, and events in history. Files are saved on the Internet ("the cloud") instead of on a personal computer. Cloud computing allows Web links to be accessed anywhere, anytime from an Internet-connected smartphone, computer, iPad, or other digital device, letting students and teachers share their history collections with schools and classrooms everywhere.

Locating, saving, and tagging resources is the bookmarking part of social bookmarking. As they locate online materials about a topic, social bookmarkers assign keywords (known as "tags") to each resource. In U.S. history, for example, broad terms—"American History," "primary sources," "teaching resources," "African Americans," and "presidents"—and more specific topics such as "Abraham Lincoln," "colonial America," "Vietnam," "Congress," or "transcontinental railroad" can all be used as keyword/tags. To locate information about a topic, computer users search for and access all the resources saved under a specific keyword/tag within a virtual file cabinet of personally chosen materials.

The social aspect of social bookmarking happens when computer users make their resources publicly available to members of online communities. This way, anyone interested in a topic can put a keyword into the Delicious, Diigo, or Pinterest search function and view all the resources that other users have tagged with that keyword. Although students and teachers have the option of making resources private or public, it is the sharing of resources that makes possible a large and diverse exchange of information among those online.

To group and share multiple resources, Delicious, Diigo, and Pinterest have features called "tag bundles," "playlists," and "education boards" that let students and teachers organize tagged resources around a theme, person, or event (Maloy & Edwards, 2012/2013). The resources are then displayed together, forming a grouped collection to be accessed and viewed in any order. In Delicious, resources are grouped into tag bundles, three or more resources for a single topic. In Diigo, resources can be displayed as a computer slideshow, creating history resource playlists. Pinterest arranges resources by broad categories, creating a collection of education boards.

Tag bundles, playlists, and education boards enable students and teachers to collect and share multimodal resources about events or concepts—for example, the Pullman Strike of 1894, the 1955 Montgomery Bus Boycott, late 19th-century nativism, or the Cold War. Instead of everyone in a class writing an individual research paper about an historical event—an activity that may tempt some students to copy information they find online—students become researchers and curators of collections of Web resources. Students locate materials that reveal information about people's lives or about critical events in the past, assemble these materials into a tag bundle, online playlist, or education board, and continue expanding each collection as they find new resources.

The goal is to identify video, audio, text, and primary source materials for each online collection. Studying ancient Rome and the Roman Republic through the lens of Shakespeare's play *Julius Caesar* one could compile links to the text of the play from the MIT's "Complete Works of William Shakespeare"; the British Council Film Collection video selection of Marc Anthony's funeral oration in Act III, Scene 2; audio of Orson Wells' 1938 radio broadcast of the play, set in Fascist Italy; the PBS website for the video series The Roman Empire in the First Century; teaching modules from the Folger Shakespeare Library; and an excerpt from Plutarch on the assassination of Julius Caesar from the Internet Ancient History Sourcebook project at Fordham University. These materials generate a multimedia collage of linked historical information that can be shared with other schools and classrooms.

Sharing Historical Biographies Online

Assembling biography tag bundles, playlists, and education boards about historical figures is another innovative way to use social bookmarking technologies in the history/social studies classroom. Every curriculum framework or school textbook includes multiple historical figures who students are expected to know. Additionally, there are hundreds and hundreds of lesser known, but compellingly interesting individuals whose stories and struggles reveal historical lives and times. Students are attracted to stories of people in the past, so constructing and sharing online historical biographies promotes the core curriculum goals—discussed in earlier chapters—of covering, uncovering, and discovering history.

Tag bundling allows students and teachers to locate, individually or as part of group projects, a wide-ranging collection of resources about historical figures. The goal here is not to create a single definitive text-based biography, but to construct a broader collage of information about an individual's life, times, and lasting legacies. In constructing these historical tag bundles, Web searchers purposefully include not only text-based primary and secondary sources, but pictures, sound, and moving images in different genres and formats, including print, media, and art.

We created a model biography tag bundle about Bessie Coleman, early 20th-century aviator and stunt flyer, and first Black woman to hold an international pilot's license (Table 6.2). Bessie Coleman's story is important for multiple ways she struggled to overcome racial and gender discrimination in the field of aviation, and for her outspoken opposition to segregation in the South where she refused to appear before White-only audiences as an aerial show performer.

In this approach, students locate a secondary source biography, one or more primary source materials, audio or visual resources, and interactive online materials as well as additional resources that the students find interesting and relevant. For Bessie Coleman, we chose secondary source biographies from the Atlanta Historical Museum and the U.S. Centennial of Flight Commission. Our primary source selections included a newspaper article and promotional billboard both from 1921. Our visual source was also a U.S. postage stamp issued in 1991 to honor Coleman's accomplishments. The interactive source was an online learning game from the PBS

Table 6.2. Social Bookmarking, Tag Bundle, and Playlist for Bessie Coleman

Biography	Bessie Coleman, 1892–1926, Atlanta Historical Museum
	Bessie Coleman, U.S. Centennial of Flight Commission
Primary source	"Aviatrix Must Sign Away Life to Learn Trade," *Chicago Defender*, October 8, 1921
	Colored Air Circus Billboard poster, 1921
Audio/visual resource	Collectible Stamp from United States Post Office Black Heritage Series (issued April 1995)
Interactive Web resource	"The Adventures of Josie True," an online learning game from the *FlyGirls* website from PBS American Experience (Bessie Coleman appears as a character in the game)
Other resources	*Essay*: "Bessie Coleman: Race and Gender Realities Behind Aviation Dreams," Amy Sue Bix in *Flight, Biographical Essays in Honor of Centennial of Flight, 1903–2003* (National Aeronautics and Space Administration, 2012). *Lesson Plan*: "Design a Campaign for Social Change" from *Black Wings: African American Pioneer Aviators* (Smithsonian Air & Space Museum

"FlyGirls" website that features Coleman as one of the game characters. Two other resources complete the bundle: an essay on Coleman and a lesson plan about Black aviators as pioneers for social change.

Students and teachers will find several advantages to creating and sharing historical biographies using social bookmarking technologies. First, it is easy to adopt or adapt our framework for organizing online information about historical figures. Everyone can use our categories—primary sources, secondary sources, audio/visual resources, interactive resources, and other materials—or they can create categories themselves. The goal is to locate a range of online resources that convey a broad portrait of a person's life in the context of her or his times.

Second, using our model of multiple social bookmarking categories expands the Internet research process from text-only to multimedia and multimodal resources. Students and teachers are expected to locate not only primary and secondary sources (which are often text-based), but visual and interactive sources as well. This process puts photographs, artwork, motion pictures, audio recordings, and other multimedia resources at the center of history learning, and does so in ways that involve much more than students listening to a teacher's voice. Multiple media makes history learning more multimodal for all involved.

Third, creating and sharing online historical biographies using playlists, tag bundles, or education boards encompasses a wide-angle perspective of people and events. The life and times of an historical figure is not compressed into the kind of short text-based account often found in a textbook or on a website, but enlarged by including different types of online resources. This process of resource identifying encourages students and teachers to view individual lives not solely in terms of a series of names, dates, and places, but through the issues and themes raised by their actions. In the bundle of sources created for Bessie Coleman, one sees not just the first Black international female pilot, but also an individual who struggled to overcome segregation and improve society, themes that resonate within the history/social studies curriculum.

Finally, creating and sharing historical biography collections using social bookmarking technologies fosters democratic teaching in democratic classrooms by promoting civic engagement among students and teachers. When an individual or a group assembles a bundle of biographical links about an historical figure, new information has been created that can potentially contribute to a widened discussion about the past and its implications for the present and the future. By sharing that information digitally, students and teachers acknowledge their membership in a wider community that can benefit from what they learned. By both adding information and sharing information digitally, students and teachers help to realize the goal of schools preparing engaged citizens for a democratic society who know how to seek and find multiple sources of information.

Conclusion

In this chapter we explored how students and teachers can use digital technologies and student research in ways that build democratic classrooms. Computers make possible unique, powerful, and transforming learning environments using methods and approaches that have not been part of traditional educational systems. It is hardly an exaggeration to say that before computers the last technology to produce a salient change in teaching was the invention of the printing press by Johannes Gutenberg around 1450. Digital technologies are just beginning to transform education by changing student–teacher relationships, redesigning how people look for and produce information, and redefining the nature of the skills and competencies that schools provide students.

It is easy to forget how new the computer revolution is in schools and society. The Macintosh computer debuted in 1984, the first mobile phone with email and Internet connectivity appeared in 1996, the Google search engine was launched in 1998. Today these tools are taken for granted by students who have never known a world without the Internet, smartphones, text messaging, and other interactive technologies (Project Tomorrow, 2012).

To build more democratic classrooms requires shifting from an older view of technology, one that stressed the importance of teachers and students learning steps and procedures for using technology hardware, to a newer focus on students and teachers co-constructing collaborative outcomes and products with technology. Learning online research skills, curating wikis and designing wikiquests, and bookmarking educational sites use technology to co-construct knowledge and build collaborative learning environments in classrooms. By its very structure, co-constructing with technology involves individuals working in groups and emphasizes collective contributions. Students and teachers, in positions as authors and editors, analyze information and make decisions while building dispositions and understandings of mutual trust and responsibility on which democratic participation can be established and sustained.

Chapter 7

Connecting

Civic Learning and Community Engagement

Most students do not look much further for information than the classroom in which they are learning. I believe it is my job as a teacher to
show them that the material they are learning is not isolated and it has
infinite connections to the "real" world they will all be entering soon."

—High School Teacher Candidate

Newcastle University (Newcastle upon Tyne, UK) professor and 2013 TED
Prize winner Sugata Mitre's research focuses on using technology to promote what he calls self-organized learning environments (SOLE) among
children and adolescents (Mitra, 2013). SOLEs emphasize peer–peer and
individual-guided learning built around students' own interests and questions. Mitre's first initiative was a series of experiments called the "Hole in
the Wall" project. Placing a computer in an inconspicuous wall in an urban
slum section of New Delhi, India, Mitre recorded the ways that children
spontaneously interacted with the technology, teaching each other how to
navigate the Internet.

Next, Mitre created a "Granny Cloud," an initiative in which a group
of grandmothers living in the United Kingdom did academic coaching and
mentoring with children in India via weekly chats on Skype (Matias, 2012).
The "Hole in the Wall" and the "Granny Cloud" are examples of SOLEs
where people collaboratively invent new uses of technology for their own
purposes (Mitra & Negroponte, 2012).

In a broad vision, Mitra calls for a "school in the cloud," inviting students and teachers to use technology as a way for widely separated communities of students to learn from each other. Mitre's work introduces *Connecting*,
our seventh C of democratic teaching. Engaging history/social studies students and teachers with wider communities of school, neighborhood, town/

city, nation, and world are the cornerstones of democratic citizenship.

Commonly labeled *community service* or *service learning*, linkages between schools and communities also have been called *civic or community engagement, place-based education, youth leadership, youth activism,* or *action civics*. All these terms refer to occasions of "community-engaged teaching" in which students and teachers encounter, analyze, and address real-world social and economic problems (Center for Teaching, 2014). Such projects can involve face-to-face interactions between students, teachers, and communities or they can use the Internet and social media as vehicles for connecting schools and communities. Engaged students and teachers have multiple opportunities to develop the attitudes and understandings of 21st-century citizenship in a context of democratic teaching and learning.

The Civic Mission of Schools

Preparing students for productive roles as members of a democratic society is a time-honored goal of history/social studies education in K–12 schools. In theory, having students learn about the rights and responsibilities of U.S. citizens as well as the structures and functions of American political institutions will ensure that the students of today will nourish and sustain the American system in the future.

Citizenship education is widely known as *civics* or *civic education*. Civic education is "central to the purposes of American education and essential to the well-being of American democracy," according to the authors of the *National Standards for Civics and Government* (Center for Civic Education, 2010, p. 15). Every member of a democratic society should have the capacity to "participate in the political process and contribute to the healthy functioning of the political system and improvement of society" (p. 13).

Family, churches, the media, and local community organizations contribute to developing the civic character of young Americans. But schools have a "special and historic responsibility," exercised through "formal instruction in civics and government that provide a basis for understanding the rights and responsibilities of citizens in American constitutional democracy and a framework for competent and responsible participation." Classes "should be augmented by related learning experiences, in both school and community, that enable students to learn how to participate in their own governance" (Center for Civic Education, 2010, p. 14).

Curriculum standards at the state level also emphasize the importance of teaching students about civic responsibility, especially the structures of the American political system, the importance of voting, and the usefulness of citizens influencing public policy decisions. Echoing a similar theme, *The Civic Mission of Schools*, a report from the Carnegie Corporation and CIRCLE (2003) stated that "competent and responsible citizens" are (a) "informed and thoughtful," (b) "participate in their communities," (c) "act politically," and (d) "have moral and civic virtues" (p. 10). Although helping young people to achieve these civic outcomes is the responsibility of every part of society, "schools are the only institution with the capacity and mandate to reach every young person in the country" (p. 12). Because children develop an interest in politics by age 9, the report urged schools to "bring together a heterogeneous population of young people—with different backgrounds, perspectives, and vocational ambitions—to instruct them in common lessons and values" (p. 12).

The State of Civic Learning

For many observers, civic learning is in a state of crisis. Standardized tests and surveys show young citizens know more about Hollywood celebrities and entertainment trends than government leaders and national policies. From school classes, most students retain only the most general understanding of world politics, geography or global issues. The 2010 National Assessment of Educational Progress (NAEP) reported that less than 50% of the nation's eighth graders knew the purpose of the Bill of Rights, 75% of high school seniors could not name a power given to Congress under the Constitution, and of the seven subjects tested—including mathematics, science, and English/language arts—students performed the worst in history (National Center for Education Statistics, 2011a, 2011b; Week in Review, 2011, p. 2).

The Association of American Colleges and Universities (AAC&U) reported that the United States ranks 139th out of 172 world democracies in voter participation, only 10% of citizens contact a public official, and only 24% of high school seniors achieved proficient or advanced scores on a national civic assessment (National Task Force on Civic Learning and Democratic Engagement, 2012). The AAC&U called on institutions of higher education to make civic learning by students an undisputed priority, noting "full civic literacies cannot be garnered only by studying books; democratic knowledge and capabilities also are honed through hands-on, face-to-face, active engagement in the midst of differing perspectives about how to address common problems that affect the wellbeing of the nation and the world" (p. 3).

Civic involvement also has less widely discussed economic and racial dimensions. As Harvard University educator Meira Levinson (2012) has documented: "African American, Hispanic and poor students perform significantly worse on standardized tests and surveys of civic knowledge than white, Asian, and middle class students" (p. 66). Local governments and community organizations struggle to find individuals who will make the commitments of time and energy needed to serve on boards and committees. Levinson reports that low-income citizens of color are less likely to belong to groups or organizations, work on a community problem, attend a community meeting, or join a political campaign.

Focusing on "institutions other than schools," an American Political Science Association report found "democracy at risk" (Macedo et al. 2005). Citizens have turned away from active participation in politics and from involvement in public and civic life. The core of the problem, say the political scientists, is that the "design of our current political institutions and politics turns citizens off" (Macedo et al., 2005). Political primaries are long and boring, most elections are not competitive, and partisan politics is "excessively ideological, nasty, and insufficiently focused on practical problem solving."

The solution is to enhance civic engagement throughout the society, for "government is legitimate only when the people as a whole participate in their own self-rule" (Macedo et al., 2005). In this view, *civic engagement includes any activity, individual or collective, devoted to influencing the collective life of the polity*" (p. 6). This means constructing "institutions that encourage the better forms of civic activity and that promote a healthy exchange of ideas without deteriorating into cantankerous and destructive polarization" (p. 14).

"Can the Internet revive democratic participation?" asked Shakuntala Banaji and David Buckingham (2013, p. xiii) in their study of online activities by young people in seven European countries—United Kingdom, Netherlands, Slovenia, Hungary, Spain, Turkey, and Sweden. Acknowledging the unprecedented power of the Internet to reach people, Banaji and Buckingham (2010, 2013) juxtapose the participatory potential of the Web with young people's deep alienation from traditional forms of political activity. In an information age marked by interactive social media and digital technologies, youth seem far distanced from the long-standing goal of individuals acting as engaged citizens in a democratic society.

Across all seven countries, young people saw politicians as "boring, or hard to understand; working only for their own interests; and far removed from the everyday needs and realities of common citizens" (Banaji & Buck-

ingham, 2010, p. 17). They reported distrusting mainstream political organizations and practices based on personal experiences with school councils,
protest demonstrations, and online petitions that generated little response
or lasting change. At the same time, efforts by Internet content providers to
build civic engagement websites generated at best only sporadic involvement
by young people. Many of these sites lacked an immediate social issue to
engage the interests of readers and viewers; other sites lacked substantive
ways to connect youth to people in power. Although some of the respondents felt positively about liking a Facebook profile or contributing to a
message board, many others recognized that few adults were paying any
attention to their efforts. One survey respondent said: "Why should we
speak if no one is listening?" (Banaji & Buckingham, 2010, p. 20).

Some examples of online civic and political participation by youth did
emerge in the surveys. "Ethical consumption or socially conscious shopping"
captured the attention of many young people, linking concern for causes
or products with a person's choice of how to use the purchasing power of
money (Banaji & Buckingham, 2010, p. 20). The Internet also enabled
some young people to be "monitorial citizens," using the Web "by tracking
elections; keeping abreast of privacy issues; discussing, photographing, and
publicizing police behavior; debating civil liberties; and getting behind the
scenes in conflict situations" (Banaji & Buckingham, 2010, p. 20). But in
general, although the Internet was valued and used by a relatively small
number of already politically involved youth, the Web has proven "much less
effective in reaching out and engaging those who are not already engaged"
(Banaji & Buckingham, 2010, p. 23).

The effect of new media on young people's political participation may
be changing. In 2012, the MacArthur Research Network on Youth and Participatory Politics surveyed 3,000 young people between the ages of 15 and
25 years. The research looked at their involvement in participatory politics,
defined as "interactive, peer-based acts through which individuals and groups
seek to exert both voice and influence on issues of public concern" such as
blogging about a political issue, posting or forwarding a video or message
on one's social network, or being part of a poetry slam (Cohen & Kahne,
2012, p. vi). Forty-one percent of respondents had been part of at least one
participatory political event during the past year and 37% participated in
both participatory and traditional face-to-face political activities. The study's
authors concluded, "participatory politics are a significant dimension in the
political life of young people" (Cohen & Kahne, 2012, p. ix).

It seems clear that schools and new media have meaningful roles to
play in shaping the habits of civic engagement among young people. Voting,

protesting, marching, lobbying, petitioning, canvassing, and talking with others are all forms of politically minded civic action. Serving in the military, participating in a neighborhood watch, volunteering in the Peace Corps or AmeriCorps, donating money to charitable organizations, protecting the environment, and learning about the political system through print and online media are additional forms of engagement that promote democracy while improving the quality of everyone's lives. School-based community service and civic engagement initiatives are part of this broader framework of improved civic life.

Citizen Action and Action Civics

Lamenting that civic education and community engagement are only "add-ons" to the curriculum in many schools, the U.S. Department of Education (2012, pp. 2, 8) has called for a renewed emphasis on preparing "all students—regardless of background or identity—for informed, engaged participation in civic and democratic life." The Department's report, *Advancing Civic Learning and Engagement in Democracy: A Road Map and Call to Action*, is intended to address the nation's persistent and troubling "civic achievement gap" by instituting next generation civic learning initiatives called "action civics." Unlike older forms of civic education, action civics would be more "ambitious and participatory," with students at the center of the learning using technology and social networking to connect across communities.

In *No Citizen Left Behind*, researcher Meira Levinson (2012, p. 68) similarly focused on addressing a civic empowerment gap, arguing that "old-school 'civics,'" with its "flowcharts, lists and lectures about the structures and functions of government institutions" must be replaced with instructional approaches that are "more hands-on, more engaged with contemporary life, more active" where the academic work of students in school follows the civic responsibilities of informed citizens in a democratic society. In this "action civics" model, students consider real-world problems that have meaning and relevance to them and to their communities. The emphasis is for students to learn "*through* citizenship and not *about* citizenship" (p. 69).

From a similar perspective, James A. Banks (2008) has proposed a "Typology of Citizen Participation" that emphasizes action by citizens in response to community problems and needs. Banks is known for his highly regarded framework for infusing multicultural content into teaching and learning in schools. In Banks' (1991) multicultural curriculum reform model, teachers are urged to move beyond either a "contributions" or "additive" approach to teaching that trivializes and negates the histories and cultures of diverse peoples to adopt "transformative" and "social action" approaches to teaching and learning. In a transformative approach, teachers infuse the experiences of diverse people into the teaching of academic content while in a social action model, students seek to address issues and problems they are learning about in school.

Banks (2008) proposes a similar progression from minimal to active involvement in his four-stage citizen participation framework:

1. *Legal citizen* is a person with rights and obligations in the society, but who does not participate in the political system.

2. *Minimal citizen* is a person who votes in local and national elections, typically for one of the major party candidates based on what are seen as the important issues of the day, but has little other involvement with the political process.

3. *Active citizen* is a person who participates politically in ways beyond voting (joining political groups, expressing political opinions verbally or in writing, contributing to campaigns and candidates) but who still supports existing structures and systems

4. *Transformative citizen* is a person who "takes action to actualize values and moral principles beyond those of conventional authority." This person expresses interest in action to "promote social justice even when those actions violate, challenge, or dismantle existing laws, conventions or structures."

The National Action Civics Collaborative has six civic action stages that teachers can embed into curriculum:

1. community assessment,

2. issue identification,

3. research,

4. power analysis,

5. strategic development, and

6. policy-oriented action.

Like Banks, the focus is on finding ways for students to look beyond class-room and schoolhouse walls to understand and begin responding to issues and problems in local communities. Civic education, in this view, is more than the academic development of the individual; it is teaching individu-als to take interest in and responsibility for larger communities of people.

Importantly, researchers have found that civic engagement and com-munity service benefits not only the communities receiving services, but students themselves, often in ways that were not initially anticipated by those doing the service. In a national study, *Engaged for Success: Service Learning as a Tool for High School Dropout Prevention*, students participat-ing in service projects indicated that such activities motivate them to work hard academically (Billig, Root, & Jesse, 2005; Bridgeland, Balfanz, Moore, & Friant, 2008). Two of three students endorsed the idea of doing service learning, but only one of three schools offer such programs. And, in many of the schools that do offer community service programs, student involve-ment in local communities is not connected to academic classes, creating a "service learning–community service gap."

Service Learning and Community Engagement

Community service and service learning—familiar terms in education today—often are how schools seek to fulfill their civic mission. Community service happens when students voluntarily participate in projects of value for people in local communities as part of a longstanding American tradi-tion of neighbors helping neighbors in combination with elements of social charity and religious good works. As an educational approach, community service holds that students should help those in need and in so doing, those students will develop the mindsets and habits of caring, connected citizens. There are many school-based examples of students' community service from donating bake sale or talent show funds to local charities to working in soup kitchens, food banks, and senior centers. Such projects, however, often remain disconnected from the rest of the school's academic curriculum.

By contrast, service learning (also called community service learning [CSL]) happens when schools and/or teachers give students the opportunity to put academic concepts learned in the classroom into practice in real-world situations. The National Service-Learning Clearinghouse (2009) defines CSL as "combining service tasks with structured opportunities that link the task to self-reflection, self-discovery, and the acquisition and comprehension of values, skills and knowledge content." CSL programs offer students opportunities to examine their own assumptions and perspectives, and allow for experiences to create new understandings about self and society.

The benefits of service-learning programs for participating students has been widely researched. In a meta-analysis of service-learning involvement by high school-age adolescents, Shelley Billig and her colleagues at Tufts University (2005) concluded that well-designed programs help reduce achievement gaps, develop civic responsibility, increase students' self-esteem and self-efficacy, and decrease disciplinary referrals and behaviors leading to pregnancy or arrest. The Tufts study compared 1,000 high school students who experienced service learning with those who did not. All were drawn from schools matched demographically and by student population; more than half of the students were Latinos.

Examining the effect of CSL programs on schools in low socioeconomic areas, a team of researchers led by Peter Scales and Eugene Roehlkepartain (Scales, Roehlkepartain, Neal, Kielsmeier, & Benson, 2006) surveyed 1,799 principals and 217,000 diverse students in grades 6 to 12 from 300 U.S. communities. Principals answered questions about the effect of service learning on academic, social, school climate, and community indicators. Students completed the Search Institute's *Profiles of Student Life: Attitudes and Behavior* survey. The researchers found positive correlations between service learning and academic success among students from lower socioeconomic backgrounds. Principals reported their perceptions that community service leads to improved attendance, engagement in school, and academic achievement. And, although schools in low socioeconomic communities engaged in service learning the least, they gained the greatest benefits in measures of academic achievement and school engagement when they did.

More recently, researchers examined how participation in service learning produced increases in political voice among college students at Ignatius University (Seider, Gillmor, & Rabinowicz, 2012). Political voice, defined as more than intending to vote in an election, included the readiness to take actions within existing political and social systems. In surveys and interviews, CSL program participants at Ignatius reported greater awareness of political and social issues, a heightened commitment to philanthropy, increased interest in socially responsible occupations, and a stronger commitment to social change.

A positive correlation between CSL activities in school and subsequent political activities is not always the case, a point acknowledged by the Ignatius study team. One 2009 study found that Teach for America graduates (individuals who ostensibly were motivated by a desire for community service and educational change) exhibited lower rates of voting, charitable giving, and civic engagement than a group of comparable non-Teach for America peers (Seider et al., 2012).

The Ignatius researchers conclude that some students may finish a service project believing that individual good acts supersede the need for ongoing political action, whereas others may conclude that political action is impossible in today's highly divided political climate. The researchers recommend that community service be "amplified by explicitly engaging students in reflection about the potential impact of other forms of direct action" (Seider et al., 2012, p. 69). That recommendation expands the reach of service learning by asking students to confront the reality of people living in an unequal society, a situation that schooling mirrors and reproduces. By challenging inequities in societal structures, students and teachers connect service learning/community engagement activities to the processes of democratic teaching and learning in schools.

Voices of Teacher Candidates: Connecting Students and Communities

In our interviews, history and social studies teacher candidates found civic engagement, service learning, and community connections to be unfamiliar territory for their teaching. Used to defining teaching as conveying academic content, the idea that teachers also build students' civic values and personal dispositions through community engagement was new and they were uncertain about how to do this within the school curriculum.

The candidates expressed a range of views about how schools and teachers might go about connecting students with communities. Some were unsure how teacher-arranged CSL projects fit into the job of a schoolteacher. As one candidate observed, "it is rare for a school to be looked at as a community institution that serves everyone around it." At the same time, this candidate recognized that teachers play roles in the out-of-school lives of students so "connecting with the larger community makes for a healthier environment inside the school."

Most candidates saw great value in connecting community resources to the school curriculum. After inviting a Black World War II veteran from a local Veterans Education Project to speak to an American history class, a high school intern concluded "it is my job as a teacher to show [the students] that the material they are learning is not isolated and it has infinite connections to the 'real' world they will all be entering soon." The guest speaker described his experiences during the war and his feelings about being part of a segregated army fighting for a country where he was not considered to be an equal member of society. The intern recalled the students looking surprised and moved because "history was sitting right in front of them."

One high school candidate stated flatly "there is no reason I can't bring community leaders and issues into curriculum and classroom." In so doing, students see that history "happens in their own backyards." For this intern, letting students stay in the classroom after school was a form of school/community connection, "not as a paid 'agent of the state' but as a member of their greater community offering them a place to hang out and get some work done." Noting that he used community connections regularly in his 12th-grade course on law and civil liberties, another high school intern remarked that "tying learning to the community is one of the most important things a teacher can do. . . . I think all teachers should teach students to be alert and active citizens and always critically examine conventional wisdom."

One candidate saw connecting communities and curriculum as a core element of her approach to teaching history. "I have countless opportunities," she noted, "to connect events in the past to modern-day issues that affect the everyday lives of students." She focuses historical study on "individuals in history who risked their lives and participated in events that led to positive social, political, religious, and economic changes." Every day, she wants students to leave class with the "understanding that regular, ordinary people can have an effective impact on improving their own lives, as well as the lives of others." However, she acknowledged that the pressure of preparing students for high-stakes tests had prevented her from incorporating CSL projects into her classes.

Another intern at the same school also linked community connections with teaching history in secondary schools. "All the issues that are discussed in a history class," he noted, "are played out on a daily basis outside the school, or even within the hallways of the school." Instead of just discussing social problems, "social studies classes should be formed around attempting to fix the problems." Guided hands-on experiences in the real world, he believed, would involve students in the community, enliven high school classes, and prepare students for life and careers after graduation.

Repeatedly, the interns discussed the difficulties of students performing community service activities outside of the school. It is one thing to bring occasional speakers to the school or to connect historical topics to present-day themes and issues, but tight budgets and daunting logistics seem to preclude having students actually volunteer in the community. As one intern noted, "many of the students play sports, have jobs and other responsibilities after school, so it would be difficult for them to participate in these types of activities." Another intern said he teaches students about the many ways they can be more active citizens, but "a lot of the messages I give to students are lost due to the fact that they are still only freshmen and 'don't really care about how the government works.'"

Connecting Strategies for Building Democracy

This chapter's "Building Democracy" activities are designed to offer students and teachers ways to do history-related community service and civic engagement initiatives, through face-to-face projects and social media technologies. Community service by schools has traditionally involved direct personal connections between students and community members and local organizations. Social media expands the potential effects of service as well as the definition of what constitutes individuals and communities receiving service. Sharing information online, students can reach more people in more places in more ways than they might ever be able to accomplish through direct service.

We begin with ideas for using community engagement activities to build school connectedness among students, particularly those who are at risk for dropping out of school. Next, we describe using local history projects as a form of community-based teaching and learning. Both these approaches emphasize person–person engagement and service learning. Then, we look at ways to use digital resources to foster civic and democratic action in the form of classroom learning networks that can use social media and social bookmarking as ways for students and teachers to share information with people and communities.

Strategy: Creating School Connectedness

In schools across the country, large numbers of youngsters find school classes boring, disengaging, uninspiring (Center for Evaluation & Education Policy, 2009). For these students, the world of the classroom seems oddly disconnected from the world outside the walls of the school building. They find that issues and concerns in their daily lives are rarely talked about in school, generating an impression that history is mostly about events that happened long ago, far away, and bear little relevance to them or their lives. Disconnected from school, students are similarly disconnected from the goals of civic and community engagement.

In recent years, researchers have explored why students become disaffected or alienated from school, some leaving before graduating, others continuing to attend classes but exerting little academic effort and showing little commitment to learning. Although graduation rates have been slowly improving since 2001, the statistical picture is still far from ideal. In 2009, 1 in 4 Americans and 4 in 10 non-White students did not complete high school with their class (Balfanz, Bridgeland, Bruce, & Fox, 2012).

Among the sizable majority of students who stay to graduation, there is a persistent sense that school is an uninteresting place to be where it is difficult to find value in the work one is asked to complete. The 2009 High School Survey of Student Engagement of more than 42,000 students across the nation found that two of three high school youngsters are bored at least every day in class and one in six are bored in every class. Four of five students cite uninteresting material as a primary source of their boredom, whereas one in three said lack of interactions with teachers caused them to withdraw their focus from schoolwork (Yazzie-Mintz, 2010a, 2010b).

Other studies have found that between 40% and 60% of all youth—urban, rural, and suburban—report being disconnected from school, that is, not liking their teachers, lacking interest in school, and not finding schoolwork meaningful or engaging. Among the students in these studies, school connectedness is high in elementary school, begins to decline in middle school, and becomes a major issue in high schools (Monahan, Oesterie, & Hawkins, 2010).

For many educators, promoting a sense of connectedness is the key to keeping students in school and focused on education. Connectedness is the "belief by students that adults and peers in the school care about their learning as well as about them as individuals" (Centers for Disease Control and Prevention [CDC], 2009). Youth who are connected to their school are less likely to engage in delinquent or violent behavior, to drink alcohol, or to use drugs. They are less likely to initiate sexual activity at young ages. Connectedness is also linked to positive mental health and emotional well-being with less physical and emotional distress and fewer depressive symptoms and suicidal thoughts. Youth who feel connected show better academic outcomes, higher motivation, lower classroom misbehavior, higher grades, and higher rates of graduation.

Re-engaging Marginalized Students

Service learning encourages students who are at risk for leaving school to reconnect with academic learning in at least three ways. First, service projects promote more positive feelings about school among students who are otherwise not attending classes. Second, students find service projects more interesting than other academic classes. Third, over time, more frequent attendance and renewed interest motivate students to work harder academically in all their classes, improving overall school performance (Bridgeland, DiIulio, & Wulsin, 2008; Bridgeland et al., 2010).

Re-engaging marginalized students through service was the focus of "Rise UP," a social studies class at a local high school organized by dropout prevention researcher Heather Batchelor (2012). The class had all the appearances of a college seminar. There were only 15 students each term, or 30 for the school year, and one teacher. The class was not open to everyone; students had to be selected by the teacher and approved by the school administration. There were no rows, seating plans, or dress codes. Students sat, stood, and moved around, contributed to discussions when they had a point to make, behaving thoughtfully and respectfully almost all the time. The class met daily for half the school year, although some of the students took a follow-up half-year course called "Leadership in Community Service."

The students in Rise UP were not part of an AP or high honors seminar, what many observers think of when the terms *small* and *select* are used to describe a high school class. Instead, these students came from the margins of the school. Most had low grade point averages, high rates of absenteeism, and constant problems with school rules and discipline procedures. School administrators regarded them as potential dropouts. Most came from low socioeconomic backgrounds, some spoke English as a new language, and others were on special education plans.

Rise Up was designed to create a very different learning experience from that offered in traditional academic classrooms. The goal, described in the lead teacher's doctoral dissertation, was to use student-driven community service projects and democratic teaching practices to re-engage disaffected and marginalized youth with education (Batchelor, 2012). In place of expected teacher presentations and worksheets, textbook reading assignments and multiple-choice exams, these students became part of a personalized learning environment where their concerns, viewpoints, and goals were placed at the center of the academic experience.

From the first day of class, students were asked to actively contribute to the direction of the course, including choosing and designing all of the CSL projects, dictating discussion topics, and setting classroom rules and expectations. As one high school student noted, "This class gave me a place to talk about things that I never thought I'd be able to talk about. I feel like I can share anything here." A second said that he "understood the work and because it was a small class I didn't really get stressed out. I felt like I had people who I could talk to about stuff if I needed to."

In the local community, Rise UP students became service providers: raking leaves in neighborhoods near the school; weeding flowers and planting spring bulbs for a family inn; baking birthday cakes for children living in shelters; planning parties for children receiving cancer treatments; and hosting a senior citizen breakfast. Year after year, the Rise Up experience transformed the attitudes of these students toward school and beliefs about themselves as individuals. After working in a Special Olympics event with elementary school youngsters, one high school student recalled, "It made me feel so happy to work with those kids. Even though I hate all sports, doing it with them wasn't bad because I knew that I was making them excited about being able to do sports."

Expressing Choice and Voice

Teachers often refer to the "real world" when discussing history/social studies topics, telling students to wait until "you are in the real world." The sentiment is meant to convey how students' current academic work is important to future success, but it has the unintended effect of saying to many youngsters "this is not real" or "school is not real." Why should students wait for some day in the future "real world" when today they can behave as responsible members of school organizations? Helping students identify areas of interest and passion and connecting them to learning experiences is another key to building school connectedness.

Students at a local middle school experienced the power of choice and voice while exploring 19th-century reform movements in an eighth-grade U.S. history class. As part of a study of social reformers and the changes they engendered in society, students were asked to consider elements of their own community and society they would want to reform today. For these eighth graders, whose classroom was a former storage area, the answer was clear, they wanted better learning conditions in their school. What began as statements about the physical environment, cramped classrooms, stalls in bathrooms hanging from hinges, and ceiling tiles rotting from mold soon expanded to include ideas about academic curriculum and school improvement. Students surveyed the student body about what would make the learning environment better for all. The results included ideas for hands-on science lab equipment to increased funding of the arts to more of a multicultural focus in core classes.

Students connected their study of the past and their work in the present, looking for strategies previous social reformers used to create change that might provide strategies for how they could change their current situation. "Who has the power to make changes in our schools and society?" they asked, before examining the structure of school decision making and the role of the school committee. They elected a group of students as spokespeople and were put on the agenda of a school committee meeting to make a presentation of what they had learned and their ideas for a school improvement plan. The presentation was a success with the school committee taking their suggestions seriously and validating their work. More importantly, these students had engaged in a process of civic action unique to their interests and passions and learned they lesson that they were a critical part of their community and society.

The democratic principles of voice, participation, and action resonate with the building of school connectedness. As Alfie Kohn (2011) noted: "Students are less interested in whatever they're forced to do, and more enthusiastic when they have some say" (p. 5). So "if choice is related to interest, and interest is related to achievement," then classrooms where students "get to participate in making decisions about what they are doing are likely to be most effective" (p. 5). Students need to believe that school is a place where *voice* and *participation* by everyone is a fundamental feature of daily experience.

As part of a comprehensive approach to adolescent health, the CDC's (2009) policy paper on school connectedness draws a similar conclusion. In recommendation 4, "Use Effective Classroom Management and Teaching Methods to Foster a Positive Learning Environment," the CDC urges teachers to: "Apply a variety of classroom management strategies and teaching methods that are conducive to the diverse needs and learning styles of students"; "Engage students in appropriate leadership positions in the classroom and provide avenues for their voices and opinions to be heard"; and "Encourage open, respectful communication about differing viewpoints." In such democratically connected classrooms, students recognize that everyone is involved in learning, all voices are heard, everyone's rights are respected, and all backgrounds, cultures, and values are affirmed.

Strategy: Developing Youth Activism

Youth activism, in history and in contemporary society, is a compelling way to connect service activities to the history/social studies classroom (Oyler,

2011; Rubin, 2011). Middle and high school students often learn to see history only as events that happen to people rather than as products of people's decisions and choices. Accordingly, they do not picture themselves as history-making individuals whose actions matter in society, rendering them feeling powerless and alienated from democratic participation at any level.

Examples of young people making a difference, affecting events in profound ways, challenge the misconception that everyday people cannot create social and political change. Teacher Greg Barrios (2009) tells the story of a student walkout at a high school in Crystal City, Texas in December 1969. The students were protesting a school board policy that said only one Mexican American girl could be a member of the cheerleading squad, although the school served a majority of Mexican American families. High school students challenged the policy, and within a few days more than 2,000 students walked out of their schools in the community. The all-White school board still refused to change the policy.

As news of the protests spread, Texas Senator Ralph Yarborough invited three of the student leaders to Washington, DC, and the federal Department of Justice became involved in the situation. Relenting to growing pressure, the cheerleading policy was changed, setting the stage for the election of all Mexican American candidates to the school board and city council the following spring. The student walkout, concluded Barrios (2009), "remains a high point in the history of student activism in the Southwest."

Local History and Service Learning

Local history projects situate broad historical themes and questions in the daily lives of students and teachers while also generating meaningful service learning and youth activism among students. George Ella Lyon's (1996) award-winning picture book *Who Came Down That Road?* is one we read aloud as an opener for local history study at multiple grade levels (Maloy & Edwards, 1995). In the story, a young boy asks his mother who came down an old road they discover while out walking in the countryside. The mother's reply highlights the long history of a passageway whose travelers form an historical timeline going backward from European settlers to Native American peoples to now-vanished animals to early life forms in a primeval sea that originally occupied the area.

Any road, river, or other well-known passageway invites investigation using local histories and primary documents, including historical artifacts and photographs, to examine "who came down that road." Members of a class can walk back in time, actually or imaginatively, to envision the historical lives of ancestors and predecessors. Students might then interview those who live on the road today, compiling oral histories of people's experiences. Oral histories can be shared in print or online within the school and the community, further explaining the history of local communities.

Oral history projects can be focused around specific themes or specific time periods. As part of a unit on post-World War II U.S. society, one teacher candidate asked high school students to interview women in the community about their educational experiences to uncover how gender roles and assumptions influenced the school and career choices of different generations. Inspired by stories in historian Christian Appy's (2004) book, *Patriots: The Vietnam War Remembered by All Sides,* another teacher candidate asked students to interview community members about their experiences during the Vietnam War era in American history so the process of collecting and publishing oral histories would connect students to community members in new and powerful ways.

Student-directed local history projects teach students that they can interpret history for themselves and add to the historical narrative. Over the years, eighth-grade classes at Amherst Regional Middle School have undertaken an investigation of the life story of the town's namesake, Jeffery Amherst. Students engage in historical inquiry to determine how the town came to be named for this colonial era figure as well as the contemporary controversies surrounding the naming of a town after someone accused of biological warfare against native populations.

Students are eager to find out for themselves the facts of this history and draw their own conclusions. Each year after students complete this inquiry-based study, a number of them become outspoken advocates for re-evaluation of the town name. Another local history project related to a study of the Civil War included learning about local Black soldiers who served in the Union Army and were buried in the cemetery near the school. Students were excited to learn of this local connection to the past and were inspired to find additional stories of local people, past and present who made an impact on society.

The scope of historically centered local service projects is adjustable to the time available within the curriculum. Teachers and students can undertake voter information efforts, create public service announcements, promote recycling or other green initiatives, provide information to the school community about exercise and healthy lifestyle choices, and post student-made videos about historical or contemporary topics. The goal is connecting service activities by students to required learning standards and the efforts of change activists who sought to achieve similar goals in the past.

More can be learned about youth activism from a C-SPAN-filmed lecture, "20th Century Political Activism," documenting political action by young people after World War II. The lecture was written and delivered by University of Maryland Baltimore County historian Kriste Lindenmeyer (2011). There is exciting new research connecting youth activism and social media by researchers at the Berkman Center for Internet & Society at Harvard University and the MIT Center for Civic Media. The Southern Poverty Law Center has teaching materials about youth activism in civil rights history, including "The Children's March" in Birmingham, Alabama in 1963.

Activating a Student and Class Learning Network

One way to promote youth activism is by creating student and class-learning networks. Through an online network, students and teachers use the Internet to obtain information, share materials, and take action for personal or academic purposes. Constructing an online network relevant and unique to the students in each class reflects the broader democratic promise of the Web as a place where everyone has a voice to be heard, everyone's contributions to an issue or an idea matter, and everyone's actions produce meaningful effects and consequences.

A student and class-learning network is a variation of the term *personal learning network* (PLN). A PLN uses "social media and technology to collect, communicate, collaborate and create with connected colleagues anywhere at any time" (Edutopia, 2013). Like a PLN, a class-learning network can include online groups, Twitter feeds, Google+ connections, topic-related chats and blogs, and project-based resources. In theory, each network is personalized to the needs and interests of different groups of students and teachers.

A student and class-learning network receives and shares online information. To illustrate, we use a student and class-learning network based on history/social studies courses being taught at the University of Massachusetts Amherst.

Table 7.1 shows both incoming and outgoing information of the network. "From the Web" (the left-side column in Table 7.1) lists sites and organizations that send the educator and students information regularly, including the "Today's Document" app from the National Archives, *The New York Times* Breaking News Alert, and updates from the New England History Teachers Association on LinkedIn. "To the Web" shows how the teacher and students generate content for online readers and followers through an

Table 7.1. Student and Class Learning Network

From the Web	To the Web
Today's Document (iPhone/iPad app from the National Archives featuring an historic document every day of the year).	*resourcesforhistoryteachers* wiki (primary source, multicultural, and multimedia resources for teaching history in K–12 schools coded to the Massachusetts History & Social Science Curriculum Framework, AP World History Key Concepts, AP U.S. History Themes, and AP Government & Politics Standards).
The Writer's Almanac (daily email alert from American Public Media featuring poetry and short summary of important people and events in history).	
New England History Teachers Association (active history-related discussions among members on LinkedIn).	
Today's TED Talk (email notice highlighting the TED video of the day).	*resourcesforhistoryteachers* Facebook group (notices of periodic updates to the *resourcesforhistoryteachers* wiki).
TeachingHistory.org (monthly e-newsletter from the National History Education Clearinghouse).	*historytime* (ongoing collection of history and social studies Web links posted on the social bookmarking sites *Delicious* and *Diigo*).
History Teachers Group (daily updates of new history-related links from the social bookmarking service, Diigo).	*Selected Works of Robert W. Maloy* (listing of open content publications and student research projects hosted by the University of Massachusetts W.E.B. Du Bois Library).
GoodReads (iPhone/iPad app providing updates on books being read by friends as well as book reviews by the *GoodReads* community).	

open content wikispace, a Facebook group, and the Delicious and Diigo social networking sites.

Using the teacher's network as a prototype, students and teachers democratically decide on the components of their network; what organizational websites and newsgroups they want to read, what Twitter feeds they want to receive, what individuals they want to connect with using Google+ or some other social networking service. This way the members of each class identify their own personalized, continuously flowing history/social studies information streams. Small groups and individuals monitor each part of the network and report new information as it arrives.

This learning network not only receives information, but produces it for others to read and view. Together, students and teachers decide how they want to share information provided by the members of the class. A teacher might register the class on a learning network platform such as Weebly, Blogger, or ThreeRing. Once the account is established, students and teachers can designate categories related to topics they are studying, upload pictures and other images, and short video clips, while maintaining anonymity for students whose faces or names are not shown. Now the student-/teacher-created network has information flowing into and out the classroom.

Integral to the development of a student and class-learning network are the terms *push* and *pull* technologies. In pull technology, computer users seek information by accessing websites; information is acquired as requested by people who want it. A Google search is an example of pull technology.

Push technology involves information that flows directly to computer users on a regular basis. Unlike pull technology where individuals seek information, push technology informs individuals through email alerts, text messages, and other forms of digital communication. Consumer customization makes push technology successful in the world of e-commerce and online business. For example, recreation-minded consumers who want the latest information about outdoor clothing and gear receive information alerts pushed to them through email or text messaging from L.L. Bean, North Face, or other clothing manufacturers. Those same outdoor enthusiasts can have weather and related recreational information sent to them through an app on their smartphone or tablet computer.

Students and teachers are in a position to accomplish similar goals as they build a student and class-learning network. First, they select the online individuals, groups, and organizations they want information from regularly, "pulling" specific sources from the vast online resources available. Those selected sources send information for use in class learning activities. Then as students post resources on a class wiki, website, or blog, they "push" information out to the Web to be accessed by other students, teachers, and community members.

How might a class-learning network support youth activism as a form of democratic teaching and learning? First, students have an authentic purpose and real audiences for their academic work as information generators posting history/social studies resources online. They add their voices to online public discussion of how historical decisions affect present-day realities as well as future policy choices as they explore historical events and contemporary issues. By offering explanations for and proposing solutions to ongoing social and political problems, students play an activist role in a democratic system as history-making individuals whose viewpoints have been expressed beyond the classroom in a wider public sphere.

Second, students practice discussing options, making thoughtful choices, and reviewing the quality and integrity of the information they receive from online sources. After choosing specific online news sites, for example, the members of a class can evaluate the depth and breadth of the coverage. If a news information source proves insufficient, that site can be dropped and other sites can be added to the network. When interests shift or a new topic of study is introduced, the group revisits and revises the network to accommodate further sources of information. Their network is an ongoing construction, changing and evolving to meet the needs of its creators.

Strategy: Engaging Communities for Social Justice

Community engagement activities that focus on social justice build frameworks for democratic teaching and learning in history/social studies classes. University of Minnesota professor Tania Mitchell (2008) has identified three crucial elements for social justice focused community engagement: a social change orientation, a more equitable redistribution of power, and authentic relationships among partners.

Critical service learning is another term for such system-challenging approaches (Donahue & Mitchell, 2010). In traditional community service programs, involvement and support tend to flow in one direction only, from service providers to service recipients. Although such projects provide important short-term assistance to those in need, existing political and social relationships are rarely altered within and between communities. Critical service learning/community engagement initiatives, by contrast, promote social justice by addressing substantive social problems, challenging unjust systems, and giving voice and agency to all participants.

Social justice–focused community engagement by students and teachers may take many forms, as in the following examples:

1. Students and teachers start an active citizens nonfiction reading group to discuss environmental issues, economic and gender inequality, and workers' rights, and post student-written reviews of social change materials on a class website or blog.

2. Following the example of the national League of Women Voters and the North Carolina student group "NC Vote Defenders," students engage in school- or community-based voter empowerment efforts, notifying classmates and citizens of upcoming voter registration and election dates.

3. Working with local food banks and shelters, students volunteer
    onsite while developing healthy eating and nutrition guides
    for community members and examining the pricing practices
    of different food stores, including large chain outlets and
    small, cooperative markets.

In these examples, students and teachers are providing services that
address important community issues and problems as they endeavor to
achieve a more socially just society. In so doing, they are learning firsthand
about interdependence and how actions in one area can have consequences
throughout local and national systems. Students and teachers can use this
framework of interdependence and critical service learning to enact a democratic vision of service learning/community engagement based on "collaboration for social justice" where students "become allies/comrades in grassroots
movements" to address inequities and inequalities (Johnson, 2014).

Taking Action While Expanding Worldviews

Every service learning/community engagement activity has the potential to
combine academic analysis and social action within its learning experiences
for students and teachers. Academically, participants explore the historical, economic, political, and social dimensions of problems or issues facing
people and communities. Through service, participants respond to those
problems or issues by providing needed assistance and support. This combination of academics and action influences the worldviews of student and
teacher participants, generating new ways for them to think about themselves as interdependent members of multiple communities whose everyday
choices and actions have local, national, and global consequences.

Identifying manageable entry points for analysis and action is a key
for successful engagement projects. The enormity of social problems facing
people and communities seem to leave little space for any meaningful intervention by members of history/social studies classes. But small initiatives
can generate significant learning, as illustrated by the ways middle school
teacher Irene LaRoche examines different regions of the world with students
as part of the school's seventh-grade World Geography curriculum.

In a unit on Africa and the environment, students explore the issue
of water use and shortage locally and globally, using the concepts of scarcity
and abundance. In the New England town of Amherst, students and families
have the luxury of plentiful access to clean water; throughout Africa, mil-
lions are not so privileged or fortunate. To engage with the issue of water

use, students first monitor and measure their personal water footprint, charting how much water they use on a daily basis as well as whether they leave the faucet running unnecessarily or neglect to recycle plastic water bottles from the school cafeteria.

Next, the class studies the watershed of a local river, going on a field study to examine the water and the surrounding environment. While at the river, students take part in a simulation where they fill empty jugs and carry them a distance to experience the reality faced by many people worldwide. As they conclude the unit, students articulate their worldview by envisioning ways they can protect water resources, including becoming more aware of their own water usage, pledging to improve their water footprint, and learning about the agencies that are working to solve water issues in the global communities they are studying in school. Students also lead a water challenge to raise money for the digging of new water wells in Africa.

To further connect analysis, action, and worldviews, seventh-grade students throughout the school conduct a World Forum final project in World Geography classes. Students identify, discuss, and develop responses to what they see as the most pressing global issues facing human societies today. The goal is to continue building worldviews in which students see themselves as members of an interdependent planet where the actions of individuals matter to everyone.

A World Forum project is unlike a model UN. In a model UN, students represent the different countries of the world, recognizing that those fortunate enough to be representatives to the UN are among a country's educated, connected, empowered elite. A World Forum is designed to give voices to all people affected by global issues, but who may not have a voice in making decisions about policies (this includes the illiterate, the poor, the disenfranchised). Participants in a World Forum speak for those whose needs and perspectives are generally not heard or are ignored in large national and international assemblies.

Students begin by listing social, political, economic, and environmental issues they regard as important and having an effect on local, national, and global well-being. Using small- and large-group brainstorming, issues are identified and written on a whiteboard or computer screen and projected for everyone to view. Students submit all issues they find compelling: global warming, clean water, human rights, rainforest destruction, drug and sex trafficking, poverty and hunger, nuclear arms control, sustainable agriculture, and so on. It is important not to limit the list or discourage anyone from submitting an issue for consideration by the forum.

Through a process of consensus decision making, problems and issues are chosen for extended study. Each student does research on the issue as well as a country where that issue is significantly affecting its people and society. Students learn about that country's geography and the position of its government on the issue. They use historical and social science evidence, including up-to-date statistics, to document how an issue affects people's everyday lives, including a character sketch of a citizen (with religion, language, education level, occupation, ethnicity/race, and social class) of the country affected by an issue. Students then formulate plans for action, locally and globally, in the best interests of people affected by an issue, giving voice to human needs and concrete proposals for change.

Creating Digital-Age Public Service Announcements

Student-made public service announcements (PSAs) can be an effective way to integrate social justice themes into service learning/community engagement initiatives. PSAs focus thinking around pressing social and political issues and problems with a goal of informing people and motivating community members to act on issues ranging from recycling, energy conservation, and environmental protection to personal health and safety, drug and alcohol awareness, and LGBT rights. While learning about issues and problems to create thoughtful and informative PSAs, students are engaging in an experiential framework for understanding that challenges inequalities, injustices, and harmful policies and practices exist in contemporary society. PSAs provide students and teachers ready-made opportunities to not only influence the present, but also to explore times in the past when citizens mobilized resources and power to create new or more socially just and democratic systems.

Developing PSAs addresses another conspicuous social justice issue, what sociologists and educators are calling a *digital participation gap*, which affects mainly low-income, non-White, and rural youngsters (Jenkins et al., 2009). Across income brackets, most students have home access to cable television, DVD players, mobile phones, and computers, but low-income families are less likely to afford the more expensive, high-speed handheld and wireless technologies commonly found among affluent families. Digitally divided from peers, youngsters from low-income backgrounds come to school having had significantly fewer opportunities to learn and create with the latest technologies outside of school.

Smartphones with video and audio recording capabilities, interactive whiteboard apps like "Educreations," "Doceri," and "ShowMe," and student-made Common Craft videos offer dramatic new possibilities for students and teachers creating visually engaging PSA presentations that can reach wider audiences while giving technology-gapped students opportunities to learn from the latest new tools. In 2014, YouTube announced that users are now able to add clickable links to their own videos, offering opportunities for students and teachers to include additional interactive resources to educational presentations. We call these technology-based presentations "digital-age PSAs" because they provide students with exposure to new digital technologies while building new media and technological literacies. Digital-age PSAs show students how to make online presentations memorable for viewers through the use of information presentation design principles: short length, recognizable imagery, integration of voice and sound, and focus on a core message.

The key to successful learning is that students are active creators of PSAs. As two literacy researchers observed more than a decade ago: "If U.S. students cannot write to the screen—if they cannot design, author, analyze, and interpret material on the Web and in other digital environments—they will have difficulty functioning effectively as literate human beings in a growing number of social spheres" (Selfe & Hawisher, 2004, p. 2).

Conclusion

Connecting curriculum content and classroom activities with people and communities beyond the schoolhouse walls can be a transformative experience for many students. These connections may be local—a neighboring elementary school, senior center, or homeless shelter—or much broader as in voter registration drives or international famine relief. The goal is to create school activities that link school activities with real-world activities, academic learning, and civic learning (Shumer & Duckenfield, 2004).

In theory, everyone benefits—community members get needed services while the students who provide the service learn real-world skills and acquire better understanding of the problems facing different groups in society. After elementary students from a school in Maryland participated in raising trout in a tank in the classroom and then helped to stock fish in a newly reclaimed local river, educator David Sobel (2011) noted: "This is school change as it should be. Children engaged in rigorous curriculum based on real environmental and community challenges. Teachers working hand-in-hand with local scientists and historians" (p. 6).

Simultaneously, involving students with communities is complicated and complex (G. Smith & Sobel, 2010). Although service learning may increase student awareness of inequalities and diversities in society, it can also serve to perpetuate stereotypes and misconceptions about people and cultures. Some service learning projects, organized from a charity or deficit model where those with privilege and power see it as their responsibility to help those less fortunate than they, serve to reinforce the idea that people are to blame for their misfortunes. Community service by students must be connected to ongoing efforts to create equity in society. By engaging students in service activities that are aimed at challenging and changing inequities in societal structures, students and teachers expand the reach of the democratic classroom beyond the walls of the school and into the society and the social problems faced by its members.

Student involvement and participation in online communities bring new possibilities and their associated complexities. Social media (including Twitter, blogs, Facebook), smartphones, and the Internet connect students to other people in ways never before possible. These connections create exciting exchanges of ideas and information and they also raise potential issues of plagiarism, cyberbullying, and online exploitation of consumers and voters by unscrupulous advertisers and political interest groups. As democratic citizens, students must learn ways of thinking and acting in digital environments, guided by ethical practices and responses, to protect themselves and others while advancing the common good.

Conclusion

Building Democratic Spaces for Teaching and Learning

> Can you ever have Democracy with a big *D* in any system if you don't have democracy with a small d in the actual experience and everyday community life of ordinary everyday citizens?
>
> —Gar Alperovtiz (2013, p. 141)

In *Role Reversal: Achieving Uncommonly Excellent Results in the Student-Centered Classroom*, author and 16-year veteran middle school teacher Mark Barnes (2013) describes his process for remaking the classroom by replacing teacher control with student autonomy. On the first day of each new school year, Barnes tells his students there will be no homework, no tests or quizzes, and no preset teacher rules. Instead, he and the students will organize the classroom together around the three basic principles of "production, feedback, and change."

Without explicitly using the terms *democracy* or *democratic classrooms*, Barnes sets forth a broad framework for democratically based teaching and learning in schools. The classroom is organized as a community where everyone's contributions matter and everyone's ideas are respected. Students actively participate in shaping their educational experiences. Instead of organizing his role around enforcing rules and monitoring behaviors, Barnes emphasizes giving students substantive responses about their written work and learning progress. Students are constantly revising and resubmitting their papers and projects as evidence of learning progress and change. Every year, students working in this way become engaged, committed learners.

Barnes' transformation of the structures and practices of the school classroom reflects the visions of earlier reformers, John Dewey, Sylvia Ashton-Warner, John Holt, George Dennison, Vivian Gussin Paley, and Herbert Kohl, as well as contemporary commentators Michael Apple, Walter C. Parker, and Alfie Kohn. To create a student-centered classroom that is also a democratic place for teaching and learning, these educators connect to students' inner motivations and daily organizational experiences to find the key to educational change. Students must discover how to learn for their own reasons and for their own purposes. Autonomy, responsibility, and intrinsic motivation, concluded Barnes (2013, p. 20), must be "taught, retaught, and emphasized from the first day of school until the last" if students are to move past traditional school structures to new, participatory forms of learning.

We too have a democratic and student-centered blueprint for educational change—a vision of instructional practices, curriculum content, and school routines that when experienced and re-experienced by students and teachers from day 1 to day 180 and from year to year transforms teaching and learning for everyone in history/social studies classrooms. We imagine students and teachers cooperating and collaborating to build learning spaces where everyone's voice and participation will prepare students for future roles in American society. Knowledge, values, and practices learned in schools will accompany students into civic lives, renewing and extending the promises of democracy for the future.

We present the 7 Cs of democratic teaching as signposts for teachers and students working together to envision, create, and sustain democratically inspired teaching and learning in K–12 schools. The 7 Cs include:

1. *Contrasting* reveals how students expand their knowledge of democracy through the infusion of hidden histories and untold stories into required history/social studies learning standards.

2. *Conducting* examines how teachers' choice of instructional methods builds democratic thinking and understanding.

3. *Collaborating* shows how students learn about democracy by the ways that decisions are made and power is shared in the classroom.

4. *Conversing* expresses a democratic commitment to establishing and sustaining student voice and participation through how language, communication, and discussion happen in classrooms.

5. *Conferring* focuses on teachers receiving, discussing, and acting on feedback from students about their learning experiences in the classroom, affirming the democratic importance of student perceptions and viewpoints.

6. *Co-constructing* presents ways that teachers and students use digital technologies and student inquiry to create knowledge in the classroom and extend democratic values and practices.

7. *Connecting* explores ways to establish democratic links between students in history/social studies classes and the larger communities of school, neighborhood, town/city, nation, and world.

The conceptual artist Sol Lewitt (nd) once said, "the idea becomes the machine that makes the art." In producing his art, Lewitt conceives designs incorporating straight and curved lines, geometric forms, and uses of color patterns that capture the eye. Then museums and other venues lease the blueprints of compositions so other artists, interns, and volunteers can implement those outlines, exercising "certain latitudes of judgment and process" so that the drawings "are never realized in exactly the same way from one venue to another" (Reynolds, 2008). More than 100 Lewitt wall-sized drawings are being displayed on three floors at the Massachusetts Museum of Contemporary Art in North Adams through 2033.

For us, guided by Lewitt's insight, the ideas within the 7 Cs of democratic teaching become a framework and a process for remaking school classrooms and changing the experiences of students in history/social studies classrooms. Schools are notoriously slow-changing institutions with an emphasis on mandated curriculum standards, high-stakes tests, and student accountabilities, all of which constrain the prospects for progressive change. Teachers and students, unfamiliar with playing active participatory roles in their own learning, mainly replicate rather than re-envision traditional practices. The 7 Cs offer a framework and an engine for transforming prevailing structures and practices through democratic teaching and learning.

We have written this book for college students who are preparing to become teachers as well as for classroom educators already working in the field, school administrators, educational policymakers, academic researchers, and everyday citizens who are committed to improving American education and democracy in the 21st century. The ideas and strategies for making teaching and learning more democratic are a catalyst for transforming elementary, middle, and high school classrooms into energetically, engaged places of learning for all students.

The students in our teacher preparation program have experienced some of these democratic transformations firsthand, within the context of becoming a teacher in schools today. Anyone entering the classroom as a new teacher has much to learn and unlearn simultaneously. One must make sense of and meet the challenges presented by educational policies, school organizations, teacher colleagues, curriculum expectations, and family involvements as well as student responses to everything one does as a teacher. Then, at the same time, much of what a new teacher assumes to be true or thinks will be a reliable guide to practice proves not to be so and must be changed. One high school history teacher candidate summarized his year of learning and unlearning this way:

> I never thought that teaching would be this difficult. I figured that if I could just memorize the material and teach it to the students in different ways, I would be good. After being in front of a class of students since the end of October, I now know that I was way off. There is so much more to teaching than just memorizing the material and presenting it to the students.

Teaching history and social studies in K–12 schools is an immense responsibility. In history, geography, government, and economics classes at various grade levels, teachers are expected to teach students about the structures, practices, histories, and challenges of democracy in U.S. society. In so doing, teachers take the academic information found in textbooks, state curriculum frameworks, and local school district lesson plans, integrate it with their own ideas and perspectives about what students need to know, and weave all that material together to generate meaningful and memorable learning experiences about the past, present, and future.

The work of history/social studies teaching is made even more complex by the different time horizons teachers must balance as they create curriculum and instruct students. First, are the short-term outcomes of daily lesson plans, week-to-week curriculum units, and half- or full-year courses and subjects. After all, K–12 students will never again take fourth-grade North American geography, eighth-grade world history or tenth-grade U.S. history. When they leave those grades, students are supposed to know the material well enough to score highly on standardized educational tests and other measures of academic achievement.

Second, resting like a massive canopy over short-term results are the longer-term goals of preparing students for a lifetime of roles as members of a democratic society. Collectively, our society expects that when students graduate from high school they will begin seamlessly functioning as caring individuals; informed voters; rational choice makers; and engaged members of local, state, and national communities.

Not as often discussed among history and social studies educators are the deeper meanings of democratic teaching: Is it primarily a process of teaching students essential factual information about democracy and democratic institutions or is it also about giving students opportunities to practice and experience democracy as a regular part of their school experience? To address this question, we have presented the 7 Cs of democratic teaching and the ways these concepts can influence how teachers and students think about democracy, democratic teaching, and schools.

For the new teachers in our program, exploring the different Cs of democratic teaching has changed how they envision themselves and their roles in the classroom. "Democratic methods bring a new teaching style to students that promote active learning," noted one high school history teacher candidate. "All of these various methods are ones that I plan on using in my own practice in the coming years in one way or another," commented another candidate. A third declared: "I believe that part of our role as history/social science teachers is to teach students to form opinions, to be advocates for themselves, and to learn to stand up for their beliefs. . . . Simply trying to impart knowledge to our students will not provide those skills."

Students' ideas and responses are essential to the process of making history/social studies classrooms more democratic places and spaces. Gar Alperovitz asserted that democracy, as a political system, cannot be sustained without people having ongoing democratic experiences in their daily lives. Alperovitz envisioned such experiences happening in workplaces and community organizations where citizens exercise voice and power over the issues they face. We have expanded that vision to classrooms where students, together with teachers, have ongoing democratic experiences in all aspects of school experience.

To generate more democratic experiences, we urge teachers to adopt what computer advocate Marc Prensky (2010) has called a "partnering pedagogy." In Prensky's view, traditional teaching methods and approaches based on adult control are less and less relevant to today's students, who are empowered by mobile digital technologies that give them anywhere, anytime access to ideas and information. Traditional methods not only fail to engage students, they fail to promote the very democratic dispositions and understandings that history/social studies classes are supposed to be teaching.

Students benefit from learning partnerships where they work together with teachers. In learning partnerships, students have a primary responsibility to ask questions, research information, practice skills, create presentations, and use technology in all facets of learning; teachers have primary responsibility for guiding student investigations, explaining the meaning and relevance of academic material, and supporting individual learners by differentiating instruction. A partnering pedagogy focuses on students answering questions about their own learning and progress, including "Am I improving? Am I learning? Are my skills getting better? What should I be working on?" (Prensky, 2010, pp. 13, 176).

The 7 Cs of democratic teaching provide practices for a more fully realized democratic pedagogy. Students and teachers together move beyond long-held assumptions about teaching and learning in school classrooms to see new, more democratic processes and practices. As a framework for democratic teaching, the 7 Cs become, in the words of one new history/ social studies teacher, "a set of progressive methods to teach students how a democratic society works, and what is expected of them as citizens." We invite you to transform classrooms into democratic places and spaces.

References

Achugar, M., & Schleppegrell, M. J. (2005). Beyond connectors: The construction of cause in history textbooks. *Linguistics and Education, 16*(3), 298–318.

Advancement Project. (2012). *Stop the schoolhouse to jailhouse track*. Washington, DC. Retrieved from http://www.stopschoolstojails.org/content/model-discipline-policies.

Albertini, A. (2011, June 20). Turners teacher among tops in the state. *The Recorder*, p. C4.

Alperovitz, G. (2011). *America beyond capitalism. Reclaiming our wealth, our liberty, and our democracy* (2nd ed.). Hoboken, NJ: Democracy Collaborative Press.

Alperovitz, G. (2013). *What then must we do? Straight talk about the next American Revolution*. White River Junction, VT: Chelsea Green Publishing.

Ambrose, S. A., Bridges, M. W., DiPietro, M., & Lovett, M. C. (2010). *How learning works: Seven research-based principles for smart teaching*. San Francisco: Jossey-Bass.

American Civil Liberties Union of Vermont. (2014). *Student rights handbook: Introduction*. Montpeller: ACLU Vermont. Retrieved from http://www.acluvt.org/pubs/students_rights/introduction.php.

Apple, M. (2004). *Ideology and curriculum*. New York: Routledge.

Apple, M. (2013). *Official knowledge: Democratic education in a conservative age* (3rd ed.). New York: Routledge.

Apple, M. W., & Beane, J. A. (Eds.). (2007). *Democratic schools: Lessons in powerful education* (2nd ed.). Portsmouth, NH: Heinemann.

Applebee, A. N., Langer, J. A., Nystrand, M., & Gamoran, A. (2003). Discussion-based approaches to developing understanding: Classroom instruction and student performance in middle and high school. *American Educational Research Journal, 40*(3), 685–730.

Appy, C. G. (2004). *Patriots: The Vietnam War remembered from all sides*. New York: Penguin Books.

Balfanz, R., Bridgeland, J. M., Bruce, M., & Fox, J. H. (2012). *Building a grad nation: Progress and challenge in ending the high school dropout epidemic—*

Annual update. Baltimore, MD: Civic Enterprises Everyone Graduates Center at Johns Hopkins University.

Baker, E. L., Barton, P. E., Darling-Hammond, L., Haertel, E., Ladd, H. F., Linn, R. L., Ravitch, D., Rothstein, R., Shavelson, R. J., & Shepard, L. A. (2010, August 29). *Problems with the use of student test scores to evaluate teachers.* Washington, DC: Economic Policy Institute.

Banaji, S., & Buckingham, D. (2010). Young people, the Internet, and civic participation: An overview of key findings from the CivicWeb project. *International Journal of Learning and Media, 2*(1), 15–24.

Banaji, S., & Buckingham, D. (2013). *The civic web: Young people, the Internet, and civic participation.* Cambridge, MA: MIT Press.

Banks, J. A. (1991). The dimensions of multicultural education. *Multicultural Leader, 4,* 3–4.

Banks, J. A. (2007). *An introduction to multicultural education.* New York: Pearson.

Banks, J. A. (2008). Diversity, group identity, and citizenship education in a global age. *Educational Researcher, 37*(3), 129–139.

Barnes, M. (2013). *Role reversal: Achieving uncommonly excellent results in the student-centered classroom.* Alexandria, VA: Association for Supervision and Curriculum Development.

Barton, K. C. (2004). *Research on students' historical thinking and learning. Perspectives on history.* Retrieved from www.historians.org/perspectives/issues/2004/0410/0410tea1.cfm.

Barton, K. C. (2005). Primary sources in history: Breaking through the myths. *Phi Delta Kappan, 86*(10), 745–753.

Barrios, G. (2009). Walkout in Crystal City. *Teaching Tolerance, 35.* Retrieved from http://www.tolerance.org/print/magazine/number-35-spring-2009/feature/walkout-crystal-city.

Baseball Writers' Association of America. (2013). *Voting FAQ.* Retrieved from http://bbwaa.com/voting-faq/.

Bass, D. B. (2010). *A people's history of Christianity: The other side of the story.* New York: HarperOne.

Batchelor, H. A. (2012). *The Rise Up and Leadership in Community Service classes and their impact on the relationships, school retention, and graduation rates of marginalized students at one level four high school.* (Unpublished doctoral dissertation). University of Massachusetts Amherst, Amherst.

Bergmann, J., & Sams, A. (2012). *Flip your classroom: Reach every student in every class every day.* Eugene, OR: International Society for Technology in Education.

Billig, S., Root, S., & Jesse, D. (2005). *The impact of service-learning on high school students' civic engagement.* Medford, MA: The Center for Information & Research on Civic Learning and Engagement, Tufts University.

Bloom, B. (1985). *Developing talent in young people.* New York: Ballantine Books.

Bollier, D. (2014). *Think like a commoner: A short introduction to the life of the commons.* Gabriola Island, British Columbia: New Society Publishing.

Bridgeland, J. M., Balfanz, R., Moore, L. A., & Friant, R. S. (2010). *Raising their voices: Engaging students, teachers, and parents to help end the high school dropout epidemic.* Washington, DC: Civic Enterprises.

Bridgeland, J. M., DiIulio, J. J. Jr., & Wulsin, S. C. (2008). *Engaged for success: Service learning as a tool for high school dropout prevention.* Washington, DC: Civic Enterprises.

Bronson, P., & Merryman, A. (2009). *Nurtureshock: New thinking about children.* New York: Twelve.

Bryan, F. M. (2003). *Real democracy: The New England town meeting and how it works.* Chicago: University of Chicago Press.

Burbules, N. C., & Callister, T. A. Jr. (2000). *Watch IT: The risks and promises of information technologies for education.* Boulder, CO: Westview Press.

Calder, L. (2006). Uncoverage: Toward a signature pedagogy for the history survey. *Journal of American History.* Retrieved from http://www.journalofamericanhistory.org/textbooks/2006/calder.html.

California Department of Education. (2005). *History-social science framework for California public schools kindergarten through grade twelve.* Sacramento, CA.

Calkins, L. (1986). *The art of teaching writing.* Portsmouth, NH: Heinemann.

Camburn, E. M. (2012). *Review of asking students about teaching.* Boulder, CO: National Education Policy Center. Retrieved from http://greatlakescenter.org/docs/Think_Twice/TT_Camburn_MET.pdf.

Carnegie Corporation and Center for Information and Research on Civic Learning and Engagement (CIRCLE). (2003). *The civic mission of schools.* New York.

Cassidy, J. (2012, October 11). PolitiFact bias: Does the GOP tell nine times more lies than left? Really? *Human Events.* Retrieved from http://blog.lib.umn.edu/hhhevent/news/8.30.12_Human_Ostermeier_Fact.pdf.

Center for Civic Education. (2010). *National standards for civics and government.* Calabasas, CA.

Center for Evaluation & Education Policy. (2009). *Charting the path from engagement to achievement: A report on the 2009 High School Survey of Student Engagement (HSSE).* Bloomington: Indiana University.

Center for Information and Research on Civic Learning and Engagement (CIRCLE). (2010). *Youth voting.* Medford, MA: Tufts University. Retrieved from http://www.civicyouth.org/quick-facts/youth-voting/.

Center for Information and Research on Civic Learning and Engagement (CIRCLE). (2011). *Why young people don't vote.* Medford, MA: Tufts University. Retrieved from http://www.civicyouth.org/why-young-people-dont-vote/.

Center for Information and Research on Civic Learning and Engagement (CIRCLE). (2012). *Youth turnout: At least 49%, 22–23 million under 30 voted.* Retrieved from http://www.civicyouth.org/youth-turnout-at-least-49-22-23-million-under-30-voted/.

Center for Survey Research & Analysis. (2002). *History research paper study*. Sudbury, MA: The Concord Review.

Center for Teaching. (2014). *A word on nomenclature*. Nashville, TN: Vanderbilt University.

Centers for Disease Control and Prevention. (2009). *School connectedness: Strategies for increasing protective factors among youth*. Atlanta, GA: U.S. Department of Health and Human Services.

Chapman, C., Laird, J., Ifill, N., & Kewalramani, A. (2011). *Trends in high school dropout and completion in the United States: 1972–2009*. Washington, DC: National Center for Education Statistics, U.S. Department of Education.

Christensen, C. M., Horn, M. B., & Johnson, C. W. (2008). *Disrupting class: How disruptive innovation will change the way the world learns*. New York: McGraw-Hill.

Clark, S., & Teachout, W. (2012). *Slow democracy: Rediscovering community, bringing decision-making back home*. White River Junction, VT: Chelsea Green Publishing.

Coffin, L. (2009). Early town meetings: 1760s–1880s. *In Times Past*. Retrieved from http://larrycoffin.blogspot.com/2009/03/early-town-meetings1760s-1880s.html.

Cohen, E. G. (1994). *Designing groupwork: Strategies for the heterogeneous classroom*. New York: Teachers College Press.

Cohen, C. J., & Kahne, J. (2012). *Participatory politics: New media and youth political action*. The MacArthur Network on Youth & Participatory Politics. Irvine, CA: University of California Irvine. Retrieved from http://ypp.dmlcentral. net/sites/all/files/publications/YPP_Survey_Report_FULL.pdf.

Coppola, E. M. (2004). *Powering up: Learning to teach well with technology*. New York: Teachers College Press.

Crews, E. (2007). Voting in early America. *CW Journal*. Retrieved from http://www. history.org/Foundation/journal/Spring07/elections.cfm.

Crow, T. (2011). The VIEW from the SEATS. *Journal of Staff Development, 32*(6), 24–26, 28, 30.

Cuban, L. (1993). *How teachers taught: Constancy and change in American classrooms, 1890–1990*. New York: Teachers College Press.

Cuban, L. (2003). *Oversold and underused: Computers in the classroom*. Cambridge, MA: Harvard University Press.

Cuban, L. (2008). *Hugging the middle: How teachers teach in an era of testing and accountability*. New York: Teachers College Press.

Dean, C. B., Hubbell, E. R., Pitlier, H., & Stone, B. J. (2012). *Classroom instruction that works: Research-based strategies for increasing student achievement* (2nd ed.). Alexandria, VA: Association for Supervision and Curriculum Development.

Donahue, D. M., & Mitchell, T. D. (2010). Critical service learning as a tool for identity exploration. *Diversity & Democracy, 13*(2), 16–17.

Donovan, M. S., & Bransford, J. D. (Eds.). (2000). *How people learn: Brain, mind, experience, and school* (Expanded ed.). Washington, DC: National Academies Press.

Donovan, M. S. & Bransford, J. D. (2005). *How students learn: History in the classroom.* Washington, DC: National Academies Press.

Doyle, T. (2008). The learner-centered classroom. *Thriving in Academe, 26*(1), 5–7.

Dweck. C. (2006). *Mindset: The new psychology of success.* New York: Random House.

Earth Conclave. (nd). *Martha's rules: A basic adaptation of an effective alternative decision-making process.* Retrieved from http://www.earthconclave.org/Marthas.htm.

Edgerton, G. R. (2001). *Ken Burns's America.* New York: Palgrave Macmillan.

EducationCounsel. (2013). *Teacher and leader evaluation—Use of student surveys/perception data.* Retrieved from http://collegeready.gatesfoundation.org/LinkClick.aspx?fileticket=A1XJzsPGr-0%3D&portalid=0.

Edutopia. (2013, November 18). *How do I get a PLN?* Retrieved from http://www.edutopia.org/blog/how-do-i-get-a-pln-tom-whitby.

Edwards, S. A., Maloy, R. W., & Verock-O'Loughlin, R. (2003). *Ways of writing with young kids: Teaching creativity and conventions unconventionally.* Boston: Allyn & Bacon.

Ellison, R. (2003). *The collected essays of Ralph Ellison.* New York: Modern Library.

Escher, M. C. (2000). *The magic of M. C. Escher.* New York: Harry N. Abrams.

Evans, R. W. (2004). *The social studies wars: What should we teach the children?* New York: Teachers College Press.

Evans, R. W. (2011a). *The hope for American school reform: The Cold War pursuit of inquiry learning in social studies.* New York: Palgrave Macmillan.

Evans, R. W. (2011b). *The tragedy of American school reform: How curriculum politics and entrenched dilemmas have diverted us from democracy.* New York: Palgrave Macmillan.

Faber, A., & Mazlish, E. (1999). *How to talk so kids will listen & how to listen so kids will talk.* New York: Harper & Row.

Faragher, J. M., Buhle, M. J., Armitage, S. H., & Czitrom, D. H. (2001). *Out of many: A history of the American people* (Brief 3rd ed.). Upper Saddle River, NJ: Prentice-Hall.

Felder, R. (2011). Hang in there! Dealing with student resistance to learner-centered teaching. *Chemical Engineering Education, 43*(2), 131–132.

Felder, R., & Brent, R. (2009). Active learning: An introduction. *ASQ Higher Education Brief, 2*(4). Retrieved from http://www4.ncsu.edu/unity/lockers/users/f/felder/public/Papers/ALpaper(ASQ).pdf.

Ferguson, R. F. (2008). *Toward excellence with equity: An emerging vision for closing the achievement gap.* Cambridge, MA: Harvard University Press.

Ferguson, R. F. (2012). Can student surveys measure teaching quality? *Phi Delta Kappan, 94*(3), 24–28.

Ferguson, R. F., & Ramsdell, R. (2011). *Tripod classroom-level student perceptions as measures of teaching effectiveness.* Cambridge, MA: The Tripod Project. Retrieved from http://www.gse.harvard.edu/ncte/news/NCTE_Conference_Tripod.pdf.

Fiester, L. (2013). *Early warning confirmed: A research update on third-grade reading.* Baltimore, MD: The Annie E. Casey Foundation.

Finn, C. E. Jr., & Porter-Magee, K. (2011). Foreword. In S. M. Stern & J. A. Stern. *The state of state U.S. History standards 2011.* Princeton, NJ: Thomas B. Fordham Institute.

Fitzgerald, F. (1980). *America revised: What history textbooks have taught children about their country and how and why those textbooks have changed in different decades.* New York: Vintage.

Flynn, N. K. (2009). Toward democratic discourse: Scaffolding student-led discussions in the social studies. *Teachers College Record, 111*(8), 2021–2054.

Foner, E. (2003). *Who owns history? Rethinking the past in a changing world.* New York: Hill & Wang.

Foner, E. (Ed.). (2010). *Voices of freedom: A documentary history* (Vols. 1 & 2, 3rd ed.). New York: W.W. Norton.

Foner, E. (2011). *The Fiery trial: Abraham Lincoln and American slavery.* New York: W.W. Norton.

Fox, A. (2013, December 27). Standing in the way of 21st century learning? *Shelburne Falls & West County Independent,* 3.

Fox, S., & Rainie, L. (2014, February 27). The Web at 25 in the U.S. *Pew Research Internet Project.* Retrieved from http://www.pewinternet.org/2014/02/27/the-web-at-25-in-the-u-s/.

Friedman, J. F. (2005). *The secret histories: Hidden truths that challenged the past and changed the world.* New York: Picador.

Gastil, J. (1993). *Democracy in small groups: Participation, decision making and communication.* Philadelphia: New Society Publishers.

Gee, J. P. (2007). *What video games have to teach us about learning and literacy* (revised and updated ed.). New York: Palgrave Macmillan.

Gibbons, P. (2009). *English learners, academic language and thinking.* Portsmouth, NH: Heinemann.

Gingrich, N. (2006). *Recovering God in America: Reflections on the role of faith in our nation's history.* Nashville, TN: Thomas Nelson.

Goodlad, J. (1984). *A place called school.* New York: McGraw-Hill.

Grant, S. G. (2003). *History lessons: Teaching, learning and testing in U.S. high school classrooms.* New York: Routledge.

Grant, S. G. (2007). High-stakes testing: How are social studies teachers responding? *Social Education, 71*(5), 250–255.

Greene, R. W. (2009). *Lost at school: Why our kids with behavior challenges are falling through the cracks and how can we help.* New York: Scribners.

Greene, R. W. (2011). Collaborative problem solving can transform school discipline. *Phi Delta Kappan, 93*(2), 25–28.

Guarino, C., & Stacy, B. (2012). *Review of gathering feedback for teaching.* Boulder CO: National Education Policy Center. Retrieved from http://greatlakescenter.org/docs/Think_Twice/TT_Guarino_MET.pdf.

Gutmann, A., & Thompson, D. (2004). *Why deliberative democracy?* Princeton, NJ: Princeton University Press.

Halpern, S. (2011). Mind control & the Internet. *The New York Review of Books, LVIII*(11), 33–35.

Harman, C. (2008). *A people's history of the world: From Stone Age to the new millennium*. New York: Verso.

Hattie, J. (2009). *Visible learning: A synthesis of over 800 meta-analyses relating to achievement*. New York: Routledge.

Hattie, J. (2011). *Visible learning for teachers: Maximizing impact on learning*. New York: Routledge.

Heflin, J. (2011, June 9). Real local history. *The Valley Advocate, 20*.

Herr, N. (2007). *Academic language—Defined by PACT*. Internet Resources to Accompany the Sourcebook for Teaching Science. Retrieved from http://www.csun.edu/science/ref/language/pact-academic-language.html.

Herzig, M., & Chasin, M. (2006). *Fostering dialog across divides: A nuts and bolts guide from the public conversations project*. Watertown, MA: Public Conversations Project.

Hess, D. E. (2009). *Controversy in the classroom: The democratic power of discussion*. New York: Routledge.

Hmelo-Silver, C. E. (2003). Analyzing collaborative knowledge construction: Multiple methods for integrated understanding. *Computers and Education, 41*, 397–420.

Hoffer, P. C. (2004). *Past imperfect: Facts, fictions, fraud—American history from Bancroft and Parkman to Ambrose, Bellesiles, Ellis, and Goodwin*. New York: Public Affairs.

Holman, P. (1997). Democratic decision making that works. *At Work, 6*(4), 7–11.

International Year of Cooperatives. (2012). *7 cooperative principles*. Retrieved from http://usa2012.coop/about-co-ops/7-cooperative-principles.

Irons, P. (2006). *A people's history of the Supreme Court: The men and women whose cases and decisions have shaped our Constitution*. New York: Penguin Books.

Ives, S., & Burns, K. (1996). Introduction. In Dayton Duncan, *The West: An illustrated history for children* (pp. vi–vii). Boston: Little, Brown.

Jackson, P. W. (1990). *Life in classrooms*. New York: Teachers College Press.

Jarvis, B. (2013). Empowered by the past: Red state co-ops go green. *Yes! Magazine*. Retrieved from http://www.yesmagazine.org/issues/how-cooperatives-are-driving-the-new-economy/empowered-by-the-past-how-red-states-grow-green-co-ops.

Jenkins, H., & Kelley, W. (2013). *Reading in a participatory culture: Rethinking Moby Dick in the English classroom*. New York: Teachers College Press.

Jenkins, H., Purushotma, R., Weigel, M., & Clinton, K. (2009). *Confronting the challenges of participatory culture: Media education for the 21st century*. Cambridge, MA: MIT Press.

Johnson, J. (2014). *Re: Rethinking service: Changing our understanding of community is not enough*. [Online forum comment]. Retrieved from https://moodle.umass.edu/mod/forum/discuss.php?d=191284.

Kelly, M. (2013). The economy under new ownership. *Yes! Magazine, 65*, 18–24.

Kentucky Department of Education. (2014). *Student voice survey*. Retrieved from http://education.ky.gov/teachers/HiEffTeach/Pages/Student-Voice-Survey.aspx.

Kohl, H. (2007). The politics of children's literature: What's wrong with the Rosa Parks myth. In W. Au, B. Bigelow, & S. Karp (Eds.). *Rethinking our classrooms* (Vol. 1, pp. 168–171). Milwaukee, WI: Rethinking Schools.

Kohn, A. (1999). *Punished by rewards: The trouble with gold stars, incentive plans, A's, praise, and other bribes.* New York: Mariner Books.

Kohn, A. (2001). Five reasons to stop saying "Good Job!" *Young Children.* Retrieved from http://www.alfiekohn.org/parenting/gj.htm.

Kohn, A. (2011). *Feel-bad education: And other contrarian essays on children and schooling.* Boston: Beacon Press.

Kohn, A. (2014). *The myth of the spoiled child: Challenging the conventional wisdom about children and parenting.* Cambridge, MA: Da Capo Press.

Koopman, B. L. (2010). From Socrates to wikis: Using online forums to deepen discussions. *Phi Delta Kappan, 92*(4), 24–27.

Kornfeld, J., & Goodman, J. (1998). Melting the glaze: Exploring student responses to liberatory social studies. *Theory Into Practice, 37*(4), 306–313.

Krane, B. (2006). Researchers find kids need better online academic skills. *University of Connecticut Advance.* Retrieved from http://advance.uconn.edu/2006/061113/06111308.htm.

Langworth, R. (Ed.). (2008). *Churchill by himself: The definitive collection of quotations.* New York: PublicAffairs.

LaRue, F. (2011). *Report of the Special Rapporteur on the promotion and protection of the right to freedom of opinion and expression.* New York: Human Rights Council, United Nations General Assembly.

Lee, L. (2012). "A learning journey for all": American elementary teachers' use of classroom wikis. *Journal of Interactive Online Learning, 11*(3), 90–102.

Lesh, B. (2011). *"Why won't you tell us the answer?" Teaching historical thinking in grades 7–12.* Portland, ME: Stenhouse.

Levinson, M. (2012). *No citizen left behind.* Cambridge, MA: Harvard University Press.

Lewitt, S. (nd). *Paragraphs on conceptual art.* Retrieved from http://www.tufts.edu/programs/mma/fah188/sol_lewitt/paragraphs on conceptual art.htm.

Lhamon, C. E., & Samuels, J. (2014, January 8). *Dear colleague letter on the nondiscriminatory administration of school discipline.* Washington, DC: U.S. Department of Justice and United States Department of Education.

Library of Congress. (2012). *Books that shaped America.* Retrieved from http://www.loc.gov/bookfest/books-that-shaped-america/.

Lindenmeyer, K. (2011). Lectures in history: 20th century political activism. *C-SPAN: Congress, Politics, Books and American History.* Retrieved from http://www.c-span.org/Events/Lectures-in-History-20th-Century-Political-Activism/10737420466-2/.

Loewen, J. W. (1999). *Lies across America: What our historic sites got wrong.* New York: Touchstone.

Loewen, J. W. (2005). *Lies my teacher told me: Everything your American history textbook got wrong.* New York: The New Press.

Loewen, J. W. (2010). *Teaching what really happened: How to avoid the tyranny of textbooks and get students excited about doing history.* New York: Teachers College Press.

Losen, D. J., & Gillespie, J. (2012). *Opportunities suspended: The disparate impact of disciplinary exclusion from school.* Los Angeles: The Center for Civil Rights Remedies, University of California Los Angeles.

Losen, D. J., Martinez, T., & Gillespie, J. (2012). *Suspended education in California.* Los Angeles: The Center for Civil Right Remedies, University of California Los Angeles.

Lyon, G. E. (1996). *Who came down that road?* New York: Orchard Books.

Macedo, S., with Yette Alex-Assensoh, et al. (2005). *Democracy at risk: How political choices undermine citizen participation and what we can do about it.* Washington, DC: Brookings Institution Press.

Maloy, R. W. & Edwards, S. A. (1995). Coming down the road: Exploring local history with six, seven and eight year olds. In H. W. Richardson (Ed.), *Social studies: Bringing the world closer to home* (pp. 44–52). Atlanta: The Georgia Council for the Social Studies.

Maloy, R. W., & Edwards, S. A. (2012/2013). Tag bundles, education boards, and Internet playlists: Constructing historical biographies using social bookmarking technologies. *New England Journal of History, 69,* 1–2, 81–95.

Maloy, R. W., & LaRoche, I. (2010). Student-centered teaching methods in the history classroom: Ideas, issues and insights for new teachers. *Social Studies Research and Practice, 5*(3), 46–61.

Maloy, R. W., Poirier, M., Smith, H. K., & Edwards, S. A. (2010). The making of a standards wiki: Covering, uncovering, and discovering curriculum frameworks using a highly interactive technology. *The History Teacher, 44*(1), 67–82.

Maloy, R. W., Verock-O'Loughlin, R. E., Edwards, S. A., & Woolf, B. P. (2014). *Transforming learning with new technologies* (2nd ed.). Boston: Allyn & Bacon.

Marino, M. P. (2011). High school world history textbooks: An analysis of content focus and chronological approaches. *The History Teacher, 44*(3), 421–446.

Massachusetts Department of Education. (2003). *Massachusetts History & Social Science Curriculum Framework.* Malden, MA.

Matias, J. N. (2012). *Is education obsolete? Sugata Mitre at the MIT Media Lab.* MIT Center for Civic Media. Retrieved from http://civic.mit.edu/blog/natematias/is-education-obsolete-sugata-mitra-at-the-mit-media-lab.

Measures of Effective Teaching Project. (2010). *Student perceptions and the MET project.* Seattle: Bill & Melinda Gates Foundation. Retrieved from http://www.metproject.org/downloads/Student_Perceptions_092110.pdf.

Measures of Effective Teaching Project. (2012a). *Asking students about teaching: Student perception surveys and their implementation.* Seattle: Bill & Melinda Gates Foundation. Retrieved from http://www.metproject.org/downloads/Asking_Students_Practitioner_Brief.pdf.

Measures of Effective Teaching Project. (2012b). *Gathering feedback for teaching: Combining high-quality observations with student surveys and achievement gains.* Seattle: Bill & Melinda Gates Foundation. Retrieved from http://www.metproject.org/downloads/MET_Gathering_Feedback_Practioner_Brief.pdf.

Measures of Effective Teaching Project. (2012c). *Learning about teaching: Initial findings from the Measures of Effective Teaching Project.* Seattle: Bill & Melinda

Gates Foundation. Retrieved from http://www.gatesfoundation.org/college-ready-education/Documents/preliminary-finding-policy-brief.pdf.

Measures of Effective Teaching Project. (2013). *Ensuring fair and reliable measures of effective teaching: Culminating findings from the MET Project's three-year study.* Seattle: Bill & Melinda Gates Foundation. Retrieved from http://metproject.org/downloads/MET_Ensuring_Fair_and_Reliable_Measures_Practitioner_Brief.pdf.

McCann, T. M., Johannessen, L. R., Kahn, E., & Flanagan, J. M. (2006). *Talking in class. Using discussion to enhance teaching and learning.* Urbana, IL: National Council of Teachers of English.

McNeil, L. N. (1988). *Contradictions of control. School structure and school knowledge.* New York: Routledge.

Minahan, A. (1986). Martha's rules: An alternative to Robert's Rules of Order. *Affilia, 1,* 53–56.

Mitchell, T. D. (2008). Traditional vs. critical service learning: Engaging the literature to differentiate two models. *Michigan Journal of Service Learning, 14*(2), 50–65.

Mitra, S. (2013). We need schools . . . not factories. *HuffPost TED Weekends.* Retrieved from http://www.huffingtonpost.com/sugata-mitra/2013-ted-prize_b_2767598.html.

Mitra, S., & Negroponte, N. (2012). *Beyond the hole in the wall: Discover the power of self organized learning.* New York: TED Books.

Monahan, K. C., Oesterie, S., & Hawkins, J. D. (2010). Predictors and consequences of school connectedness: The case for prevention. *The Prevention Researcher, 17*(3), 3–6.

Moreau, J. (2004). *Schoolbook nation: Conflicts over American history textbooks from the Civil War to the present.* Ann Arbor: University of Michigan Press.

Montessori, M. (1964). *Dr. Montessori's own handbook.* Cambridge, MA: R. Bentley.

Mullgardt, B. (2008). Introducing and using the discussion (aka Harkness) table. *Independent Teacher.* Retrieved from http://www.nais.org/Magazines-Newsletters/ITMagazine/Pages/Introducing-and-Using-the-Discussion-(AKA-Harkness)-Table.aspx.

National Center for Education Statistics. (2011a). *The nation's report card: Civics 2010* (NCES 2011-466). Washington DC: Institute of Education Sciences, U.S. Department of Education.

National Center for Education Statistics. (2011b). *The nation's report card: U.S. History 2010* (NCES 2011-468). Washington DC: Institute of Education Sciences, U.S. Department of Education.

National Commission on Writing in America's Families, Schools, and Colleges. (2006, May). *Writing and school reform.* Princeton, NJ: College Entrance Examination Board.

National Cooperative Business Association. (2011). *Co-op types.* Retrieved from http://www.ncba.coop/ncba/about-co-ops/co-op-types.

National Council for the Social Studies. (1994). *Expectations for excellence: Curriculum standards for the social studies.* Washington, DC.

National Council for the Social Studies. (2010). *National curriculum standards for social studies: A framework for teaching, learning, and assessment*. Washington, DC.

National Council for the Social Studies. (2013). *The college, career, and civic life (C3) framework for social studies state standards—Guidance for enhancing the rigor of K–12 civics, economics, geography, and history*. Washington, DC.

National Council of Teachers of English. (2012). *Position statement on teacher evaluation*. Urbana, IL.

National Oceanic and Atmospheric Administration. (2013). *The seven seas include the Arctic, North Atlantic, South Atlantic, North Pacific, South Pacific, Indian, and Southern Oceans*. Washington, DC: U.S. Department of Commerce.

National Service Learning Clearinghouse. (2009). What is service learning? Retrieved from http://gsn.nylc.org/clearinghouse.

National Task Force on Civic Learning and Democratic Engagement. (2012). *A crucible moment: College learning and democracy's future*. Washington, DC: Association of American Colleges and Universities.

NPR Staff. (2013, December 28). *Teaching democracy through jazz, perfecting party playlists*. Retrieved from http://www.npr.org/2013/12/28/257672489/teaching-democracy-through-jazz-perfecting-party-playlists.

Obama, B. (2012, July 26). *Executive order—White House Initiative on educational excellence for African Americans*. Washington, DC: The White House. Retrieved from http://www.whitehouse.gov/the-press-office/2012/07/26/executive-order-white-house-initiative-educational-excellence-african-am.

Oregon State Board of Education. (2011). *Oregon social science academic content standards*. Retrieved from http://www.ode.state.or.us/teachlearn/subjects/socialscience/standards/adoptedsocialsciencesstandards8-2011.pdf.

Oyler, C. (2011). *Actions speak louder than words: Community activism as curriculum*. New York: Routledge.

Papert, S. (1994). *The children's machine: Rethinking school in the age of the computer*. New York: Basic Books.

Pariser, E. (2011). *The filter bubble: What the Internet is hiding from you*. New York: Penguin.

Parker, W. C. (2002). *Teaching democracy: Unity and diversity in public life*. New York: Teachers College Press.

Partnership for 21st Century Skills. (2008). *Framework for 21st century learning*. Retrieved from www.21stcenturyskills.org/index.php?option=com_content&task=view&id=254&Itemid=120.

Pesick, S. L. (2011). *Building a conversation between textbooks, students, and teachers*. National History Educational Clearinghouse. Retrieved from http://teachinghistory.org/best-practices/teaching-with-textbooks/24278.

Phillips Exeter Academy. (nd). *The amazing Harkness philosophy*. Retrieved from https://www.exeter.edu/admissions/109_1220.aspx.

Poplin, M., Rivera, J., Durish, D., Hoff, L., Kawell, S., Pawlak, P., Hinman, I. S., Straus, L., & Veney, C. (2011). Highly effective teachers in low-performing urban schools. *Phi Delta Kappan, 92*(5), 39–43.

Porter-Magee, K., Leming, J., & Ellington, L. (2003). *Where did social studies go wrong?* Washington, DC: Thomas B. Fordham Foundation.

Prensky, M. (2010). *Teaching digital natives. Partnering for real learning.* Thousand Oaks, CA: Corwin Press.

Project Tomorrow. (2008). *Speak up 2007 for students, teachers, parents & school leaders: Selected national findings.* Irvine, CA.

Project Tomorrow. (2012). *Mapping a personalized learning journey—K–12 students and parents connect the dots with digital learning.* Retrieved from http://www.tomorrow.org/speakup/pdfs/SU11_PersonalizedLearning_Students.pdf.

Project Tomorrow. (2013). *From chalkboard to tablets: The emergence of the K–12 digital learner.* Retrieved from http://tomorrow.org/speakup/SU12_DigitalLearners_StudentReport.html.

Purcell, K., Rainie, L., Heaps, A., Buchanan, J., Friedrich, L., Jackin, A., Chen, C., & Zickuhr, K. (2012). *How teens do research in the digital world.* Pew Internet & American Life Project. Retrieved from http://pewinternet.org/~/media//Files/Reports/2012/PIP_TeacherSurveyReportWithMethodology110112.pdf.

Rainie, L., & Wellman, B. (2012). *Networked: The new social operating system.* Cambridge, MA: MIT Press.

Raphael, R. (2002). *A people's history of the American Revolution: How common people shaped the fight for independence.* New York: HarperPerennial.

Raphael, R. (2004). *Founding myths: Stories that hide our patriotic past.* New York: The New Press.

Raphael, R. (2009). *Founders: The people who brought you a nation.* New York: The New Press.

Raphael, R. (2011). *The first American Revolution: Before Lexington and Concord.* New York: The New Press.

Raphael, R. (2013). *Constitutional myths: What we get wrong and how to get it right.* New York: The New Press.

Ravitch, D. (2003). *The language police: How pressure groups restrict what students know.* New York: Knopf.

Ravitch, D. (2010). *The death and life of the great American school system: How testing and choice are undermining education.* New York: Basic Books.

Ravitch, D. (2013). *Reign of error: The hoax of the privatization movement and the danger to America's public schools.* New York: Knopf.

Reynolds, J. (2008). *Massachusetts Museum of Contemporary Art Gallery Guide.* North Adams: Massachusetts Museum of Contemporary Art.

Reznitskaya, A. (2012). Dialogic teaching: Rethinking language use during literature discussions. *The Reading Teacher, 65*(7), 446–456.

Richards, L. L. (2000). *The slave power: The free north and southern domination, 1780–1860.* Baton Rouge: Louisiana State University Press.

Richardson, W. (2010). *Blogs, wikis, podcasts, and other powerful Web tools for classrooms.* (3rd ed.). Thousand Oaks, CA: Corwin Press.

Ricketts, G., Wood, P. W., Balch, S. H., & Thorne, A. (2011). *The vanishing west 1964–2010: The disappearance of Western civilization from the American undergraduate curriculum.* Princeton, NJ: National Association of Scholars.

Rideout, V. J., Foehr, U. B., & Roberts, D. F. (2010). *Generation M2: Media in the lives of 8- to 18-year-olds*. Menlo Park, CA: Henry J. Kaiser Family Foundation.

Roark, J. L. (2013). Faculty letter to President Wagner. *The Emory Wheel*. Retrieved from http://www.emorywheel.com/faculty-letter-to-president-wagner/.

Roberts, S. L. (2013). "Georgia on my mind": Writing the "new" state history textbook in the post-Loewen world. *The History Teacher, 47*(1), 41–60.

Robertson, L. A. (2006). Why are there so few female physicists? *The Physics Teacher, 44*, 177–180.

Robinson, D. L. (2011). *Town meeting: Practicing democracy in rural New England*. Amherst: University of Massachusetts Press.

Rodriguez, R., Weinstein, K. R., Hanson, V. D., & Mead, W. R. (2003, August). *Terrorists, despots, and democracy: What children need to know*. Washington, DC: Thomas B. Fordham Foundation.

Rogers, E. M. (2003). *Diffusion of innovations* (5th ed.). New York: Free Press.

Rothstein, J., & Mathis, W. J. (2013). *Review of two culminating reports from the MET Project*. Boulder, CO: National Education Policy Center. Retrieved from http://nepc.colorado.edu/thinktank/review-MET-final-2013.

Rothstein, R., Ladd, H, F., Ravitch, D., Baker, E. L., Barton, P. E., et al. (2010), Problems with the use of student test scores to evaluate teachers. Economic Policy Institute. Retrieved from http://www.epi.org/publication/bp278/.

Rubin, B. C. (2011). *Making citizens: Transforming civic learning for diverse social studies*. New York: Routledge.

Russell, W.B. III. (2010). Teaching social studies in the 21st century: A research study of secondary social studies teachers' instructional methods and practices. *Action in Teacher Education, 32*(1), 65–72.

Sarason, S. B. (1982). *The culture of the school and the problem of change* (2nd ed.). Boston: Allyn & Bacon.

Sarason, S. B. (1996). *Revisiting "the culture of the school and the problem of change."* New York: Teachers College Press.

Saxe, D. W. (2006). *Land and liberty I: A chronology of traditional American history*. Boca Raton, FL: BrownWalker Press.

Scales, P. C., Roehlkepartain, E. C., Neal, M., Kielsmeier, J. C., & Benson, P. L. (2006). Reducing academic achievement gaps: The role of community service and service learning. *Journal of Experiential Education, 29*, 38–60.

Schimmel, D. (2002). Legal miseducation? The Bill of Rights and the school curriculum. *Insights on Law & Society, 3*(1), 10–12.

Schimmel, D. (2003). Collaborative rule-making and citizenship education: An antidote to the undemocratic hidden curriculum. *American Secondary Education, 31*(3), 16–35.

Schul, J. E. (2010). Revisiting an old friend: The practice and promise of cooperative learning for the twenty-first century. *The Social Studies, 102*(2), 88–93.

Schultz, E. B., & Tougias, M. J. (2000). *King Philip's war: The history and legacy of America's forgotten conflict*. Woodstock, VT: Countryman Press.

Schur, J. B. (2007). *Eyewitness to the past: Strategies for teaching American history in grades 5–12*. Portland, ME: Stenhouse.

Selfe, C. L., & Hawisher, G. E. (2004). *Literate lives in the information age: Narratives of literacy from the United States*. Mahwah, NJ: Lawrence Erlbaum.

Seider, S. C., Gillmor, S., & Rabinowicz, S. (2012). The impact of community service learning upon the expected political voice of participating college students. *Journal of Adolescent Research, 27*(1), 44–77.

Shumer, R., & Duckenfield, M. (2004). Service-learning: Engaging students in community-based learning. In F. P. Schargel & J. Smink (Eds.), *Helping students graduate: A strategic approach to dropout prevention* (pp. 155–163). Larchmont, NY: Eye on Education.

Simon, H. A. (1983). *Computers in education: Realizing the potential*. Retrieved from http://digitalcollections.library.cmu.edu/awweb/awarchive?type=file&item=33980.

Simpson, K. (2012). *Reforms pitched for Colorado schools' zero-tolerance rules*. DenverPost.com. Retrieved from http://www.denverpost.com/news/ci_19756112.

Smith, G. A., & Sobel, D. (2010). *Place- and community-based education in schools*. New York: Routledge.

Sobel, D. (2011). When the community becomes the classroom. *Harvard Education Letter, 27*(5), 8, 6–7.

South Carolina Department of Education. (2011). *South Carolina social studies academic standards*. Columbia, S.C.

Stahl, R. J., VanSickle, R. L., & Stahl, N. N. (2009). *Cooperative learning in the social studies classroom* (Second edition). Washington, DC: National Council for the Social Studies.

Stanford History Education Group. (2013). *Beyond the bubble: A new generation of history assessments*. Stanford, CA: Stanford University. Retrieved from http://beyondthebubble.stanford.edu/.

Stern, S. M., & Stern, J. A. (2011). *The state of state U.S. History standards 2011*. Princeton, NJ: Thomas B. Fordham Institute.

Stitzlein, S. M. (2011). Democratic education in an era of town hall protests. *Theory and Research in Education, 9*(1), 73–86.

Suter, K. (nd). *The way you say it*. Chatswood, AU: Conflict Resolution Network. Retrived from http://www.crnhq.org/pages.php?pID=15.

Takaki, R. (2008). *A different mirror: A history of multicultural America*. Boston: Little, Brown.

Teaching Tolerance. (2014). *Teaching the movement 2014: The state of civil rights education in the United States*. Montgomery, Alabama: Southern Poverty Law Center.

Teachout, T. (2009). *Pops: A life of Louis Armstrong*. New York: Mariner Books.

Teachout, T. (2012). *Author's note to Satchmo at the Waldorf*. Lenox, MA: Shakespeare and Company.

Toloson, I. A., McGee, T., & Lemmons, B. P. (2013). *Reducing suspensions among academically disengaged Black males*. Los Angeles: The Civil Rights Project, University of California Los Angeles.

Tough, P. (2013). *How children succeed: Grit, curiosity, and the hidden power of character*. New York: Mariner Books.

U.S. Department of Education. (2011). *Teaching American History*. Retrieved from http://www2.ed.gov/programs/teachinghistory/index.html.

U.S. Department of Education. (2012, January). *Advancing civic learning and engagement in a democracy: A road map and call to action*. Retrieved from http://www.ed.gov/sites/default/files/road-map-call-to-action.pdf.

U.S. Department of Education. (2014). *Expansive survey of America's public schools reveals troubling racial disparities*. Retrieved from http://www.ed.gov/news/press-releases/expansive-survey-americas-public-schools-reveals-troubling-racial-disparities.

van Dijck, J. (2013). *The culture of connectivity: A critical history of social media*. New York: Oxford University Press.

Vanneman, A., Hamilton, L., Baldwin Anderson, J., & Rahman, T. (2009). *Achievement gaps: How Black and White students perform in math and reading on the National Assessment of Educational Progress* (NCES 2009-455). Washington, DC: National Center for Education Statistics, Institute for Education Sciences, U.S. Department of Education.

Vogler, K. (2005). Impact of a high school graduation examination on social studies teachers' instructional practices. *Journal of Social Studies Research, 29*(2), 19–33.

Vogler, K. (2008). Comparing the impact of accountability examinations on Mississippi and Tennessee social studies teachers' instructional practices. *Educational Assessment, 13*, 1–32.

Wagner, J. (2013, Winter). From the President . . . As American as compromise. *Emory Magazine*. Retrieved from http://www.emory.edu/EMORY_MAGAZINE/issues/2013/winter/register/president.html.

Wang, T. A. (2012). *The politics of voter suppression: Defending and expanding Americans' right to vote*. Ithaca, NY: Cornell University Press.

Ward, K. (2010). *Not written in stone: Learning and unlearning American history through 200 years of textbooks*. New York: The New Press.

Watters, A. (2011). Why wikis still matter. *Edutopia*. Retrieved from http://www.edutopia.org/blog/wiki-classroom-audrey-watters.

Week in Review. (2011, May 8). An "F" in civics. *The New York Times*, 2.

Wessling, S. B. (2012). *"They are the experts": A national teacher of the year talks about student surveys*. Measures of Effective Teaching Project. Retrieved from http://education.ky.gov/teachers/hieffteach/documents/met%20studentsurveys%20q%20and%20a.pdf.

Westheimer, J. (2007). *Pledging allegiance: The politics of patriotism in America's schools*. New York: Teachers College Press.

Wiggins, G. P., & McTighe, J. (2005). *Understanding by design*. Alexandria, VA: Association for Supervision and Curriculum Development.

Wills, G. (2005). *"Negro President": Jefferson and the slave power*. New York: Mariner Books.

Williams, J. K. & Maloyed, C. L. (2013). Much ado about Texas: Civics in the social studies curriculum. *The History Teacher, 47*(1), 25–40.

Wilson, B. L., & Corbett, H. D. (2001). *Listening to urban kids: School reform and the teachers they want*. Albany: SUNY Press.

Wineburg, S. (2001). *Historical thinking and other unnatural acts: Charting the future of teaching the past*. Philadelphia: Temple University Press.

Wineburg, S., Martin, D., & Monte-Sano, C. (2011). *Reading like a historian: Teaching literacy in middle and high school history classrooms*. New York: Teachers College Press.

Wineburg, S., & Monte-Sano, C. (2008). "Famous Americans": The changing pantheon of American heroes. *The Journal of American History*. Retrieved from http://www.journalofamericanhistory.org/textbooks/2008/wineburg.html.

Wineburg, S., Mosburg, S., Porat, D., & Duncan, A. (2007). *Forrest Gump* and the future of the teaching the past. *Phi Delta Kappan, 89*(3), 168–177.

Wolff, R. D. (2012). *Democracy at work: A cure for capitalism*. Chicago: Haymarket Books.

Wolk, S. (2008, October). School as inquiry. *Phi Delta Kappan, 90*(2), 115–122.

Woods Hole Oceanographic Institution Information Office. (1997). *What are the seven seas?* Woods Hole, MA: Woods Hole Oceanographic Institution.

Yazzie-Mintz, E. (2010a). *Charting the path from engagement to achievement. A Report on the 2009 High School Survey of Student Engagement*. Bloomington: Center for Evaluation & Education Policy, Indiana University.

Yazzie-Mintz, E. (2010b). Leading for engagement. *Principal Leadership*. Retrieved from http://ceep.indiana.edu/hssse/images/Yazzie-Mintz%20Principal%20Leadership%20March%202010.pdf.

Zemelman, S., Daniels, H., & Hyde, A. (2012). *Best practice: Bringing standards to life in American classrooms* (4th ed.). Portsmouth, NH: Heinemann.

Zinn, H. (2002). *You can't be neutral on a moving train: A personal history of our times*. Boston: Beacon Press.

Zinn, H. (2009). *The Zinn Reader: Writings on Disobedience and Democracy* (2nd ed.). New York: Seven Stories Press.

Zinn, H. (2010). *A people's history of the United States: 1492 to present*. New York: HarperCollins.

Zinn, H., & Arnove, A. (2004). *Voices of a people's history of the United States*. New York: Seven Stories Press.

Zinn, H., Konopacki, M., & Buhle, P. (2008). *A people's history of the American empire: A graphic adaptation*. New York: Metropolitan Books.

Zinn, H., & Stefoff, R. (2007). *A young people's history of the United States, Vols. 1 & 2*. New York: Seven Stories Press.

Zirin, D. (2009). *A people's history of sports in the United States: 250 years of politics, protest, people, and play*. New York: The New Press.

Index

Made in the USA
Middletown, DE
03 February 2020

84113499R00146